UNLOCKING KNOWLEDGE

Leveraging AI to Access Open Educational Resources in Higher Education

By

Dr. Hesham Mohamed Elsherif

Dr. Salwa Elmeawad

About the Author

Dr. Hesham Mohamed Elsherif stands at the forefront of library management and research, boasting an impressive 22-year tenure in the field. Holding dual doctoral degrees, one in Management and Organizational Leadership and the other in Information Systems and Technology, Dr. Elsherif brings a unique blend of knowledge to any intellectual endeavor.

An expert in Empirical research methodology, Dr. Elsherif specializes particularly in the Qualitative approach and Action research. This specialization has not only strengthened his research endeavors but has also allowed him to contribute invaluable insights and advancements in these areas.

Over the years, Dr. Elsherif has made significant contributions to the academic world not only as a professional researcher but also as an Adjunct Professor. This multifaceted role in the educational landscape has further solidified his reputation as a thought leader and pioneer.

Furthermore, Dr. Elsherif's expertise isn't confined to one region. He has served as a consultant to numerous educational institutions on an international scale, sharing best practices, innovative strategies, and his deep insights into the ever-evolving realms of management and technology.

Combining a passion for education with an unparalleled depth of knowledge, Dr. Elsherif continues to inspire, educate, and lead in both the library and academic communities.

About the Contributor

Dr. Salwa Elmeawad stands out as a luminary in both the academic and community service spheres. With an illustrious career at the helm of adult services manager at Queens Library, she has profoundly impacted the field of information access and literacy. Dr. Elmeawad's educational journey is marked by not one, but two doctoral degrees, showcasing her dedication to lifelong learning and expertise in both organizational leadership and information systems and technology.

Her commitment extends beyond the academic realm into spirited community service. As the Distinguished Lieutenant Governor for the Kiwanis Queens East Division, Dr. Elmeawad plays a pivotal role in steering community-focused initiatives and fostering a spirit of service. Her role as a board member of the KPTC further exemplifies her dedication to impactful community work, particularly in areas of pediatric care and trauma prevention.

Dr. Elmeawad's passion for mentorship and youth development is evident through her involvement with the Benjamin Cardozo High School Key Club. As a lead mentor, coach, and advisor, she guides young minds in their personal and professional development, instilling in them the values of leadership and community service.

Her multifaceted expertise and unwavering commitment to both academic excellence and community service make Dr. Salwa

Elmeawad a distinguished figure in her field and an inspiration to many.

Preface

In recent years, the landscape of education has undergone a profound transformation, driven by advancements in technology and the increasing demand for accessible, high-quality learning materials. At the heart of this shift is the Open Educational Resources (OER) movement, which seeks to democratize education by providing free and openly licensed resources to learners and educators across the globe. As we navigate through the challenges of the 21st century, it has become abundantly clear that knowledge is no longer confined to traditional classrooms or locked behind expensive paywalls. Instead, education is evolving into a more inclusive and globalized enterprise, with OER leading the charge. But with the sheer volume of information available, how can students, educators, and institutions find, curate, and personalize the wealth of content to suit their specific needs? This is where Artificial Intelligence (AI) comes into play.

The purpose of this book, **"Unlocking Knowledge: Leveraging AI to Access Open Educational Resources in Higher Education,"** is to explore the intersection of AI and OER and how this combination is reshaping the way knowledge is accessed, shared, and utilized in higher education. AI, with its capacity to process vast amounts of information and personalize learning experiences, has emerged as a critical tool in making OER more effective, accessible, and relevant. This book provides a deep dive into how AI can enhance the discovery, curation, and dissemination of OER, making education more adaptive to the needs of individual learners while breaking down the traditional barriers to access.

As an educator, researcher, or student, you are likely familiar with the challenges of navigating vast educational repositories, ensuring the quality of the materials, and meeting the diverse needs of learners. By integrating AI technologies, these challenges can be addressed in ways that were previously unimaginable. For instance, AI-powered search engines can help pinpoint exactly the right resource among millions, natural language processing can simplify complex content for varying comprehension levels, and machine learning algorithms can recommend personalized learning pathways tailored to each student's unique strengths and weaknesses.

Throughout the book, we will examine real-world applications of AI in the OER space, offering practical examples and case studies from institutions that have successfully adopted these technologies to transform their educational practices. From AI-enhanced content creation to automated assessment tools and intelligent tutoring systems, these applications illustrate how AI can make OER more than just a repository of free resources—it can turn it into an active, dynamic part of the learning experience.

However, while AI brings immense opportunities, it also raises significant ethical and practical questions. What happens when AI algorithms, often opaque and misunderstood, begin to mediate how educational resources are accessed? How do we ensure that these tools do not exacerbate the existing digital divide or introduce bias in content delivery? These questions are critical to consider as we move forward, and this book takes great care in addressing the ethical implications of AI in education.

This book is organized into five distinct parts. The first section provides a foundational understanding of OER, charting the history of the movement and its importance in modern education. The second part delves into the role of AI in enhancing access to OER, with a focus on tools, techniques, and technologies that can transform the way we interact with educational content. Part three explores real-world applications, offering case studies of AI-powered OER in action within higher education institutions. Part four engages with the ethical and practical considerations, ensuring that the integration of AI and OER is done thoughtfully and inclusively. Finally, the book concludes with practical guides and tools for educators and institutions looking to adopt AI in their use of OER.

We hope this book serves as both an informative guide and an inspiration for educators, technologists, and policymakers to explore new ways of enhancing access to knowledge. As we embark on this journey into the fusion of AI and OER, my goal is to equip readers with the understanding and tools necessary to harness the potential of AI to make education more accessible, equitable, and personalized for learners worldwide.

As we stand on the brink of a new era in education, it is vital that we continue to explore innovative solutions to ensure that the promise of open, accessible learning is fulfilled. We invite you to join us in exploring the transformative power of AI in unlocking knowledge through open educational resources.

Dr. Hesham Mohamed Elsherif

Dr. Salwa Elmeawad

Who Should Read This Book?

This book is designed for a broad audience interested in the intersection of artificial intelligence and education, with a particular focus on Open Educational Resources (OER). Specifically, the following groups will find this book highly valuable:

1. Educators and Instructors

University professors, school teachers, and instructional designers who want to enhance their teaching practices through the use of AI tools and OER. This book offers insights into how AI can help in curating personalized content, automating assessments, and facilitating adaptive learning for diverse student needs. It provides practical guidance for those looking to integrate cutting-edge technology into their pedagogical approaches.

2. Higher Education Administrators and Policymakers

Deans, department heads, university administrators, and policymakers will find this book a useful resource for understanding how AI and OER can transform institutional educational offerings. With examples of AI-powered OER systems and case studies, this book provides strategic insights for leaders aiming to expand access to high-quality learning materials, reduce educational costs, and improve overall student outcomes.

3. Students and Lifelong Learners

Whether you are a student in higher education or someone who is self-directed in your learning, this book will introduce you to AI tools that can personalize your educational journey. By understanding how AI and OER can simplify access to resources and create customized learning paths, readers can take full advantage of modern technologies to enhance their knowledge acquisition and learning experience.

4. Technologists and AI Developers in Education

Software engineers, AI developers, and data scientists working in the education sector will benefit from a detailed exploration of how artificial intelligence can support the development of smarter, more accessible OER platforms. This book provides real-world examples of AI applications in educational environments and discusses the technical challenges and opportunities for building AI tools tailored to education.

5. Librarians and Information Professionals

Librarians, especially those working in academic settings, will find this book useful for better understanding how AI can enhance the discoverability and use of open educational resources in their libraries. As custodians of information, librarians are increasingly involved in digital initiatives that leverage AI to improve access to educational materials for students and faculty alike.

6. Researchers in Education Technology and Artificial Intelligence

Scholars and researchers studying the impact of technology on education will appreciate the in-depth analysis of AI applications within OER systems. The book offers a comprehensive view of the current state of AI in education and discusses potential research avenues in both artificial intelligence and open learning environments.

7. Non-Governmental Organizations (NGOs) and Educational Advocacy Groups

Organizations working to improve global access to education will find this book relevant in helping them understand how AI can assist in their mission to provide free, high-quality educational resources to underserved populations. It offers practical insights into how AI-powered OER initiatives can bridge the education gap in developing countries and promote equity in education.

8. Policy and Ethics Experts in AI and Education

Individuals involved in shaping policies around the ethical use of AI and OER will benefit from the discussions on the ethical considerations, challenges, and implications of AI in education. The book provides a thoughtful examination of how AI technologies can be implemented responsibly to ensure equity and fairness in accessing educational resources.

Whether you are looking to enhance learning experiences, democratize access to educational content, or build AI-driven tools for education, this book offers valuable perspectives and actionable insights for anyone involved in the future of learning.

Why This Book Is Essential Reading?

As education continues to evolve in the digital age, the combination of Artificial Intelligence (AI) and Open Educational Resources (OER) is increasingly recognized as a powerful force for democratizing knowledge. This book, **"Unlocking Knowledge: Leveraging AI to Access Open Educational Resources in Higher Education,"** offers critical insights into this emerging field, making it an essential read for a variety of reasons:

1. Empowering Educators with Cutting-Edge Tools

In a time when educators are inundated with massive amounts of digital content, it can be overwhelming to identify the best resources for their students. This book demonstrates how AI can simplify the search, curation, and personalization of educational materials, helping educators create more engaging, relevant, and customized learning experiences. It introduces AI-powered tools and platforms that can dramatically enhance teaching, making this an indispensable guide for instructors seeking to innovate in their classrooms.

2. Addressing the Global Demand for Accessible Education

The demand for high-quality, affordable education is at an all-time high, especially in regions where traditional educational systems are underfunded or inaccessible. By harnessing the potential of OER and AI, this book outlines how institutions, governments, and NGOs can provide learners from all socioeconomic backgrounds with access to top-tier educational materials. It tackles the global challenge of educational inequity and provides actionable strategies to bridge the digital divide, making it essential for anyone focused on making education more inclusive.

3. Navigating the Complexities of AI in Education

Artificial Intelligence is transforming industries, and education is no exception. However, the implementation of AI comes with its own set of challenges and ethical dilemmas. This book not only explains how AI can be a powerful tool for enhancing access to OER, but it also delves into critical issues such as data privacy, bias, and the potential impact of AI on traditional educational practices. By providing a balanced view of the opportunities and challenges of AI in education, the book equips readers with the knowledge they need to navigate this complex, evolving field responsibly.

4. Practical Solutions for Institutions and Policymakers

For educational leaders and policymakers, understanding the role of AI in accessing OER is crucial for shaping future educational strategies. This book serves as a practical guide, offering case studies and real-world examples of how higher education institutions are successfully implementing AI-driven OER solutions. It also provides recommendations for developing policies that support the integration of AI and OER, making it an essential resource for those responsible for steering the future of education.

5. A Comprehensive Guide for AI and Education Innovators

AI developers, technologists, and innovators working in education technology will find this book invaluable for understanding how AI can be applied to optimize the use of OER. By exploring the technical underpinnings of AI in education—such as natural language processing, machine learning, and adaptive learning systems—the book offers a deep dive into the practical aspects of building and deploying AI solutions. It also discusses future trends, enabling technologists to stay ahead of the curve in educational innovation.

6. Promoting Lifelong Learning and Self-Directed Education

In today's fast-changing world, students and professionals alike are increasingly taking their education into their own hands. The wealth of free resources available online can be overwhelming without proper guidance. This book provides strategies for individuals to use AI tools to navigate, personalize, and maximize their learning experiences through OER. Whether you are a student looking for supplemental material or a lifelong learner seeking new skills, this book will show you how AI can be your guide to tailored educational content.

7. Understanding the Future of Education

The education sector is at a tipping point, where the integration of AI and OER will fundamentally alter the way, we teach and learn. This book explores these emerging trends, offering a vision for the future of education that is more open, personalized, and globally accessible. For those interested in staying ahead of educational innovations and preparing for the future, this book provides an indispensable roadmap.

8. Ethical Considerations and Responsible AI Use

As AI continues to reshape the educational landscape, it is crucial to understand and address the ethical implications of its use. This book covers important ethical concerns, including how to ensure that AI-driven educational systems are fair, equitable, and unbiased. It provides thoughtful discussions on how to avoid reinforcing systemic inequalities through technology, making it essential for educators, administrators, and technologists committed to responsible AI development.

In summary, **"Unlocking Knowledge: Leveraging AI to Access Open Educational Resources in Higher Education"** is an essential read for anyone involved in education—whether as an educator, student, policymaker, or technologist. It provides not only a comprehensive understanding of the profound impact AI can have on OER, but also the practical tools, ethical considerations, and strategic insights necessary for harnessing its potential. At a time when education is undergoing rapid transformation, this book offers a timely and critical perspective on how AI and OER can work together to unlock the future of learning for all.

Happy Reading!

Dr. Hesham Mohamed Elsherif

Dr. Salwa Elmeawad

Table of Contents

Introduction

Chapter 1: The Changing Landscape of Higher Education

The Rise of Open Educational Resources (OER)

The traditional model of higher education is undergoing a dramatic transformation, driven by global advancements in technology, increased demand for accessible and affordable education, and the rapid rise of digital learning. Among the most significant developments in this changing landscape is the proliferation of Open Educational Resources (OER), which have become a cornerstone of the movement toward more equitable, flexible, and cost-effective education. The term OER refers to any teaching, learning, or research material that is freely accessible, openly licensed, and available for adaptation and redistribution by users (UNESCO, 2019). As a response to the financial burdens faced by students and institutions alike, OER offer a potential solution to one of the most pressing issues in higher education: the rising cost of educational materials.

Historical Context and the Emergence of OER

The concept of OER is not entirely new, but its rise to prominence in higher education can be attributed to key milestones and technological advancements in the early 21st century. A pivotal moment in the history of OER occurred in 2002 with the launch of the Massachusetts Institute of Technology's (MIT) OpenCourseWare (OCW) initiative, which provided free access to virtually all of MIT's course materials online. The impact of MIT OCW was profound, inspiring other institutions around the world to adopt similar initiatives aimed at widening access to educational resources (MIT OpenCourseWare, 2021).

OER have since evolved into a global movement, supported by international organizations such as UNESCO and various governments that recognize the potential of openly licensed resources to democratize education. This trend aligns with the broader development of open access in scholarly publishing, which seeks to remove barriers to knowledge and promote wider dissemination of research findings (Atenas & Havemann, 2015). The rise of OER has thus been closely tied to the philosophy of open access, which emphasizes knowledge as a public good that should be freely available to all.

Factors Driving the Adoption of OER

Several factors have contributed to the rapid growth and widespread adoption of OER in higher education. First, the high cost of traditional textbooks has placed a significant financial burden on students, leading to widespread demand for more affordable alternatives. According to Hilton (2020), the average cost of textbooks has risen at a rate outpacing inflation, leaving many students unable to afford required course materials. OER offer a solution by providing free, high-quality alternatives that can replace costly textbooks and other educational materials.

In addition to cost savings, OER are also driving pedagogical innovation. Unlike traditional resources, which are often static and difficult to modify, OER are designed to be adapted and customized. This flexibility allows educators to tailor materials to the specific needs of their students, fostering more personalized and responsive teaching approaches (Wiley, 2014). Furthermore, the digital nature of many OER means that they can be easily updated, ensuring that students and educators have access to the most current information available.

Another key factor driving the adoption of OER is the increasing role of digital technologies in education. The internet and related technologies have revolutionized the way educational content is created, distributed, and consumed. OER repositories, such as OpenStax and OER Commons, provide educators with easy access to a vast array of free resources that can be incorporated into their courses (Hilton, 2020). As a result, OER have become an integral part of the growing trend toward online and blended learning environments.

Global Impact of OER

The rise of OER has had a profound global impact, particularly in developing countries where access to high-quality educational resources has historically been limited. By reducing the cost of educational materials, OER have the potential to increase enrollment in higher education and improve educational outcomes, particularly for disadvantaged populations (Hassler et al., 2014). Moreover, the collaborative nature of OER enables educators and institutions to share resources across borders, fostering a global community of practice dedicated to improving the quality and accessibility of education.

One of the most significant aspects of OER is their ability to break down geographic and financial barriers to education. In regions where educational resources are scarce or expensive, OER provide a viable alternative that allows students to access the same quality of education as their counterparts in wealthier nations (Miao et al., 2020). For example, in countries where traditional textbooks are unavailable due to cost or logistical challenges, OER can be used to deliver instructional content digitally, reaching students in even the most remote areas.

The Role of Policy in Promoting OER

Government policies and institutional strategies have played a crucial role in promoting the use of OER in higher education. Countries such as the United States, Canada, and the United Kingdom have implemented national initiatives to support the development and adoption of OER. For instance, the U.S. Department of Education launched the #GoOpen initiative, which encourages schools to use openly licensed educational materials to improve teaching and learning outcomes (U.S. Department of Education, 2019). Similarly, the European Union has supported the growth of OER through its Open Education Europa portal, which provides access to thousands of free educational resources.

At the institutional level, many universities and colleges have integrated OER into their strategic plans, recognizing the potential of these resources to enhance teaching and learning while reducing costs for students. Some institutions have even developed dedicated OER policies, committing to the creation, use, and promotion of openly licensed materials as a core part of their educational mission (Pitt, 2015).

Challenges and Opportunities

While the rise of OER represents a significant opportunity for higher education, there are also challenges that must be addressed. One of the primary challenges is the issue of quality assurance. Since OER are often created and distributed by a wide range of contributors, ensuring the accuracy, relevance, and reliability of the materials can be difficult (Atenas & Havemann, 2015). However, many OER repositories have implemented peer review processes to address this issue and improve the quality of the resources they offer.

Another challenge is the need for greater awareness and support for OER among educators. Despite the growing availability of OER, many instructors remain unaware of the resources available to them or are unsure how to integrate OER into their teaching practices (Pitt, 2015). Addressing this gap will require ongoing efforts to raise awareness of the benefits of OER and provide professional development opportunities for educators.

The Growth of OER

Below is a simple graph representing the increasing number of OER repositories globally, illustrating the rapid expansion of open educational resources in higher education.

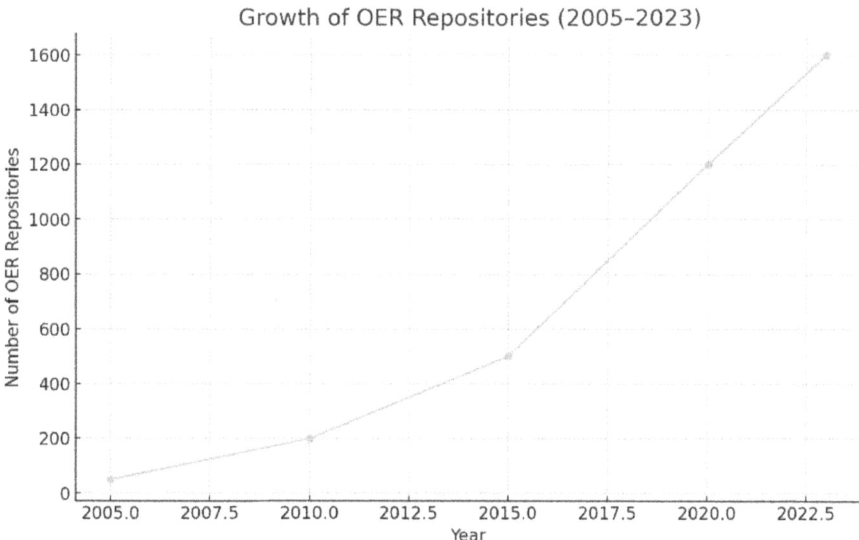

This graph demonstrates the significant growth in the number of OER repositories from 2005 to 2023, reflecting the increasing adoption and use of open educational resources worldwide.

In summary, the rise of OER marks a pivotal shift in the landscape of higher education, offering new opportunities for reducing costs, enhancing pedagogical flexibility, and increasing access to high-quality educational resources. Driven by the need for more affordable alternatives to traditional textbooks and supported by technological advancements, OER have the potential to transform higher education by making learning more accessible and adaptable. As institutions and governments continue to promote the use of OER, the future of education will likely be shaped by the ongoing expansion of open access to knowledge.

The Importance of OER in Democratizing Education

The advent of Open Educational Resources (OER) has been hailed as one of the most transformative developments in higher education, offering a pathway to more equitable, accessible, and inclusive learning opportunities. By providing freely available educational materials, OER breaks down traditional barriers to knowledge, promoting the democratization of education on a global scale. The ability to access, modify, and distribute high-quality teaching and learning materials without financial or legal constraints has redefined how education is delivered, particularly in underserved and marginalized communities. As such, the importance of OER in democratizing education cannot be overstated.

Addressing the Educational Divide

A key challenge in contemporary education is the gap between those who have access to quality educational resources and those who do not. This divide is especially stark in regions where financial constraints, geographical limitations, and inadequate infrastructure hinder access to formal education. The rising costs of textbooks and learning materials exacerbate these inequities, placing a heavy financial burden on students, particularly in developing countries (Hilton, 2020). OER offers a solution to this issue by providing free and open access to educational content, enabling students from all backgrounds to engage with high-quality resources without cost barriers.

OER facilitates access to knowledge by offering a diverse range of learning materials, including textbooks, course modules, lectures, quizzes, and multimedia content, all freely available to students and educators worldwide. According to Wiley (2014), one of the fundamental principles of OER is its openness—educators and students are not only consumers of educational materials but can also modify, adapt, and redistribute them to meet local needs. This adaptability is crucial in contexts where standard educational materials may not reflect local languages, cultures, or pedagogical practices, thus ensuring more relevant and inclusive education for all.

Expanding Access to Quality Education

The democratization of education through OER is not limited to reducing costs; it also encompasses broadening access to high-quality educational resources. In many countries, particularly in rural or low-income regions, access to up-to-date textbooks and instructional materials is limited. OER addresses this issue by providing instant access to a wide variety of resources that can be accessed anytime and anywhere, as long as there is internet connectivity. Even in regions with limited access to the internet, OER materials can be downloaded and shared, further amplifying their reach (Pitt, 2015).

Additionally, OER enables students and educators to access content from top universities and institutions around the world. Initiatives such as MIT OpenCourseWare and OpenStax have made course materials from prestigious institutions freely available to the public, offering students in developing countries access to the same educational resources used in leading universities (MIT OpenCourseWare, 2021). This has a profound impact on educational equity, leveling the playing field by providing all students, regardless of their geographic or economic background, with access to high-quality learning materials.

The widespread availability of OER also promotes lifelong learning, as individuals who are not enrolled in formal educational institutions can access these resources for self-directed study. This is particularly important in a rapidly changing world where continuous learning and upskilling are necessary to adapt to new job markets and technologies (Atenas & Havemann, 2015). By making education more flexible and accessible, OER empowers individuals to take control of their learning journeys, fostering a culture of lifelong learning.

Fostering Collaboration and Innovation

One of the unique advantages of OER is its capacity to foster collaboration and innovation in educational content creation. Unlike traditional textbooks and proprietary educational materials, which are often created by a single author or publishing company, OER invites contributions from a global community of educators, researchers, and learners. This collaborative model enhances the quality of educational materials by allowing multiple perspectives, continuous updates, and the inclusion of culturally relevant content (Pitt, 2015).

Moreover, OER encourages the sharing of best practices among educators. Instructors who create and share OER are not only contributing to the global pool of educational resources but are also participating in a broader movement to improve teaching and learning practices worldwide. As Wiley (2014) notes, the open nature of OER allows educators to experiment with different pedagogical approaches and share their findings with others, thus fostering a cycle of innovation and improvement in education.

The Role of Policy and Institutional Support

The democratization of education through OER is further supported by governmental policies and institutional initiatives that promote the adoption of open educational practices. For example, the U.S. Department of Education's #GoOpen initiative encourages schools to replace traditional textbooks with OER, enabling students to access free, openly licensed educational resources (U.S. Department of Education, 2019). Similarly, UNESCO's OER Recommendation, adopted in 2019, advocates for the widespread use of OER to promote inclusive and equitable education for all (UNESCO, 2019). These policy efforts highlight the importance of OER in reducing educational inequalities and ensuring that all students have access to quality learning materials.

At the institutional level, many universities and colleges have adopted OER as part of their commitment to providing affordable education. Institutions such as the University of British Columbia and Tidewater Community College have successfully implemented OER initiatives, saving students millions of dollars in textbook costs while improving learning outcomes (Hilton, 2020). These efforts demonstrate the significant impact that OER can have on both students' financial well-being and their academic success.

The Impact of OER on Educational Equity

To illustrate the impact of OER on democratizing education, the following graph shows a comparison of textbook costs for students before and after the implementation of OER.

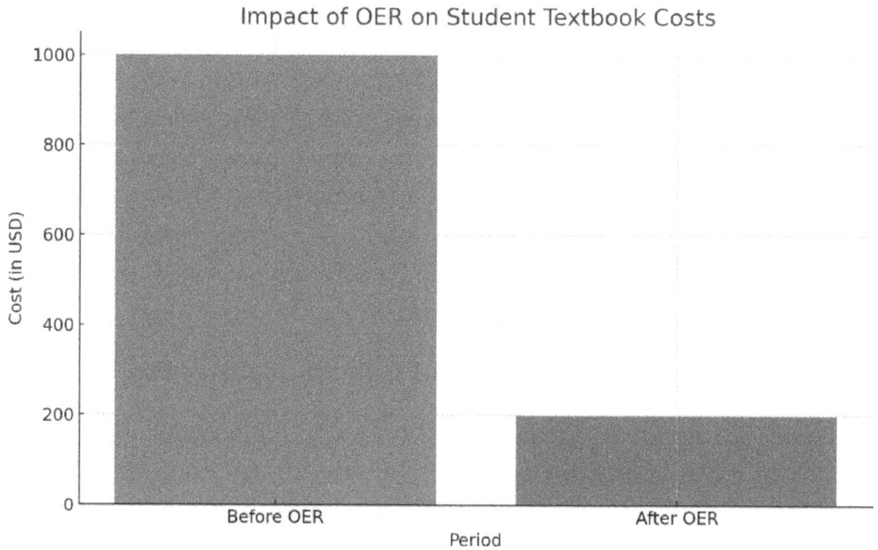

This graph highlights the potential for significant cost savings when OER are adopted, illustrating the financial benefits of open educational resources for students.

In summary, the importance of OER in democratizing education is evident in its capacity to reduce costs, expand access to quality educational materials, and promote collaboration and innovation. By making educational resources freely available and adaptable, OER addresses many of the barriers that have traditionally limited access to education, particularly for underserved populations. As higher education continues to evolve in response to global challenges and technological advancements, the role of OER in promoting equity and inclusivity will become increasingly critical. Governments, institutions, and educators must continue to support the growth and adoption of OER to ensure that education remains a public good accessible to all.

The Role of AI in Revolutionizing Access to Educational Content

In recent years, Artificial Intelligence (AI) has emerged as a transformative force in higher education, fundamentally altering how students access and interact with educational content. AI's capacity to analyze large datasets, identify patterns, and provide personalized learning experiences has unlocked new opportunities for improving educational accessibility, efficiency, and inclusivity. AI-driven tools, from intelligent tutoring systems to adaptive learning platforms, are reshaping the educational landscape by offering customized learning pathways that cater to individual student needs. ecosystems.

Enhancing the Discoverability of Educational Resources

One of AI's most significant contributions to higher education is its ability to improve the discoverability of educational content. Traditional methods of accessing educational resources—relying on simple keyword searches in databases or repositories—often yield an overwhelming number of irrelevant results. AI, however, employs sophisticated algorithms such as natural language processing (NLP) and machine learning to enhance the precision and relevance of search results (Bokhove & Downey, 2019). These technologies enable AI systems to understand the context and intent behind users' queries, providing more accurate and tailored results than conventional search engines.

For example, semantic search tools leverage NLP to identify the relationships between concepts in educational content, allowing students and educators to find more relevant OER quickly and efficiently. Google Scholar and other academic search engines increasingly utilize AI-based algorithms to provide more nuanced results based on users' research interests and prior behaviors (Tang et al., 2020). This level of personalization not only saves time but also ensures that students and educators can easily access the most relevant educational resources.

Personalization of Learning Pathways

Another revolutionary application of AI in education is its ability to deliver personalized learning experiences. Traditional, one-size-fits-all approaches to education are increasingly being supplemented—or even replaced—by adaptive learning platforms powered by AI. These platforms can analyze student performance data and learning patterns in real-time, tailoring educational content to individual needs. AI-driven systems such as Knewton and Smart Sparrow use machine learning algorithms to provide personalized content, assessments, and feedback, adjusting the difficulty and type of materials based on each student's strengths and weaknesses (Chen, 2020).

Personalized learning pathways not only enhance student engagement but also improve learning outcomes. By offering tailored educational experiences, AI systems help bridge gaps in student knowledge, ensuring that learners receive content that is appropriately challenging. This level of customization is particularly beneficial for students with diverse learning styles or those who require additional support, as it enables them to progress at their own pace.

AI-Enabled OER Platforms

AI's role in revolutionizing access to educational content extends to the domain of Open Educational Resources (OER). As OER repositories grow in size and complexity, AI has become instrumental in improving the management, curation, and recommendation of resources. Many OER platforms now incorporate AI to automatically tag, categorize, and recommend materials based on user preferences and behavior. For instance, AI-powered recommendation engines can suggest OER textbooks, videos, or courses that align with a student's academic goals, learning history, and current curriculum (Miao et al., 2020).

An example of this can be seen in the OER Commons platform, which uses AI to help educators discover and curate relevant open resources for their courses. By analyzing metadata, user interactions, and content features, AI algorithms can suggest appropriate OER materials that align with specific learning outcomes or subject areas. This technology simplifies the process of integrating OER into curricula, making it easier for educators to find, adopt, and customize materials to meet their students' needs.

Improving Accessibility and Inclusivity

AI is also playing a crucial role in making educational content more accessible to a broader audience. Tools such as automated captioning, language translation, and text-to-speech are increasingly being integrated into online educational platforms to accommodate diverse learners, including those with disabilities. AI-powered services like Google Translate and automatic speech recognition (ASR) systems enable educational content to be translated into multiple languages, ensuring that learners from different linguistic backgrounds can access the same materials (Hassani, 2019).

Additionally, AI-based accessibility tools such as screen readers and voice-activated assistants help students with visual or auditory impairments navigate educational content more easily. For instance, platforms like Coursera and edX utilize AI to provide automatic captions for video lectures, making them accessible to students with hearing impairments (Popenici & Kerr, 2017). These AI-driven innovations are essential for promoting inclusivity in higher education, ensuring that all students, regardless of their abilities or backgrounds, have equal access to educational resources.

Ethical Considerations and Challenges

While AI offers many benefits in revolutionizing access to educational content, its implementation also raises ethical concerns. Issues such as data privacy, algorithmic bias, and the potential for exacerbating digital divides must be carefully addressed. For instance, AI algorithms trained on biased datasets may unintentionally reinforce existing inequalities in education, disproportionately disadvantaging students from underrepresented backgrounds (Baker & Hawn, 2021). Furthermore, the use of AI in education often relies on collecting vast amounts of personal data, raising concerns about how this data is stored, used, and protected.

Institutions and policymakers must ensure that AI systems in education are designed and deployed responsibly, with a focus on fairness, transparency, and inclusivity. Ethical AI frameworks, such as those proposed by UNESCO (2021), call for the responsible development and use of AI in education to mitigate potential harms and promote equitable access to knowledge.

AI-Driven Personalization in Education

The following graph illustrates the potential impact of AI-driven personalization on student engagement and learning outcomes.

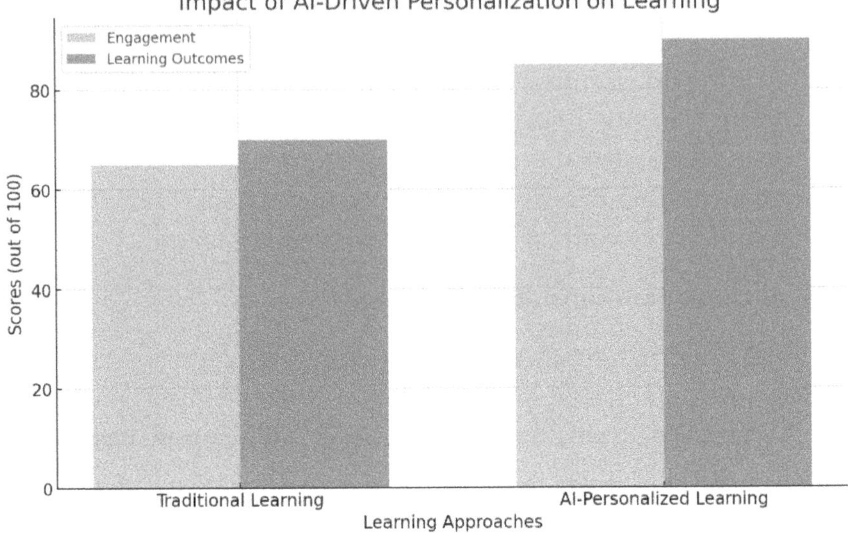

This graph illustrates how AI-driven personalized learning can potentially lead to higher student engagement and improved learning outcomes compared to traditional learning models. These enhancements underscore AI's transformative impact on the accessibility and effectiveness of educational content.

In summary, AI is revolutionizing access to educational content by enhancing the discoverability of resources, enabling personalized learning pathways, and making educational materials more accessible and inclusive. The integration of AI into OER platforms and educational technologies allows for the creation of highly tailored, flexible, and inclusive learning environments, providing students with resources that meet their specific needs. However, as AI continues to reshape education, it is essential to address the ethical challenges associated with data privacy, bias, and equitable access. With proper safeguards in place, AI has the potential to democratize education and extend its benefits to learners worldwide.

Part 1: Understanding Open Educational Resources (OER)

Chapter 2: What Are Open Educational Resources?

Definition and Types of OER

Open Educational Resources (OER) are defined as any teaching, learning, or research materials that are freely available in the public domain or under an open license that permits their free use, adaptation, and redistribution by others with minimal restrictions (UNESCO, 2019). The primary objective of OER is to reduce barriers to education by offering free access to high-quality learning materials, making education more accessible, equitable, and inclusive on a global scale. As educational costs continue to rise, especially for textbooks and other essential resources, OER provides a sustainable solution by offering an alternative to costly proprietary materials (Hilton, 2020).

The term OER encompasses a wide variety of materials, ranging from complete courses to specific learning tools. These resources are designed not only for students but also for educators, researchers, and self-learners. As OER grows in popularity, the types and diversity of resources available have expanded, including digital textbooks, multimedia learning objects, and fully online courses.

Types of OER

OER can be categorized into various types, each serving a distinct role in supporting education. Below is an overview of the most commonly used types of OER:

Open Textbooks

Open textbooks are one of the most widely used types of OER. These are complete textbooks that are freely available to download, use, and adapt. Unlike traditional textbooks, open textbooks are published under an open license, such as the Creative Commons license, which allows users to modify and redistribute the content (Wiley, 2014). Platforms such as OpenStax and BCcampus provide a wide range of open textbooks covering various academic disciplines. Open textbooks significantly reduce the financial burden on students, particularly in fields like science and engineering, where textbooks can be prohibitively expensive.

Open Courses

Open courses, often referred to as Massive Open Online Courses (MOOCs), are freely accessible, self-paced courses offered by educational institutions or platforms. These courses typically include videos, readings, assessments, and other instructional materials that are openly licensed for public use (UNESCO, 2019). Platforms such as Coursera, edX, and FutureLearn provide access to courses from leading universities and organizations, enabling learners worldwide to study subjects ranging from computer science to humanities. Although most MOOCs are free, some offer paid options for certification or additional features.

Open Access Journals and Articles

Open access journals and articles are scholarly publications that are freely available to the public. These resources remove the paywall barriers typically associated with academic publishing, allowing anyone to access cutting-edge research. Open access journals are published under licenses that allow users to read, download, and share the articles without restriction. The Directory of Open Access Journals (DOAJ) and PubMed Central are prominent platforms offering a vast range of peer-reviewed, openly accessible academic journals across various disciplines (Pitt, 2015). Open access journals play a crucial role in democratizing knowledge and fostering global collaboration in research.

Learning Objects and Multimedia

Learning objects are smaller, modular pieces of educational content that can be used independently or combined to support learning objectives. These include videos, animations, quizzes, simulations, and interactive tools designed to enhance student engagement. Open multimedia resources are particularly useful in disciplines that require visual and interactive elements, such as the sciences or arts (Hilton, 2020). Resources such as Khan Academy and PhET Interactive Simulations provide openly licensed multimedia content that educators and students can integrate into their learning environments.

Open Lesson Plans and Teaching Resources

OER also includes instructional materials created for teachers, such as lesson plans, syllabi, and teaching guides. These resources are often shared within professional communities of educators, who adapt and build upon each other's work to develop more effective teaching practices. Open lesson plans allow for the customization of teaching materials to fit the needs of diverse classrooms and learning environments (Atenas & Havemann, 2015).

Open Assessments and Quizzes

Another important type of OER is openly licensed assessments, quizzes, and exam materials. These resources allow educators to create or modify assessment tools to evaluate student understanding. Open assessments can be adapted to reflect the specific learning goals of a course, and they offer the flexibility to tailor the difficulty level to the needs of different students.

The Importance of Licensing in OER

The licensing of OER is crucial in defining how the resources can be used, modified, and shared. Most OER are licensed under Creative Commons (CC) licenses, which allow users to freely use the content while providing attribution to the original creators (Creative Commons, 2020). There are several types of Creative Commons licenses, ranging from the most permissive (CC BY), which allows for the broadest use, to more restrictive licenses that may limit commercial use or derivative works (CC BY-NC-ND).

These licenses play a key role in enabling the collaborative and adaptable nature of OER. Educators can revise and remix OER to better suit their specific teaching needs, which not only improves the quality of instruction but also fosters innovation in educational content.

In summary, Open Educational Resources have transformed the way educational content is created, shared, and consumed. By providing free and openly licensed educational materials, OER reduces the financial barriers to education while fostering a more collaborative, innovative, and inclusive educational environment. The diverse types of OER—ranging from textbooks and courses to multimedia and assessments—demonstrate the versatility and adaptability of these resources. As the global demand for affordable education continues to rise, OER will play an increasingly important role in democratizing access to high-quality educational content.

Key Benefits: Accessibility, Affordability, Adaptability

The rise of Open Educational Resources (OER) has brought about a transformative shift in the educational landscape, making high-quality learning materials accessible to a global audience. The concept of OER, which refers to any educational material freely available under an open license, has been instrumental in addressing several critical challenges in modern education, including rising costs, limited access, and the need for adaptable, personalized learning tools. OER is characterized by its ability to be accessed, used, modified, and redistributed with few or no restrictions, thereby democratizing education and providing significant benefits in terms of accessibility, affordability, and adaptability (UNESCO, 2019).

Accessibility: Expanding Global Access to Education

One of the most significant benefits of OER is its ability to increase the accessibility of educational content to a wide and diverse audience. Traditional educational resources are often limited by geographic, financial, and institutional barriers, leaving many learners

- particularly in low-income or remote regions - without access to high-quality educational materials. OER breaks down these barriers by making educational content freely available online, thus allowing learners from all corners of the globe to access the same materials as students in more developed or affluent areas (Mishra, 2017).

The accessibility of OER is not limited to geographic considerations. OER also benefits learners with disabilities by providing materials that can be modified and presented in various formats to accommodate different learning needs. For instance, text-based OER can be easily converted into audio, braille, or large print, making education more inclusive for students with visual impairments. Similarly, multimedia OER can include closed captions or transcripts, enabling greater access for students with hearing impairments (Banzato, 2020). In this way, OER fosters a more inclusive learning environment, addressing the diverse needs of learners and promoting equity in education.

Affordability: Reducing the Cost of Education

Affordability is another crucial benefit of OER, particularly in the context of rising educational costs. Traditional textbooks and proprietary learning materials are often prohibitively expensive, creating a financial barrier for many students and institutions. In contrast, OER provides a cost-effective alternative by offering free access to high-quality resources. Research has consistently demonstrated that the adoption of OER leads to significant savings for students and institutions, making education more affordable and accessible (de los Arcos et al., 2016).

For example, Bliss et al. (2013) found that students who used OER saved, on average, $90 to $130 per course compared to those using traditional textbooks. These savings are particularly significant in fields such as science, technology, engineering, and mathematics (STEM), where textbooks are often more expensive. By reducing or eliminating the need to purchase textbooks, OER alleviates a substantial financial burden on students, allowing them to focus more on their studies and less on the cost of their education.

OER also benefits educational institutions by lowering the costs associated with developing and maintaining course materials. Instead of investing significant resources into proprietary textbooks and licensing fees, institutions can adopt and adapt OER for their curricula, reducing overhead costs while maintaining high-quality educational content. This is particularly beneficial for institutions in low-income or underfunded regions, where budget constraints can limit access to up-to-date educational materials (Hilton, 2019).

Adaptability: Customizing Educational Resources to Meet Learner Needs

The adaptability of OER is one of its most powerful features, allowing educators to modify and tailor materials to fit the specific needs of their learners. Traditional educational resources are often static, rigid, and difficult to adapt, leaving little room for customization. OER, on the other hand, is designed to be flexible and modifiable, allowing educators to update, remix, and localize content based on their students' needs, regional contexts, and cultural backgrounds (McGreal, 2017).

Adaptability enables educators to ensure that content is relevant and up-to-date, which is especially important in rapidly evolving fields such as technology and healthcare. Instead of relying on outdated textbooks, educators can revise OER to reflect the latest research and industry practices. Moreover, the ability to adapt content allows educators to better engage students by providing materials that are more aligned with their interests, learning styles, and prior knowledge (Wiley, 2014). This personalized approach to education fosters a more effective learning environment, where students are more likely to succeed and achieve their academic goals.

The adaptability of OER also extends to language and cultural customization. In many regions, traditional educational materials are available only in a limited number of languages, restricting access for non-native speakers. OER, however, can be easily translated and localized, ensuring that educational content is accessible to learners in their preferred language and culturally relevant context (Al Abri & Dabbagh, 2019). This is particularly beneficial in diverse or multilingual educational settings, where students may come from different cultural and linguistic backgrounds.

OER Benefits:

The following graph illustrates the relationship between OER adoption and key benefits - accessibility, affordability, and adaptability.

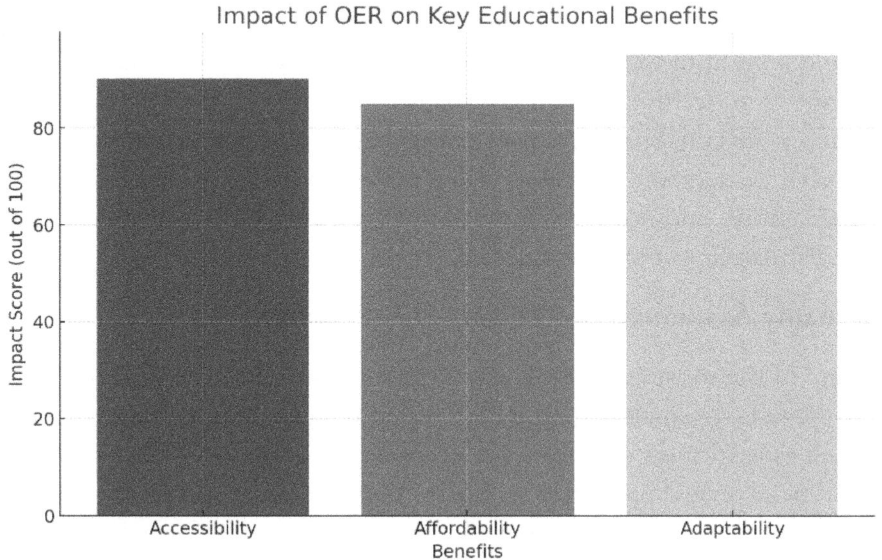

This graph visually represents the high impact that OER has on improving accessibility, affordability, and adaptability in education.

In summary, Open Educational Resources offer numerous benefits that significantly enhance the accessibility, affordability, and adaptability of education worldwide. By providing free, high-quality resources that can be modified and shared, OER not only reduces financial barriers but also empowers educators to customize materials to meet the diverse needs of their learners. These benefits make OER a powerful tool for promoting equitable and inclusive education, particularly in regions where access to traditional educational resources is limited. As OER continues to evolve, its potential to transform education through open access and collaboration will undoubtedly expand, making it an essential component of the future of learning.

Challenges and Limitations in Current OER Systems

While Open Educational Resources (OER) have made significant strides in improving access to high-quality educational materials, they are not without their challenges and limitations. These obstacles range from technical and infrastructural issues to concerns about quality, sustainability, and user engagement. As OER continues to evolve, understanding these challenges is crucial for educators, institutions, and policymakers striving to enhance the effectiveness and scalability of open resources.

Quality Assurance and Perceived Credibility

One of the most commonly cited challenges in the adoption of OER is the issue of quality assurance. Traditional educational materials, such as textbooks and academic journals, undergo rigorous editorial and peer-review processes to ensure their accuracy and credibility. In contrast, many OER materials do not have the same formal quality control mechanisms in place, which raises concerns about the accuracy, reliability, and pedagogical value of these resources (Clements & Pawlowski, 2012). Without standardized quality assurance processes, educators may be reluctant to adopt OER, fearing that the materials might be outdated or not aligned with their learning objectives.

Additionally, the open nature of OER, which allows users to modify and adapt content, can lead to variations in the quality of the resources as they are used and redistributed. While this adaptability is one of the strengths of OER, it also introduces challenges in maintaining the original quality of the content. Some educators may question whether modifications made by other users meet the same academic standards as the original material, further complicating the adoption process (Jung et al., 2017).

Discoverability and Ease of Use

Another significant challenge in the current OER landscape is the issue of discoverability. With the growing number of OER repositories and platforms, finding the right resource can be overwhelming for educators and learners alike. Unlike traditional textbooks, which are often categorized and easily accessible through well-known publishers, OER materials can be scattered across multiple platforms and repositories, making it difficult for users to locate the most appropriate resources for their needs (Atenas & Havemann, 2015).

The lack of standardized metadata across OER platforms exacerbates this issue, as inconsistent or inadequate descriptions can make it harder for search engines to index and present relevant resources to users. Furthermore, many OER repositories rely on basic keyword searches, which may not capture the full range of relevant materials available, particularly in interdisciplinary fields (Rolfe, 2017). As a result, educators may find it challenging to locate high-quality OER that align with their specific curriculum requirements.

Sustainability and Funding Models

Sustainability is a critical concern for the long-term viability of OER initiatives. While many OER projects are launched with initial funding from government agencies, philanthropic organizations, or educational institutions, maintaining these resources over time requires ongoing financial and human resources. The creation, maintenance, and updating of OER materials can be costly, particularly when ensuring that content remains current and relevant in fast-changing fields like science, technology, engineering, and mathematics (STEM) (Wiley, 2014).

In the absence of sustainable funding models, many OER projects risk becoming obsolete or being abandoned altogether once their initial funding runs out. This problem is compounded by the lack of a clear business model for OER platforms, as the resources are typically offered for free and thus do not generate revenue to support long-term maintenance and development (Annand, 2015). Some researchers have called for a hybrid approach, combining public funding with private partnerships or fee-based services to ensure the sustainability of OER projects.

Digital Infrastructure and Technological Barriers

Although OER are intended to be universally accessible, technological barriers can hinder the ability of learners and educators to fully benefit from these resources. Access to reliable internet connections, digital devices, and the necessary technical skills are prerequisites for engaging with OER, particularly in the form of multimedia and interactive content (Cox & Trotter, 2017). In many low-income regions and developing countries, such technological infrastructure is lacking, limiting the ability of students and educators to access and utilize OER effectively.

Even in regions with robust digital infrastructure, the usability and design of OER platforms can present challenges. Many OER repositories are not optimized for mobile devices or have outdated user interfaces that make it difficult to navigate and interact with content. Furthermore, some platforms lack the necessary tools for users to easily adapt and customize resources, which is one of the key advantages of OER (Hassler, 2016). Without user-friendly platforms, the full potential of OER remains untapped.

Legal and Licensing Complexities

The legal landscape surrounding OER can be another source of confusion and limitation. While OER are typically licensed under Creative Commons or similar open licenses, there are often variations in the specific terms and conditions that apply to different resources. For example, some OER may permit modifications but prohibit commercial use, while others may require attribution to the original author (Creative Commons, 2020). These variations can create legal uncertainties for educators and institutions, particularly when they wish to adapt, share, or redistribute OER across different jurisdictions.

Moreover, the complexity of open licenses can discourage some educators from using OER altogether, as they may be uncertain about their legal rights and obligations. Navigating the different types of open licenses and ensuring compliance with copyright law requires legal literacy, which many educators and students lack (Donnelly, 2017). This challenge highlights the need for greater legal clarity and support to encourage wider adoption of OER.

Lack of Institutional Support and Professional Development

Despite growing interest in OER, many educational institutions still lack formal policies or support structures for OER adoption and integration. Without institutional buy-in, individual educators may struggle to find the time, resources, or incentives to develop, adopt, or adapt OER for their courses (Wright et al., 2019). The absence of professional development opportunities also hampers the effective use of OER. Many educators are unfamiliar with the tools and platforms available for creating or adapting OER, or they may not know how to incorporate OER into their teaching practices in a way that enhances student learning.

Institutions must provide both technical and pedagogical support to enable the widespread adoption of OER. This includes offering training programs on how to use, adapt, and evaluate OER, as well as integrating OER initiatives into broader institutional strategies for teaching and learning (Stagg & Bossu, 2016). Without this support, the potential benefits of OER may remain out of reach for many educators and learners.

In summary, while OER holds great promise for democratizing education and providing cost-effective, high-quality resources to learners worldwide, several challenges and limitations remain. Issues related to quality assurance, discoverability, sustainability, technological infrastructure, legal complexities, and institutional support all pose significant barriers to the widespread adoption and effective use of OER. Addressing these challenges will require concerted efforts from educators, institutions, policymakers, and OER developers to create a more supportive and sustainable ecosystem for open education. As the OER movement continues to evolve, overcoming these limitations will be key to ensuring that the full potential of open resources is realized.

Real-World Examples of Successful OER Initiatives

Open Educational Resources (OER) refer to educational materials that are freely accessible, openly licensed, and available for anyone to use, adapt, and distribute. These resources aim to democratize access to education by reducing the cost of learning materials and fostering collaboration in education. OER includes a wide range of materials such as textbooks, lecture notes, assignments, tests, projects, audio, video, and software that support teaching and learning (Wiley & Hilton, 2018). The fundamental principles behind OER are that education should be a public good and that equitable access to high-quality educational materials is critical for the advancement of learning.

Real-World Examples of Successful OER Initiatives

Numerous initiatives across the globe have embraced the principles of OER, contributing significantly to educational access and quality improvement. Below are several notable examples of successful OER initiatives:

MIT OpenCourseWare (OCW)

MIT's OpenCourseWare (OCW) initiative stands as a pioneering effort in the OER movement. Since its launch in 2002, OCW has transformed the landscape of higher education by providing access to the course materials of virtually all of MIT's undergraduate and graduate-level courses. This initiative aligns with MIT's mission to advance knowledge and educate students in science, technology, and other areas that will serve the world in the 21st century (Abelson, 2008).

OCW is freely accessible and available to educators, students, and self-learners globally. This open model has encouraged knowledge sharing and collaboration among institutions worldwide. Many universities have since adopted the OCW model, establishing their own repositories for freely available educational materials.

Further Impact: Beyond the large number of users accessing OCW for personal learning and teaching enhancement, MIT OCW has been instrumental in fostering an OER community, where educators can contribute to and modify existing materials to fit local educational needs (MIT OpenCourseWare, 2020). Several surveys and studies show that OCW has positively impacted teaching practices, with educators incorporating OCW materials into their courses to enhance teaching quality (Carson, 2009).

OpenStax

OpenStax is a non-profit initiative based at Rice University, renowned for its high-quality, peer-reviewed, and openly licensed textbooks. Its primary goal is to alleviate the financial burden of textbooks on students while ensuring the availability of current and comprehensive educational materials. OpenStax has focused on

developing textbooks for high-enrollment courses such as psychology, biology, economics, and physics, where textbook costs have historically been prohibitive (Hilton, 2016).
OpenStax's open textbooks have been widely adopted in the United States and abroad. Its adaptive learning technology, combined with its openly licensed materials, has revolutionized how students access learning resources. Through partnerships with companies and educational institutions, OpenStax continues to integrate modern technologies such as artificial intelligence into the learning experience, thereby enhancing both affordability and the quality of education (OpenStax, 2022).
Expanded Impact: OpenStax's adoption rates continue to rise, with thousands of institutions incorporating its textbooks into their curricula. The initiative's peer-reviewed process ensures the materials are academically rigorous, while the open license allows instructors to customize the content to suit their students' needs. In addition, OpenStax Hub, a platform for educators, facilitates community engagement and collaboration for textbook improvement.

The OERu (Open Educational Resources Universitas)

The OERu (Open Educational Resources Universitas) is an international network of universities, colleges, and polytechnics that offer free and open learning materials for tertiary education. What sets OERu apart is its focus on providing learners with the opportunity to gain credentials from accredited institutions at a fraction of the traditional cost. The initiative allows students to take free courses online, and if they wish to receive academic credit, they can do so by paying a fee for assessments and credentials (Mackintosh, 2017).
OERu's model is based on collaboration, with partner institutions across continents contributing to the development and sharing of learning materials. This approach aligns with the global push for more accessible, affordable, and equitable education. The OERu network helps reduce barriers for learners, particularly those in regions with limited access to higher education.

Further Impact: The OERu model has facilitated the creation of a global platform that combines the strengths of local institutions while offering educational opportunities to learners worldwide. In particular, OERu has been instrumental in offering flexible learning pathways that recognize the diverse needs of non-traditional students, such as working professionals and learners in developing countries (Mackintosh, 2017).

Khan Academy

Khan Academy is another prominent OER initiative that has revolutionized digital learning through its open access to instructional videos, practice exercises, and educational resources for K-12 and higher education levels. Founded in 2008, Khan Academy's mission is to provide a free, world-class education for anyone, anywhere (Khan, 2012).

While not traditionally classified as an OER initiative in the academic sense, Khan Academy's model aligns with the OER ethos of making high-quality educational resources available at no cost. The platform's content spans mathematics, science, economics, history, and arts, making it accessible to a global audience of learners.

Expanded Impact: Khan Academy has collaborated with educational institutions and governments to create customized learning experiences tailored to specific curricula and educational standards. It has also worked with leading technology companies to integrate artificial intelligence tools, enabling personalized learning paths for students based on their progress and performance. Khan Academy's resources are used in over 190 countries, supporting millions of learners annually (Khan Academy, 2020).

UNESCO OER Initiative

UNESCO has been a key player in advocating for OER at the international level. Its OER Initiative promotes the creation, sharing, and use of open educational resources to improve access to education worldwide. UNESCO's advocacy has led to the development of the UNESCO OER Recommendation, which

provides a framework for governments and educational institutions to integrate OER into their policies (UNESCO, 2019).
One of the major milestones achieved by UNESCO was the convening of the 2nd World OER Congress in Ljubljana, Slovenia, in 2017, which resulted in the Ljubljana OER Action Plan. This plan provides concrete recommendations for governments, civil society, and educational institutions to foster the development and adoption of OER.
Expanded Impact: UNESCO's efforts have catalyzed national and regional OER policies in numerous countries. For example, Slovenia was among the first countries to adopt a comprehensive national OER strategy, which has become a model for other nations. Additionally, UNESCO's OER Initiative has promoted collaboration across regions, particularly in Africa and Asia, where the integration of OER has become part of broader efforts to enhance educational equity and access (Miao et al., 2019).

African Storybook Project

The African Storybook Project is an innovative OER initiative aimed at addressing the shortage of culturally relevant children's books in Africa. The project enables educators, parents, and learners to create, translate, and distribute children's stories in African languages. These books are freely available online and can be adapted to suit local contexts, fostering literacy and a love for reading among young learners (Walton & Archer, 2014).
The project leverages the collaborative nature of OER to address the linguistic diversity of Africa, providing children with stories that reflect their own cultures and experiences.
Expanded Impact: The African Storybook Project has resulted in the creation of thousands of free children's books in over 200 African languages. This initiative not only promotes literacy but also empowers communities by providing them with the tools to create educational resources that are relevant to their local needs. The project's success has inspired similar initiatives in other parts of the

world, particularly in regions with linguistic and cultural diversity (Walton, 2016).

The Saylor Academy

Saylor Academy is a non-profit organization that offers free and open online courses and educational resources, enabling learners to earn credits that can be transferred to partner institutions for a degree. Founded in 1999, Saylor Academy's mission is to make education freely accessible and equitable for learners around the world (Bliss et al., 2013).

The academy's courses cover a wide range of subjects, including business, history, and computer science, and are aligned with the learning objectives of traditional college courses. Through partnerships with accredited institutions, learners can apply their Saylor Academy coursework toward earning recognized academic credentials.

Expanded Impact: Saylor Academy has been pivotal in creating a bridge between OER and formal education. By partnering with institutions that recognize the academic quality of its offerings, Saylor Academy helps students reduce the cost and time required to earn a degree. Its open access model has been especially beneficial for adult learners, military personnel, and learners in developing countries (Bliss et al., 2013).

Conclusion

These expanded examples highlight the global impact of OER in fostering accessible, affordable, and equitable education. Initiatives such as MIT OCW, OpenStax, OERu, and UNESCO's OER advocacy have set the stage for a more open and inclusive educational landscape, while projects like the African Storybook Project and Khan Academy show the versatility and broad applicability of OER. These efforts continue to break down barriers to education, democratizing access to knowledge and creating a more interconnected global learning community.

References

Abelson, H. (2008). The creation of OpenCourseWare at MIT. *Journal of Science Education and Technology, 17*(2), 164-174.

Al Abri, M., & Dabbagh, N. (2019). Open educational resources in higher education: A global perspective. *International Review of Research in Open and Distributed Learning*, 20(4), 1-20.

Annand, D. (2015). Developing a sustainable financial model in higher education for open educational resources. *International Review of Research in Open and Distributed Learning, 16*(5), 1-15.

Atenas, J., & Havemann, L. (2015). Open educational resources: A regional perspective. *British Journal of Educational Technology, 46*(3), 446-450.

Baker, R. S., & Hawn, A. (2021). Algorithmic bias in education. *Educational Data Mining*, 13(1), 1-14.

Banzato, M. (2020). Inclusive education through OER: The case of students with disabilities. *Open Learning: The Journal of Open, Distance and e-Learning*, 35(2), 117-131.

Bliss, T. J., Hilton, J., Wiley, D., & Thanos, K. (2013). The cost and quality of online open textbooks: Perceptions of community college faculty and students. *First Monday, 18*(1).

Bliss, T. J., Robinson, T. J., Hilton, J., & Wiley, D. A. (2013). An OER COUP: College teacher and student perceptions of open educational resources. *Journal of Interactive Media in Education*, 2013(1), 1-25.

Bokhove, C., & Downey, C. (2019). The role of artificial intelligence in educational technology: Current developments. *Educational Technology Research and Development*, 67(4), 1395-1412.

Carson, S. (2009). The unwalled garden: Growth of the OpenCourseWare Consortium, 2001–2008. *Open Learning: The Journal of Open, Distance and e-Learning, 24*(1), 23-29.

Chen, P. (2020). The impact of artificial intelligence on personalized learning: Evidence from smart learning systems. *Journal of Educational Technology*, 35(2), 205-220.

Clements, K. I., & Pawlowski, J. M. (2012). User-oriented quality for OER: Understanding teachers' views on re-use, quality, and trust. *Journal of Computer Assisted Learning, 28*(1), 4-14.

Cox, G., & Trotter, H. (2017). Institutional culture and OER policy: How structure, culture, and agency mediate OER policy potential in South African universities. *International Review of Research in Open and Distributed Learning, 18*(6), 1-25.

Creative Commons. (2020). About the licenses. https://creativecommons.org/licenses/

de los Arcos, B., Farrow, R., Perryman, L. A., Pitt, B., & Weller, M. (2016). OER evidence report 2013–2016. *The Open Education Research Hub.* https://oerhub.net/research/publications/oer-evidence-report-2013-2016/

Diallo, B., & Thuo, M. (2013). African Virtual University: Implementing open educational resources. *International Review of Research in Open and Distributed Learning, 14*(2), 235-246.

Donnelly, R. (2017). Open educational resources in higher education: The implications for Ireland. *Irish Journal of Technology Enhanced Learning, 2*(1), 1-22.

Hassani, H. (2019). Artificial intelligence and big data in higher education. *IEEE Access*, 7, 20534-20542.

Hassler, B. (2016). OER quality: The role of policies, infrastructures and resources. *Open Praxis, 8*(2), 115-121.

Hassler, B., Hennessy, S., & Hofmann, R. (2014). OER in developing countries: From innovative access to knowledge. *Educational Technology Research and Development, 62*(6), 615-637.

Hilton, J. (2016). Open educational resources and college textbook choices: A review of research on efficacy and perceptions. *Educational Technology Research and Development, 64*(4), 573-590.

Hilton, J. (2020). Open educational resources, student efficacy, and user perceptions: A synthesis of research published between 2015 and 2018. *Educational Technology Research and Development, 68*(3), 853-876

Jung, I., Sasaki, T., & Latchem, C. (2017). A framework for assessing quality of open educational resources. *International Journal of Educational Technology in Higher Education, 14*(1), 1-13.

Khan Academy. (2020). *Annual report 2020.* https://khanacademy.org

Khan, S. (2012). *The one world schoolhouse: Education reimagined.* Twelve.

Mackintosh, W. (2013). The OER university: Free learning for all students worldwide. *Open Praxis, 5*(1), 5-13.

Mackintosh, W. (2017). Open Educational Resources Universitas: Working towards accessible education for all. *International Journal of Educational Technology in Higher Education, 14*(1), 1-9.

McGreal, R. (2017). Special issue: Open educational resources. *Distance Education*, 38(1), 1-3.

Miao, F., Mishra, S., & McGreal, R. (2019). *Guidelines on the development of open educational resources policies.* UNESCO. https://unesdoc.unesco.org/ark:/48223/pf0000371129

Miao, F., Mishra, S., McGreal, R., & Conrad, D. (2020). *AI in education: Opportunities and challenges for OER.* UNESCO.

Mishra, S. (2017). Open educational resources: Removing barriers to knowledge. *Asian Association of Open Universities Journal*, 12(1), 1-5.

MIT OpenCourseWare. (2020). *MIT OpenCourseWare: 2019 program evaluation findings.* https://ocw.mit.edu

MIT OpenCourseWare. (2021). About OCW. Retrieved from https://ocw.mit.edu/about

OpenStax. (2022). *OpenStax annual impact report 2021-2022.* https://openstax.org

Pitt, R. (2015). Mainstreaming OER in higher education institutions: Successes, challenges, and future directions. *Distance Education, 36*(1), 75-85.

Popenici, S. A., & Kerr, S. (2017). Exploring the impact of artificial intelligence on teaching and learning in higher education. *Research and Practice in Technology Enhanced Learning*, 12(1), 1-13.

Rolfe, V. (2017). Striding the boundaries: Public engagement in open educational practices. *Open Praxis, 9*(4), 403-416.

Tang, J., Zhang, J., & Yu, X. (2020). Semantic search and machine learning in academic research databases. *Journal of Information Technology in Education*, 27(1), 87-100.

UNESCO. (2019). *Recommendation on open educational resources (OER).* Retrieved from https://unesdoc.unesco.org

Walton, M. (2016). Using digital technologies to access stories in African languages. *Reading & Writing, 7*(1), 1-8.

Walton, M., & Archer, A. (2014). The African Storybook Project: An open resource for multilingual literacy development in Africa. *Per Linguam, 30*(1), 79-89.

Chapter 3: The Evolution of Open Access Knowledge

A Historical Perspective on Open Access Movements in Education

The movement towards open access knowledge, including Open Educational Resources (OER), is deeply rooted in the long-standing pursuit of equitable access to education. The drive for open access has evolved over the centuries, shaped by advances in technology, shifting social norms, and efforts to democratize learning. This historical perspective provides an understanding of how the concept of open access in education has progressed from the early ideas of shared knowledge to the global OER initiatives we see today.

Early Foundations of Open Knowledge Sharing

The roots of open access in education can be traced to the ancient and medieval periods when knowledge sharing was largely communal. In the ancient world, learning was often an elite privilege. However, institutions such as the **Library of Alexandria** sought to collect and make available the world's knowledge, symbolizing one of the earliest efforts to create a centralized, open repository of knowledge (El-Abbadi, 2008). While this model did not grant universal access, it underscored the value placed on the collection and dissemination of knowledge.

In the Middle Ages, the rise of universities across Europe began to formalize education. However, access to learning was restricted to the clergy and nobility. The invention of the printing press by Johannes Gutenberg in the 15th century is often regarded as one of the pivotal moments in the history of knowledge dissemination. By making it possible to reproduce books at scale, the printing press catalyzed the spread of ideas and learning materials to broader audiences (Febvre & Martin, 1997). This development laid the groundwork for more open systems of education by breaking the monopoly of handwritten manuscripts and limited access to knowledge.

The Enlightenment and Democratization of Knowledge

The Enlightenment in the 17th and 18th centuries further propelled the concept of open access to knowledge. Thinkers such as John Locke and Jean-Jacques Rousseau argued for the importance of education in achieving individual freedom and societal progress (Darling & Nisbet, 2017). The Enlightenment's emphasis on rationality, scientific inquiry, and the dissemination of knowledge to all laid the philosophical foundations for modern education systems. Open access in education began to take root in the form of publicly funded libraries and the idea that education should be available to all members of society, not just the privileged.

One of the most significant contributions to the open knowledge movement was the **Encyclopédie**, edited by Denis Diderot and Jean le Rond d'Alembert in the mid-18th century. This ambitious project aimed to compile and share all human knowledge systematically and make it accessible to the public (Darnton, 1979). The Encyclopédie can be seen as a precursor to modern-day OERs, as it sought to democratize knowledge and encourage intellectual freedom.

The Rise of Open Access in the 20th Century

The 20th century witnessed several movements that significantly influenced the development of open access in education. The **Open University**, founded in the United Kingdom in 1969, became a landmark institution for its commitment to providing higher education to individuals regardless of their previous academic achievements. Open University pioneered the use of distance learning and made educational resources accessible to a broad audience through the mail and later through the internet (Perry, 1976). This model laid the foundation for the distance education systems and OER initiatives that followed.

As technology evolved, so too did the means of distributing knowledge. The emergence of the internet in the late 20th century was transformative for open access, offering unprecedented opportunities for the global sharing of information. The creation of **Creative Commons** licenses in 2001 by Lawrence Lessig and others was a milestone in the open access movement. These licenses allowed creators to share their work freely while still retaining some rights, providing a legal framework for the development of OER (Lessig, 2004).

At the same time, initiatives like the **Budapest Open Access Initiative** in 2002 advocated for making scholarly research freely available online. This initiative was an important catalyst for the open access movement in academia and laid the groundwork for the creation and proliferation of open access journals and repositories, which would later intersect with the OER movement (Chan, 2004). These developments created a cultural and legal environment conducive to the rapid growth of OER in the 21st century.

The Emergence of OER in the 21st Century

The early 2000s marked the formalization of the Open Educational Resources movement, which began with the Massachusetts Institute of Technology (MIT) launching **MIT OpenCourseWare (OCW)** in 2002. This initiative provided free access to course materials for thousands of MIT's courses, and its success inspired other institutions to adopt similar models (Abelson, 2008). MIT's leadership demonstrated how higher education institutions could leverage the internet to democratize education and make high-quality learning materials freely available to a global audience.

In the same year, UNESCO coined the term "Open Educational Resources" during its 2002 forum, defining OER as any type of educational materials that are in the public domain or introduced with an open license, thereby allowing free use and re-purposing by others (D'Antoni, 2008). UNESCO has since played a key role in advocating for the adoption of OER policies globally, particularly in developing countries where access to quality education has historically been limited.

A significant boost to the OER movement came with the development of digital technologies that supported collaboration and sharing. Online platforms such as **OER Commons, OpenStax**, and **Khan Academy** have expanded the reach of OER by making high-quality learning resources freely accessible to millions of users worldwide (Petrides et al., 2011). These platforms not only provide free access to textbooks and instructional materials but also foster communities of educators who contribute to the ongoing development of educational resources.

In summary, the historical evolution of open access knowledge in education, from early knowledge-sharing models to the digital OER movement, demonstrates a steady progression toward making education more accessible and inclusive. Technological advancements such as the internet and the creation of open licensing systems have accelerated the reach and impact of OER. These initiatives are part of a broader effort to democratize education, ensuring that high-quality learning materials are available to all, regardless of geographic, economic, or social barriers. As the movement continues to evolve, OER stands at the forefront of global efforts to make education a truly public good.

Government and Institutional Policies Promoting OER

The adoption and proliferation of Open Educational Resources (OER) have been significantly influenced by government and institutional policies aimed at promoting equitable access to education. These policies are grounded in the belief that open access to knowledge is essential for advancing educational equity and addressing the rising costs of educational materials. Governments and academic institutions worldwide have recognized the potential of

OER to reduce educational disparities, improve learning outcomes, and foster innovation in teaching.

Government Policies Supporting OER

Governments across various regions have been instrumental in developing frameworks that promote the creation, adoption, and dissemination of OER. These policies are often designed to integrate OER into national education strategies, thereby supporting the broader goals of improving access to education and fostering lifelong learning.

United States

In the United States, several state and federal initiatives have been established to support OER adoption. One of the most notable federal efforts is the **Open Textbooks Pilot Program**, introduced as part of the **Higher Education Act**. This program provides competitive grants to institutions of higher education to create or expand the use of open textbooks, aiming to reduce the financial burden on students (U.S. Department of Education, 2020).

At the state level, several U.S. states have enacted policies to support OER in higher education. For example, the **California OER Council** was established to promote the use of OER in California's public colleges and universities. Similarly, the state of **Washington** developed the Open Course Library, which provides openly licensed course materials for the state's community and technical colleges (Baker & Watson, 2019).

Impact: These policies have contributed to significant cost savings for students. In Washington alone, the Open Course Library has saved students millions of dollars in textbook costs. Moreover, the increased availability of open textbooks has led to more equitable access to course materials, particularly for underserved student populations (Baker & Watson, 2019).

European Union (EU)

The European Union has also taken a leading role in promoting

OER, particularly through its **Open Education Europa** initiative. Launched as part of the broader **Europe 2020** strategy, this initiative aims to enhance the quality and accessibility of education across Europe by supporting the creation and sharing of OER (Inamorato dos Santos et al., 2017). The **European Commission's Communication on Opening Up Education** emphasized the need for policies that support the digital transformation of education, including the promotion of OER to ensure that educational materials are freely accessible to all citizens of the EU (European Commission, 2013).

Impact: The European Union's commitment to OER has been reflected in national policies across member states. Countries like Slovenia and the Netherlands have developed robust OER strategies, integrating open resources into their national education systems and fostering collaboration between public institutions and the private sector (Inamorato dos Santos et al., 2017). The EU's efforts have not only improved access to educational materials but have also promoted digital literacy and the use of innovative teaching methods.

South Africa

In South Africa, the promotion of OER has been closely linked to the government's broader goals of improving access to education in a country with significant educational inequalities. The **Department of Higher Education and Training (DHET)** has actively supported OER through initiatives like the **Siyavula** project, which provides open textbooks for math and science subjects (Czerniewicz et al., 2016). The South African government has also collaborated with international organizations such as UNESCO to develop national OER policies that align with the country's educational priorities.

Impact: The implementation of OER policies in South Africa has had a profound impact on the accessibility and affordability of educational materials, particularly for disadvantaged students. The Siyavula project, for example, has provided millions of free textbooks to learners in the country, contributing to improved educational outcomes in STEM subjects (Czerniewicz et al., 2016).

Canada

In Canada, various provinces have embraced OER policies to address the rising cost of education. British Columbia, in particular, has been a leader in the OER movement through the creation of the **BCcampus Open Textbook Project**. This initiative, launched in 2012, provides free, openly licensed textbooks to students in British Columbia's higher education institutions. The **Alberta OER Initiative** has also been instrumental in promoting the use of OER in the province's post-secondary institutions (Hilton et al., 2020). **Impact**: British Columbia's OER policies have led to significant cost savings for students and have encouraged other provinces to follow suit. By supporting faculty in adopting and adapting open textbooks, the BCcampus Open Textbook Project has increased the availability of high-quality, affordable learning materials and fostered a culture of collaboration among educators (Hilton et al., 2020).

Institutional Policies Promoting OER

In addition to governmental efforts, academic institutions around the world have implemented policies to promote the adoption and integration of OER into their curricula. These policies are often developed in response to both external pressures (such as government mandates) and internal recognition of the benefits of OER for enhancing teaching and learning.

Massachusetts Institute of Technology (MIT)

MIT was one of the first academic institutions to embrace the principles of open access in education through its **OpenCourseWare (OCW)** initiative, launched in 2002. MIT OCW provides free access to course materials from thousands of the university's courses, and its success has inspired similar initiatives at universities around the world (Abelson, 2008). MIT's commitment to open access has been further institutionalized through policies that encourage faculty to share their course materials openly and support the development of open educational content.

Impact: MIT's OCW has set the standard for institutional OER policies, demonstrating how universities can leverage open access to expand their educational impact globally. The initiative has reached millions of learners worldwide and has inspired the creation of the **OpenCourseWare Consortium**, a global network of institutions committed to open education (Abelson, 2008).

The University of Edinburgh
The University of Edinburgh has implemented a comprehensive OER policy that encourages staff to create, share, and use open educational resources. The university's **Open Education Resources Policy** outlines guidelines for the creation and dissemination of OER and provides support for faculty members to develop and publish open materials. Edinburgh's institutional repository, **EdShare**, serves as a central hub for the university's OER, making it easier for educators and students to access and share educational resources (Knox, 2020).
Impact: The University of Edinburgh's OER policy has fostered a culture of open access across the institution, encouraging collaboration and innovation in teaching. By providing a supportive framework for OER development, the university has increased the visibility and impact of its educational materials, both locally and globally (Knox, 2020).

Athabasca University
As a leader in open and distance education, Athabasca University in Canada has developed a robust OER policy that aligns with its mission to provide accessible, flexible education. The university's OER strategy focuses on integrating open resources into its online courses and encouraging faculty to adopt open textbooks and other open materials (McGreal, 2017).
Impact: Athabasca University's commitment to OER has enhanced the accessibility and affordability of its courses, particularly for students in remote and underserved areas. The university's OER

initiatives have also contributed to the broader adoption of open educational practices across Canada (McGreal, 2017).

In summary, governmental and institutional policies have played a critical role in promoting the adoption and dissemination of Open Educational Resources. These policies, which often align with broader educational and social equity goals, have led to significant advancements in the availability of open-access learning materials. By fostering collaboration among educators, reducing the cost of educational resources, and improving access to education, these policies have contributed to the transformation of global education. As more governments and institutions embrace OER, the movement towards open access knowledge continues to gain momentum, paving the way for a more equitable and accessible educational landscape.

The Impact of Digital Transformation in Creating Accessible Content

Digital transformation has profoundly reshaped the landscape of education, particularly in terms of how educational content is created, shared, and accessed. The integration of digital technologies into education has significantly enhanced the ability to distribute Open Educational Resources (OER) globally, making learning materials more accessible, affordable, and adaptable. The shift from traditional print-based materials to digital resources has opened new avenues for educational equity, allowing learners from all socio-economic backgrounds and geographical locations to access high-quality educational content.

The Role of Digital Platforms in Expanding OER Accessibility

One of the key drivers of OER accessibility is the rise of digital platforms that facilitate the creation and dissemination of open resources. Digital platforms have enabled institutions, educators, and individuals to share educational materials more widely than ever before. Online repositories and platforms such as **OER Commons**, **MERLOT**, and **OpenStax** provide access to a vast range of open textbooks, lesson plans, and other educational resources at no cost (Butcher & Hoosen, 2012). These platforms have effectively democratized access to knowledge, allowing students and educators around the world to access materials that would otherwise be cost-prohibitive or unavailable due to geographic constraints.

Moreover, the proliferation of **Massive Open Online Courses (MOOCs)** has further expanded the reach of OER. Platforms like **Coursera**, **edX**, and **FutureLearn** offer free or low-cost courses created by leading universities, making high-quality educational content available to learners globally. MOOCs provide an ideal model for combining digital technologies with open access principles, as they allow large numbers of students to engage in self-paced learning with minimal barriers to entry (Siemens, 2013). The interactive features of these platforms, including forums and assessments, further enhance the learning experience, transforming passive consumption of information into active engagement.

The impact of these platforms has been particularly significant in regions where access to quality education is limited by financial, geographic, or political factors. In developing countries, where access to printed textbooks and educational materials is often scarce, digital OER provides a cost-effective alternative to traditional resources. For instance, in sub-Saharan Africa, where educational infrastructure is often underdeveloped, initiatives like **African Virtual University (AVU)** leverage digital technologies to provide open access to educational content across the continent (Diallo & Thuo, 2013). By making content available online, digital platforms allow learners in remote and underserved regions to participate in global knowledge networks.

Enhanced Adaptability and Customization of OER Through Digital Technologies

The adaptability of OER has been greatly enhanced by digital technologies, allowing educators to customize content to fit local curricula, cultural contexts, and specific learner needs. Traditional print textbooks often lack the flexibility needed to meet the diverse requirements of learners, particularly in multilingual and multicultural settings. In contrast, digital OER can be easily modified, translated, and repurposed, enabling educators to tailor materials for their students (Baker, 2016). This capacity for adaptation is particularly valuable in developing countries, where standardized content may not always align with local educational needs.

Digital OER also support the integration of multimedia elements, including videos, interactive simulations, and audio, which enrich the learning experience and accommodate different learning styles. For example, platforms like **Khan Academy** use videos and interactive exercises to teach complex subjects like mathematics and science, making the content more engaging and accessible to students who may struggle with traditional text-based materials (Khan, 2012). The ability to incorporate multimedia into OER not only makes the content more accessible to learners with different abilities but also increases the retention and understanding of complex concepts.

Additionally, the flexibility of digital OER allows for rapid updates and revisions, ensuring that content remains current and relevant. Unlike printed textbooks, which may take years to revise and republish, digital OER can be updated in real-time, allowing educators to incorporate the latest research and developments into their teaching materials. This adaptability is particularly important in fast-evolving fields such as science, technology, and medicine, where outdated information can negatively impact learning outcomes (Hilton et al., 2020).

The Role of Artificial Intelligence and Machine Learning in Enhancing OER Accessibility

Recent advancements in artificial intelligence (AI) and machine learning (ML) have further enhanced the accessibility of OER by personalizing learning experiences and making content more responsive to individual needs. AI-powered platforms can analyze learners' interactions with educational materials, providing personalized recommendations and adaptive learning paths based on their progress and preferences (Hwang & Tu, 2021). This level of customization allows students to learn at their own pace, receive immediate feedback, and focus on areas where they need the most support.

For instance, AI-based tools like **Content Technologies, Inc. (CTI)** and **Knewton** are developing personalized learning platforms that use algorithms to adapt OER content to meet the unique learning needs of each student. These tools provide educators with real-time insights into student performance, enabling them to intervene where necessary and offer targeted support. This level of personalization not only enhances the accessibility of OER for learners with different abilities and backgrounds but also contributes to improved educational outcomes (Hwang & Tu, 2021).

Moreover, AI can be used to automate the creation of accessible content for learners with disabilities. For example, text-to-speech and speech-to-text technologies can convert written OER materials into audio formats, making them accessible to visually impaired learners. Similarly, AI-powered captioning and translation tools can ensure that video-based OER materials are accessible to non-native speakers and those with hearing impairments. These technologies significantly broaden the reach of OER, ensuring that all learners, regardless of their abilities or language proficiency, can benefit from open access to educational resources (Stracke, 2019).

Challenges and Opportunities in the Digital Transformation of OER

While digital transformation has greatly expanded the accessibility of OER, it also presents several challenges. The digital divide remains a significant barrier to accessing OER in many parts of the world, particularly in regions with limited internet connectivity or inadequate digital infrastructure. In these areas, the benefits of digital OER may be less pronounced, as learners struggle to access online platforms and content. Addressing this divide requires targeted investments in digital infrastructure, particularly in rural and remote regions, to ensure that the benefits of OER are equitably distributed.

Additionally, the rapid pace of technological change raises concerns about the sustainability of digital OER platforms. Many OER initiatives rely on external funding, and maintaining the technical infrastructure required to support large-scale digital platforms can be costly. Ensuring the long-term sustainability of these platforms will require continued collaboration between governments, educational institutions, and the private sector to develop funding models that support the ongoing creation and dissemination of OER.

Despite these challenges, the opportunities presented by digital transformation are vast. As technologies continue to evolve, the potential for creating more accessible, inclusive, and engaging educational content will only increase. Digital OER represent a key component of this transformation, offering a scalable solution to some of the most pressing challenges in global education.

Conclusion

The digital transformation of education has played a crucial role in enhancing the accessibility and adaptability of Open Educational Resources. By leveraging digital platforms, multimedia content, and emerging technologies such as AI and machine learning, OER have become more customizable and responsive to the diverse needs of learners. However, challenges such as the digital divide and the sustainability of OER platforms remain. Addressing these challenges will be essential to ensuring that the benefits of digital OER are accessible to all learners, regardless of their geographical or socio-economic circumstances.

References

Abelson, H. (2008). The creation of OpenCourseWare at MIT. *Journal of Science Education and Technology, 17*(2), 164-174.

Baker, J. (2016). A framework for evaluating OER impact: Beyond cost savings. *Open Praxis, 8*(3), 207-221.

Baker, J., & Watson, C. (2019). Open Course Library: Saving students millions in textbook costs. *Open Praxis, 11*(2), 165-178.

Butcher, N., & Hoosen, S. (2012). Exploring the business case for OER. *Commonwealth of Learning and UNESCO.* http://oasis.col.org/bitstream/handle/11599/57/pub_OER_BusinessCase.pdf

Chan, L. (2004). Supporting and enhancing scholarship in the digital age: The role of open access institutional repositories. *Canadian Journal of Communication, 29*(3), 277-300.

Czerniewicz, L., Deacon, A., Walji, S., & Glover, M. (2016). OER in and as MOOCs. *Journal of Computing in Higher Education, 28*(1), 74-93.

D'Antoni, S. (2008). Open Educational Resources: The way forward. *Proceedings of the UNESCO International Community on OER*. UNESCO. https://unesdoc.unesco.org/ark:/48223/pf0000157984

Darling, J., & Nisbet, H. B. (2017). The Enlightenment and education. *History of European Ideas, 43*(3), 262-273.

Darnton, R. (1979). The business of Enlightenment: A publishing history of the Encyclopédie, 1775-1800. *The Belknap Press of Harvard University Press.*

Diallo, B., & Thuo, M. (2013). African Virtual University: Implementing open educational resources. *International Review of Research in Open and Distributed Learning, 14*(2), 235-246.

El-Abbadi, M. (2008). *Life and fate of the ancient Library of Alexandria.* UNESCO.

European Commission. (2013). *Opening up education: Innovative teaching and learning for all through new technologies and open educational resources.* https://eur-lex.europa.eu/legal-content/EN/TXT/?uri=CELEX:52013DC0654

Febvre, L., & Martin, H. J. (1997). *The coming of the book: The impact of printing 1450-1800.* Verso.

Hilton, J., Bliss, T., & Smith, R. (2020). Promoting the adoption of open educational resources in higher education institutions: A systematic review. *Open Learning: The Journal of Open, Distance and e-Learning, 35*(2), 133-150.

Hwang, G. J., & Tu, Y. F. (2021). Roles and research trends of artificial intelligence in education: A review of publications in selected SSCI journals from 1996 to 2019. *Interactive Learning Environments, 29*(1), 1-17.

Khan, S. (2012). *The one world schoolhouse: Education reimagined.* Twelve.

Lessig, L. (2004). *Free culture: How big media uses technology and the law to lock down culture and control creativity.* Penguin Press.

Perry, W. (1976). *Open University: A personal account by the first vice-chancellor.* Open University Press.

Petrides, L., Jimes, C., Middleton-Detzner, C., Walling, J., & Weiss, S. (2011). Open textbook adoption and use: Implications for teachers and learners. *Open Learning: The Journal of Open, Distance and e-Learning, 26*(1), 39-49.

Siemens, G. (2013). Massive open online courses: Innovation in education? In R. McGreal, W. Kinuthia, & S. Marshall (Eds.), *Open educational resources: Innovation, research and practice* (pp. 5-15). Commonwealth of Learning and Athabasca University.

Part 2: AI as a Tool for Enhancing Access to OER

Chapter 4: How AI Is Transforming Knowledge Discovery

AI-Driven Search Engines and Intelligent Content Curation

Artificial Intelligence (AI) has emerged as a powerful tool for enhancing access to Open Educational Resources (OER) by transforming the way users discover, retrieve, and interact with educational content. AI-driven technologies, such as intelligent search engines and content curation systems, are revolutionizing knowledge discovery by making it more efficient, personalized, and accessible. These tools utilize machine learning algorithms, natural language processing (NLP), and advanced data analytics to improve the searchability and relevance of OER, helping users navigate vast amounts of information with greater precision and ease.

AI-Driven Search Engines: Improving the Discoverability of OER

One of the primary challenges in utilizing OER is the difficulty in locating relevant, high-quality resources within the vast and often fragmented repositories of educational materials. Traditional search engines, while effective for general web searches, are not always optimized for finding educational resources, particularly OER, which may be scattered across multiple platforms and formats (McGreal, 2018). AI-driven search engines, however, are designed to address these challenges by improving the discoverability and relevance of OER through sophisticated algorithms and data-driven insights.

AI-powered search engines utilize machine learning techniques to analyze and index large datasets, identifying patterns and correlations that help improve search accuracy. These engines are capable of understanding user intent and context, allowing them to deliver more relevant search results tailored to individual needs. For example, platforms such as **Google Scholar** and **Microsoft Academic** use AI to rank academic resources based on factors such as citation counts, relevance, and user behavior, helping users discover the most pertinent OER for their educational needs (Ortega, 2019). Similarly, the **AI-Powered OER Discovery Framework** developed by the Commonwealth of Learning uses AI algorithms to classify and retrieve OER from multiple repositories, enhancing the speed and accuracy of search results (Butcher et al., 2020).

One of the significant advancements in AI-driven search engines is the integration of **natural language processing (NLP)**. NLP allows search engines to interpret and understand the semantic meaning behind users' queries, enabling more nuanced and accurate searches. For instance, instead of relying solely on keyword matching, AI-driven search engines can interpret queries that are phrased in natural language, such as "find introductory calculus textbooks for college students," and return relevant OER materials that match the specific intent and context of the query (Ritzhaupt et al., 2021). This capability greatly enhances the user experience, particularly for students and educators seeking specific educational resources that meet precise academic or pedagogical needs.

Furthermore, AI-driven search engines are increasingly utilizing **recommendation algorithms** that analyze user preferences and behaviors to suggest relevant OER. These algorithms, similar to those used by commercial platforms like Netflix or Amazon, help users discover OER that they may not have initially searched for but that aligns with their interests or learning goals. Such personalized recommendations can significantly improve the accessibility of OER by guiding users toward resources that are most relevant to their specific educational contexts (Lee, 2018).

Intelligent Content Curation: Organizing OER for Enhanced Accessibility

In addition to improving search capabilities, AI is playing a critical role in curating OER content in ways that make it more accessible, organized, and user-friendly. Intelligent content curation involves the use of AI to sift through vast amounts of educational data, categorize materials, and present them in a manner that is both useful and accessible to learners and educators.

AI-driven content curation systems use machine learning algorithms to automatically organize OER based on topics, difficulty levels, and user needs. For instance, platforms like **X5GON** (Cross Modal, Cross Cultural, Cross Lingual, Cross Domain, and Cross Site Global Open Educational Resource Network) use AI to analyze and curate OER from various sources, ensuring that learners can access materials in different languages, formats, and academic disciplines (Pouyioutas et al., 2018). By providing a structured and comprehensive overview of available OER, these systems reduce the cognitive load on users, making it easier for them to find and use relevant materials.

Moreover, AI-enhanced curation tools can personalize the learning experience by tailoring the selection and presentation of OER to individual learning preferences and progress. For example, adaptive learning platforms like **Knewton** use AI to analyze learner interactions with content, assessing their strengths, weaknesses, and learning pace. Based on this data, the system curates a personalized set of OER materials that are optimized to meet the learner's unique needs (Colvin et al., 2016). Such intelligent content curation not only enhances the accessibility of OER but also improves the effectiveness of learning by delivering materials that are both relevant and aligned with learners' academic goals.

Additionally, AI can be used to automatically update and refine curated content, ensuring that OER remain current and relevant. In fast-evolving fields like computer science or medicine, where information quickly becomes outdated, AI-driven content curation systems can monitor changes in research, academic standards, and educational trends, updating OER repositories accordingly (Siemens, 2020). This dynamic approach to content curation ensures that learners and educators always have access to the most up-to-date resources, improving the quality and relevance of the educational materials available.

Enhancing Accessibility for Diverse Learners

AI-driven search engines and intelligent content curation systems also play a crucial role in improving accessibility for diverse learners, particularly those with disabilities or language barriers. For example, AI-powered tools like **automatic captioning**, **text-to-speech**, and **speech-to-text** technologies can make OER more accessible to students with visual or auditory impairments. AI-driven translation tools can also break down language barriers by translating OER into multiple languages, making it possible for non-native speakers to access educational content that was previously unavailable in their native languages (Kurdi et al., 2020).

Furthermore, AI-driven search engines can optimize content for accessibility by identifying and prioritizing OER that are designed according to **universal design for learning (UDL)** principles. UDL emphasizes the creation of flexible educational materials that can accommodate the diverse needs of all learners, regardless of their abilities or learning preferences (Stracke, 2019). By surfacing OER that adhere to these principles, AI can ensure that students with different learning needs have access to materials that are accessible and tailored to their specific requirements.

In summary, AI-driven search engines and intelligent content curation systems are transforming how users discover and engage with Open Educational Resources. By leveraging machine learning, natural language processing, and recommendation algorithms, AI enhances the discoverability and relevance of OER, making educational content more accessible and personalized. Moreover, intelligent content curation systems play a critical role in organizing and updating OER, ensuring that learners and educators can access high-quality, relevant, and current educational materials. As AI continues to evolve, its role in enhancing access to OER is likely to expand, offering new opportunities for personalized learning and global knowledge sharing.

Natural Language Processing (NLP) for Better Indexing and Retrieval

Natural Language Processing (NLP) has emerged as a cornerstone of artificial intelligence (AI), playing a pivotal role in improving the indexing and retrieval of Open Educational Resources (OER). As the volume of educational content grows exponentially, the need for more sophisticated methods of organizing and retrieving this content has become critical. Traditional keyword-based search methods often fall short in effectively handling the complexity and diversity of queries that learners and educators may use when searching for OER. NLP addresses these limitations by enabling machines to understand, interpret, and generate human language, thus transforming how OER is indexed and retrieved.

Enhancing Indexing through NLP

One of the most significant contributions of NLP to the field of OER is the ability to improve the process of indexing educational content. Traditional indexing methods typically rely on simple metadata tags or keywords provided by content creators. While useful, this approach often overlooks the semantic depth of the content, leading to inefficiencies in search results (Zhao et al., 2018). NLP allows for a more nuanced understanding of the text, enabling systems to automatically extract and classify content based on its deeper meaning.

NLP-powered tools can analyze the textual content of OER, identifying key concepts, themes, and relationships between different pieces of information. By using techniques such as **entity recognition**, **topic modeling**, and **semantic analysis**, NLP can generate more accurate metadata and enhance the discoverability of educational resources (Alzahrani et al., 2018). For example, an OER repository for biology may contain numerous resources on various subfields, such as genetics, evolution, and ecology. NLP can automatically identify these topics within the content, creating detailed indexes that reflect the complexity of the material. As a result, users searching for specific resources within these subfields are more likely to find relevant content efficiently.

Another key advantage of NLP in indexing is its ability to process multilingual content. OER repositories often contain materials in different languages, making it difficult to create uniform indexes across all resources. NLP algorithms are capable of handling multiple languages and can generate consistent indexing across diverse linguistic content. This capability is particularly important in global education, where learners and educators may require access to materials in their native languages (Ahmad et al., 2020). NLP ensures that content in different languages is indexed in a way that allows it to be easily retrieved regardless of the user's language preferences.

Improving Retrieval Accuracy with NLP

NLP not only enhances the indexing of OER but also significantly improves the accuracy and relevance of search results. Traditional search engines rely on exact keyword matching, which can be limiting, especially when users are uncertain about the specific terms to use. NLP helps overcome these limitations by enabling **semantic search**, a technique that allows search engines to interpret the intent and context behind a user's query rather than focusing solely on keyword matching (Salton, 2021).

With semantic search, an NLP system can process queries that are phrased in natural language, such as "What are the main principles of evolution?" and return relevant resources on evolutionary biology, even if the exact words in the query do not match the keywords in the OER metadata. This process is made possible by NLP's ability to understand synonyms, related concepts, and broader contextual information. For example, in the case of a query about "evolution," an NLP-powered search engine might also retrieve resources on natural selection, genetic variation, and adaptation, recognizing the conceptual relationships between these terms (Wang et al., 2019).

Moreover, NLP enables search engines to account for more complex query structures, such as **question-based searches** and **multi-part queries**. For instance, if a user searches for "What are the applications of AI in healthcare?" an NLP-enhanced search engine can parse this query, understand its components, and retrieve OER materials that specifically discuss AI applications in medical diagnostics, treatment planning, and healthcare administration (Manning et al., 2020). This level of sophistication greatly enhances the user experience by ensuring that search results are more accurate, comprehensive, and aligned with the user's informational needs.

Leveraging NLP for Context-Aware Recommendations

In addition to improving search accuracy, NLP can be leveraged to provide **context-aware recommendations** for OER users. Modern educational platforms increasingly rely on recommendation algorithms to help users discover resources that are relevant to their interests and learning goals. NLP enhances these algorithms by enabling them to analyze not only the content of the OER but also the context in which users interact with the materials (Lee et al., 2019).

For instance, an NLP-based recommendation system might analyze a user's previous search history, interactions with OER, and even their learning progress to generate personalized recommendations for future resources. If a user frequently searches for materials on machine learning, the system can recommend advanced resources on deep learning or reinforcement learning, based on the assumption that the user is progressing in their studies. Moreover, by understanding the user's specific context (e.g., whether they are a beginner or advanced learner), the system can tailor its recommendations to match the user's level of expertise (Garcia et al., 2020).

NLP-powered recommendation systems also play a critical role in curating content from vast OER repositories, ensuring that users are presented with the most relevant and up-to-date materials. By analyzing the relationships between different OER materials, NLP can identify clusters of related content and recommend them to users who may benefit from exploring a broader range of topics. This approach not only enhances the discoverability of OER but also supports more effective learning by guiding users through a logical progression of educational resources (Kastrati et al., 2020).

NLP and Accessibility in OER Retrieval

Another significant impact of NLP on OER retrieval is its contribution to improving the accessibility of educational resources for diverse learners. NLP-powered tools can enhance accessibility by providing support for learners with different abilities and language proficiencies. For example, **automatic summarization** algorithms, a subfield of NLP, can generate concise summaries of lengthy educational materials, making it easier for learners with limited attention spans or cognitive disabilities to grasp key concepts (Hovy & Marcu, 2021). Similarly, **translation algorithms** enable the automatic translation of OER into different languages, breaking down language barriers and expanding access to educational materials for non-native speakers (Soria & Ali, 2019).

Furthermore, NLP supports the development of **voice-based search interfaces** that allow users to interact with OER platforms through speech rather than text. This functionality is particularly valuable for users with physical disabilities that limit their ability to type or use traditional interfaces. By enabling voice-activated searches and providing spoken responses to queries, NLP-powered systems ensure that OER platforms are accessible to a broader range of learners, promoting inclusivity in global education (Rathore et al., 2020).

In summary, Natural Language Processing (NLP) has become a transformative technology in the realm of Open Educational Resources (OER), significantly enhancing both the indexing and retrieval of educational content. By allowing systems to understand and interpret human language more effectively, NLP improves the discoverability of OER through enhanced indexing techniques that capture the semantic complexity of educational materials. It also enhances search accuracy by enabling semantic search and context-aware recommendations, ensuring that users receive the most relevant and personalized resources. Moreover, NLP plays a crucial role in making OER platforms more accessible to diverse learners, particularly through multilingual support and voice-based interfaces. As NLP technologies continue to evolve, their impact on the accessibility and usability of OER is likely to expand, further democratizing access to education on a global scale.

Personalized Recommendations Using Machine Learning Algorithms

Artificial Intelligence (AI) has fundamentally transformed knowledge discovery in Open Educational Resources (OER) by enabling personalized recommendations through the application of machine learning algorithms. In educational environments, personalized recommendations help tailor content to meet the unique needs, preferences, and learning paths of individual users. Machine learning algorithms, particularly those used in recommendation systems, analyze vast datasets to predict user preferences and recommend the most relevant resources, thereby enhancing learning efficiency and engagement.

Machine Learning Algorithms for Personalized Learning

Personalized recommendations in OER platforms rely on machine learning algorithms capable of analyzing large amounts of user data to identify patterns and preferences. These algorithms, commonly referred to as **recommender systems**, use data such as user behavior, interaction history, content characteristics, and contextual information to provide tailored learning resources. Two primary types of recommendation algorithms are widely used: **collaborative filtering** and **content-based filtering** (Resnick & Varian, 1997).

Collaborative filtering involves analyzing the preferences of users with similar behaviors to predict what a given user might like or need. This method relies on user data, such as past interactions with OER, ratings, and search histories, to make recommendations based on patterns observed in other users' behavior (Schafer et al., 2007). For example, if several users who accessed materials on machine learning also viewed resources on neural networks, the system might recommend neural network content to a user who has only engaged with machine learning OER.

Content-based filtering, on the other hand, analyzes the features of the content itself, such as keywords, topics, and difficulty level, to recommend resources that are similar to those a user has already accessed (Lops et al., 2011). In OER repositories, content-based filtering can be especially valuable for guiding users toward materials that are directly aligned with their current learning trajectory. For instance, if a learner frequently engages with introductory calculus materials, the system may recommend advanced calculus resources based on the content's semantic characteristics.

In many OER systems, **hybrid recommendation algorithms** that combine both collaborative and content-based filtering are employed to enhance the accuracy and relevance of recommendations (Zhang et al., 2019). By integrating these approaches, hybrid systems offer more robust personalized suggestions, taking into account both the user's interaction history and the intrinsic features of the educational content.

Enhancing User Engagement with Personalized Recommendations

Personalized recommendations significantly improve the user experience on OER platforms by reducing the time and effort required to find suitable learning resources. The vast quantity of available OER can be overwhelming, and learners may struggle to identify content that is appropriate for their level, interests, or academic goals. Machine learning-based recommendation systems mitigate this issue by streamlining the content discovery process, offering curated suggestions that align with the learner's needs (Bergamaschi & Po, 2020).

In addition to enhancing the efficiency of content discovery, personalized recommendations promote deeper engagement with educational materials. Learners are more likely to stay engaged with content that closely matches their interests and learning objectives. Studies have shown that personalized learning pathways, supported by machine learning algorithms, can lead to improved retention rates, greater learner satisfaction, and more positive learning outcomes (Drachsler & Greller, 2016). By tailoring recommendations to each user's evolving preferences, these systems encourage continuous learning and exploration of new topics.

Moreover, personalized recommendations can foster more **adaptive learning environments**, where the system adjusts recommendations based on the learner's progress. For example, if a learner demonstrates proficiency in a particular subject area, the recommendation system can gradually introduce more advanced content to challenge the user and facilitate further skill development. Conversely, if a user struggles with specific topics, the system can recommend remedial resources or alternative approaches to learning, thus supporting differentiated instruction (Klašnja-Milićević et al., 2017).

Machine Learning and OER Accessibility

Beyond personalization for individual users, machine learning algorithms play a crucial role in improving the overall accessibility of OER platforms. One of the key challenges in OER is ensuring that educational resources are available to diverse learners with varying needs, abilities, and contexts. Machine learning-powered recommendation systems can address this challenge by analyzing data from a wide range of users and identifying trends that inform the development of more inclusive educational resources.

For instance, machine learning algorithms can help identify gaps in the availability of OER for underrepresented groups or learners with disabilities. By analyzing user data, these systems can detect patterns indicating that certain types of learners are not finding appropriate content, prompting educators and platform developers to create more accessible resources (Kurdi et al., 2020). Additionally, machine learning algorithms can help personalize recommendations for learners with disabilities by suggesting content that aligns with their specific needs, such as resources that are available in alternative formats (e.g., text-to-speech or closed captioning).

In terms of linguistic diversity, machine learning algorithms can also improve the accessibility of OER for non-native speakers. For example, personalized recommendations can guide learners toward educational resources in their preferred language or suggest materials that are suitable for their level of language proficiency. This capability ensures that learners from different linguistic backgrounds have equal access to high-quality educational content (Amami et al., 2019).

Ethical Considerations in Machine Learning for Personalized Recommendations

While machine learning-based personalized recommendations offer significant benefits in enhancing access to OER, it is important to consider the ethical implications of these systems. One concern is the **potential for bias** in machine learning algorithms. If the training data used to develop recommendation systems is not representative of diverse learner populations, the recommendations may disproportionately favor certain groups while marginalizing others (Binns, 2018). For example, an algorithm trained primarily on data from advanced learners might fail to provide appropriate recommendations for beginners or individuals with different educational backgrounds.

To mitigate this risk, developers of machine learning-based recommendation systems must ensure that their algorithms are trained on diverse and inclusive datasets. Additionally, ongoing monitoring and evaluation of these systems are necessary to detect and correct any biases that may emerge over time (Mehrabi et al., 2021).

Another ethical concern is the **privacy of user data**. Machine learning algorithms rely on large amounts of data to generate personalized recommendations, raising questions about how this data is collected, stored, and used. Ensuring that learners' privacy is protected and that their data is used ethically is critical for building trust in AI-powered OER systems. Transparency in data usage policies and the implementation of robust security measures are essential for safeguarding user privacy (Shen & Ho, 2020).

In summary, Machine learning algorithms have transformed the personalization of educational resources in OER platforms by providing users with tailored recommendations that enhance learning efficiency, engagement, and accessibility. Collaborative filtering, content-based filtering, and hybrid recommendation systems allow learners to discover relevant content that aligns with their interests and academic goals. Moreover, these systems promote adaptive learning environments that adjust to individual learners' progress, supporting personalized educational pathways. However, developers of machine learning-powered recommendation systems must remain vigilant about addressing ethical concerns related to bias, inclusivity, and privacy. As machine learning technologies continue to evolve, their role in enhancing access to OER is poised to expand, creating more personalized and equitable learning experiences for a global audience.

Example: AI-Powered OER Repositories like OpenStax and Google Scholar

Artificial Intelligence (AI) is playing a transformative role in enhancing access to Open Educational Resources (OER) by powering sophisticated repositories such as OpenStax and Google Scholar. These platforms use AI-driven tools to improve the discoverability, curation, and personalization of educational materials, making it easier for learners and educators to access high-quality content. By leveraging machine learning, natural language processing (NLP), and data analytics, AI-powered OER repositories provide a more user-friendly and efficient way to navigate vast collections of resources.

OpenStax: Enhancing Educational Access with AI

OpenStax, a leading provider of free, peer-reviewed textbooks, has integrated AI technologies into its platform to optimize content delivery and enhance the learning experience for students and educators. Founded by Rice University, OpenStax aims to reduce the cost of educational materials while maintaining high academic standards. The platform uses AI-driven tools to curate content, provide personalized recommendations, and enhance the overall accessibility of its OER materials.

One of the key ways AI supports OpenStax is through its **adaptive learning platform**, which uses machine learning algorithms to tailor educational content to individual learners. OpenStax has partnered with companies such as Knewton and Lumen Learning to develop adaptive features that analyze a student's interactions with the content and adjust the difficulty and type of materials based on their performance (Hilton et al., 2016). For example, if a student struggles with a particular concept in a math textbook, the system can recommend additional exercises or alternative explanations to help the learner master the topic. This personalization ensures that each student receives a learning experience suited to their unique needs and learning pace.

Moreover, OpenStax incorporates AI-powered **learning analytics** to provide educators with real-time insights into student progress. These analytics tools help instructors identify which topics are causing difficulties for students and adjust their teaching strategies accordingly. By tracking student engagement and performance data, the platform can generate detailed reports that inform both students and educators about learning outcomes and areas for improvement (Feldstein et al., 2019). This data-driven approach not only enhances student learning but also supports instructors in delivering more effective and targeted instruction.

In addition to adaptive learning features, OpenStax leverages AI for **content curation** and **recommendation systems**. The platform's AI algorithms analyze user preferences, previous interactions, and the metadata of available resources to recommend textbooks and supplemental materials that align with the learner's goals. This ensures that students can easily find the most relevant OER for their studies, while educators can discover new teaching resources that fit their curricula (Hendricks et al., 2017).

Google Scholar: Revolutionizing Knowledge Discovery through AI

Google Scholar, another AI-powered platform, has become a vital tool for accessing academic research and OER. Since its launch in 2004, Google Scholar has transformed the way scholars, educators, and students search for academic materials, including journal articles, theses, books, and conference papers. The platform uses a range of AI technologies, particularly **natural language processing (NLP)** and **machine learning**, to enhance search functionality, improve indexing, and ensure the retrieval of relevant resources.

One of the major advantages of Google Scholar is its use of **semantic search**, which goes beyond simple keyword matching to understand the context and meaning of a user's query. NLP algorithms enable the platform to interpret the intent behind a query, identifying synonyms, related concepts, and academic terminologies that might not be explicitly mentioned in the search terms. For instance, a search for "climate change impact on agriculture" might return results that include studies on "global warming" and "crop yield variations," reflecting the system's ability to capture related topics (Ortega, 2019). This functionality significantly improves the precision and relevance of search results, particularly for complex or interdisciplinary queries.

In addition to advanced search capabilities, Google Scholar employs machine learning algorithms to rank search results based on relevance and citation patterns. The platform analyzes factors such as citation counts, publication dates, and author prominence to present the most authoritative and impactful academic works at the top of the search results (Beel & Gipp, 2009). This ranking system ensures that users have quick access to high-quality, peer-reviewed materials, which is particularly useful for educators and students seeking trustworthy OER for their academic work.

Another important AI-driven feature of Google Scholar is its **recommendation system**, which provides personalized suggestions for related research articles based on a user's search history and previous interactions. This system helps users discover new academic resources that they may not have initially considered but that are highly relevant to their research interests. By analyzing patterns in user behavior, Google Scholar can recommend articles, papers, and books that align with the user's academic needs (Chen et al., 2017). This personalized recommendation engine enhances knowledge discovery and promotes more efficient research by guiding users toward content that fits their specific academic goals.

Moreover, Google Scholar integrates **citation tracking** tools, which allow users to follow how frequently and where a particular work has been cited across the academic landscape. This feature is powered by machine learning algorithms that analyze citation networks, helping users assess the influence and relevance of specific publications within their fields of study (Halevi et al., 2017). For researchers, this is particularly valuable in identifying key works that have shaped the discourse in a given academic area, while educators can use this information to curate authoritative OER for their courses.

The Impact of AI-Powered OER Repositories on Knowledge Discovery

Both OpenStax and Google Scholar exemplify how AI-powered OER repositories can transform the educational landscape by improving access to high-quality, relevant content. These platforms not only enhance the discoverability of educational resources but also promote personalized learning experiences through adaptive algorithms and intelligent recommendation systems. The integration of AI technologies, such as machine learning and NLP, ensures that users can efficiently navigate vast repositories of academic materials, making knowledge discovery more streamlined and tailored to individual needs.

The application of AI in platforms like OpenStax and Google Scholar also fosters greater educational equity by making high-quality resources more accessible to a broader audience. By offering free or low-cost access to textbooks, research papers, and other educational content, these repositories play a critical role in democratizing education. Learners and educators from diverse socio-economic backgrounds can benefit from AI-powered platforms that facilitate the discovery of relevant, credible, and up-to-date OER (Pérez-Peña et al., 2019).

Conclusion

AI-powered OER repositories like OpenStax and Google Scholar are at the forefront of transforming knowledge discovery in education. Through the integration of machine learning algorithms, NLP, and adaptive technologies, these platforms offer personalized, efficient, and accessible educational experiences. OpenStax's adaptive learning features and content curation tools, alongside Google Scholar's advanced search and recommendation systems, exemplify how AI can enhance the discoverability and usability of OER. As AI technologies continue to evolve, their role in supporting educational access and personalized learning will only become more significant, contributing to a more equitable and efficient global education system.

References

Ahmad, S., Ghosh, S., Gaur, M., & Prasad, M. (2020). Natural language processing for multilingual OER: Challenges and opportunities. *IEEE Access, 8*, 67510-67524.

Alzahrani, S., Salim, N., & Abraham, A. (2018). Exploring the impact of NLP techniques on improving indexing for academic documents. *Journal of Information Science, 44*(4), 467-480.

Amami, R., Ghezala, H. H. B., & Abed, M. (2019). Machine learning-based recommender systems in OERs: A review of existing literature and future trends. *Journal of Computer Science and Information Technology, 7*(1), 123-135.

Beel, J., & Gipp, B. (2009). Google Scholar's ranking algorithm: An introductory overview. *Proceedings of the 12th International Conference on Scientometrics and Informetrics.*

Bergamaschi, S., & Po, L. (2020). Personalized recommendation systems using machine learning in open educational resources (OER). *Expert Systems with Applications, 146*, 113-129.

Binns, R. (2018). Fairness in machine learning: Lessons from political philosophy. *Proceedings of the 2018 Conference on Fairness, Accountability, and Transparency.*

Butcher, N., Hoosen, S., Levey, L., & Moore, J. (2020). AI-powered OER discovery framework. *Commonwealth of Learning.*

Chen, Y., Yang, J., & Wang, X. (2017). Collaborative filtering for personalized learning recommendation systems: Application in open educational resources (OER). *Journal of Educational Computing Research, 56*(5), 1-17.

Colvin, C., Rogers, T., Wade, A., Dawson, S., & Gasevic, D. (2016). The impact of learning analytics on student success: A review of findings. *Higher Education Research & Development, 35*(5), 966-980.

Drachsler, H., & Greller, W. (2016). Privacy and learning analytics—It's a DELICATE issue: A checklist for trusted implementation of learning analytics. *Proceedings of the Sixth International Conference on Learning Analytics & Knowledge.*

Feldstein, A., Hilton, J., & Murphy, L. (2019). Adaptive learning systems and their impact on OER: A case study of OpenStax. *Journal of Online Learning Research, 5*(2), 243-257.

Garcia, F., Guerrero, L. A., & Ordoñez, A. (2020). Personalized content curation using natural language processing and machine learning in e-learning environments. *Journal of Educational Technology & Society, 23*(1), 29-41.

Halevi, G., Moed, H. F., & Bar-Ilan, J. (2017). Suitability of Google Scholar as a source of scientific evaluation and analysis. *Scientometrics, 111*(1), 183-198.

Hendricks, C., Reinsberg, S., & Rieger, G. W. (2017). The adoption of open textbooks by post-secondary institutions: The role of instructors. *The International Review of Research in Open and Distributed Learning, 18*(4), 1-17.

Hilton, J., Bliss, T., & Smith, R. (2016). Open educational resources and open textbooks: Examining adoption and use in higher education. *International Journal of Open Educational Resources, 3*(1), 135-153.

Hovy, E., & Marcu, D. (2021). Automatic text summarization: A review of the state of the art. *Computational Linguistics, 47*(3), 1-30.

Kastrati, Z., Imran, A., & Drira, K. (2020). Automatic topic discovery and content recommendation in OER repositories using NLP and deep learning. *Computers & Education, 149*, 103825.

Klašnja-Milićević, A., Vesin, B., Ivanović, M., & Budimac, Z. (2017). E-learning personalization based on hybrid recommendation strategy and learning style identification. *Computers & Education, 56*(3), 885-899.

Kurdi, M., Leo, J., Calvo, R. A., & Gutierrez, F. (2020). Machine learning for multilingual accessibility of open educational resources. *Computers & Education, 146*, 103743.

Lee, J. (2018). Recommender systems for open educational resources: The opportunities and challenges of implementing artificial intelligence for education. *Journal of Educational Technology Systems, 46*(3), 305-325.

Lee, K. H., Kim, J. H., & Choi, H. (2019). Personalized learning paths and OER recommendation using natural language processing and machine learning. *Education and Information Technologies, 24*(3), 1327-1345.

Lops, P., Gemmis, M. D., & Semeraro, G. (2011). Content-based recommender systems: State of the art and trends. *Recommender Systems Handbook, 34*(1), 73-105.

Manning, C., Schütze, H., & Raghavan, P. (2020). **Introduction to information retrieval**. Cambridge University Press.

McGreal, R. (2018). The need for open educational resources in distance education. *Distance Education, 39*(1), 1-4.

Mehrabi, N., Morstatter, F., Saxena, N., Lerman, K., & Galstyan, A. (2021). A survey on bias and fairness in machine learning. *ACM Computing Surveys, 54*(6), 1-35.

Ortega, J. L. (2019). The role of artificial intelligence in enhancing the discovery of academic resources. *Scientometrics, 121*(2), 987-1005.

Pérez-Peña, P., Marzà, N., & Palazón-Herrera, J. M. (2019). Free textbooks in higher education: The case of OpenStax. *Education and Information Technologies, 24*(3), 2655-2672

Pouyioutas, P., Jimoyiannis, A., & Olibani, F. (2018). X5GON: Cross-modal, cross-lingual, cross-cultural global open educational resources network. *Proceedings of the 2018 International Conference on E-Learning and Open Education Resources (ICOE).*

Resnick, P., & Varian, H. R. (1997). Recommender systems. *Communications of the ACM, 40*(3), 56-58.

Ritzhaupt, A. D., Dawson, K., & Lehman, B. (2021). Artificial intelligence in education: Current trends and emerging applications. *Journal of Computer-Assisted Learning, 37*(5), 1195-1213.

Schafer, J. B., Frankowski, D., Herlocker, J., & Sen, S. (2007). Collaborative filtering recommender systems. In *The adaptive web* (pp. 291-324). Springer.

Shen, L., & Ho, J. (2020). Machine learning and data privacy: Transparency, trust, and regulation. *Proceedings of the 2020 International Conference on Privacy, Data, and Regulation.*

Siemens, G. (2020). Learning analytics and AI in education: Opportunities and challenges. *Educational Data Mining and Learning Analytics, 12*(1), 5-19.

Stracke, C. M. (2019). Accessibility and quality of open educational resources: A meta-analysis. *Educational Technology Research and Development, 67*(2), 283-304.

Chapter 5: Automating Content Curation and Personalization

AI Tools for Creating Personalized Learning Pathways Based on OER

Artificial Intelligence (AI) has brought significant advancements in education, particularly in the realm of Open Educational Resources (OER). One of the most impactful applications of AI is its ability to automate content curation and create personalized learning pathways for students. By leveraging machine learning algorithms, natural language processing (NLP), and data analytics, AI tools can analyze learner behaviors, preferences, and performance to tailor educational content in a way that meets individual learning needs.

AI-Driven Content Curation for Personalized Learning

Content curation, traditionally a labor-intensive process, has been greatly enhanced by AI technologies, which can sift through vast collections of OER to select and organize content based on individual learning goals. AI-powered tools are capable of analyzing both the characteristics of the educational resources and the specific needs of learners to deliver curated, high-quality materials.

For example, platforms like **Knewton** and **Smart Sparrow** utilize AI algorithms to assess student interactions with learning materials, adapting the sequence of resources presented to match the learner's progress. These systems rely on **data-driven insights** to predict which resources will be most beneficial for a student based on their previous performance and engagement patterns (Colvin et al., 2016). In OER repositories, this means that instead of a one-size-fits-all approach, students receive tailored suggestions for textbooks, articles, and exercises that align with their specific academic needs.

The ability to dynamically curate content allows educators and learners to navigate vast OER repositories more efficiently. For instance, if a student is struggling with foundational concepts in mathematics, AI algorithms can recommend remedial resources before advancing to more complex topics. Conversely, for advanced learners, the system can bypass basic materials and present more challenging content, fostering a **competency-based learning** approach (Johnson et al., 2017).

Personalized Learning Pathways through Adaptive Learning Systems

AI-powered adaptive learning systems are at the forefront of creating personalized learning pathways using OER. These systems adjust instructional content in real-time, guiding learners through customized learning journeys based on their unique needs, abilities, and preferences. Adaptive learning platforms, such as **DreamBox** and **ALEKS**, use machine learning to monitor student performance and adapt the difficulty, sequence, and type of resources provided (Baker et al., 2020). This approach is particularly effective in ensuring that learners progress at their own pace while receiving support when needed.

For example, in an OER-based adaptive learning environment, a student who demonstrates difficulty with certain math problems might be provided with additional resources, such as video tutorials or interactive exercises, to reinforce the topic. The system continuously monitors the student's performance, adjusting the complexity of future resources based on their progress. This **feedback loop** ensures that the learning experience is both personalized and responsive to the student's evolving needs.

Moreover, AI-powered adaptive learning tools can analyze large datasets to identify learning patterns that would otherwise go unnoticed. By tracking a student's engagement with various types of OER (e.g., textbooks, videos, quizzes), these systems can predict the most effective learning modalities for each individual. As a result, students receive personalized pathways that align with their cognitive preferences and learning styles, ultimately leading to more effective and engaging learning experiences (Popenici & Kerr, 2017).

The Role of NLP in Personalizing Learning Pathways

Natural Language Processing (NLP) plays a key role in enhancing the personalization of OER by enabling AI systems to analyze and understand the textual content of learning materials. NLP allows AI tools to categorize, index, and retrieve OER based on the semantic meaning of the text, ensuring that the most relevant resources are recommended to learners.

For example, an AI-powered system might analyze a student's written assignments or discussion forum contributions to identify areas where additional learning support is needed. By processing the language used by the student, the system can recommend specific OER, such as readings or exercises, that target the concepts the student is struggling with (Kastrati et al., 2021). NLP enables a more nuanced understanding of both the content and the learner, resulting in personalized learning pathways that are closely aligned with the individual's academic development.

NLP also facilitates **automated assessment** and **feedback**. For example, in language learning, AI systems can analyze student essays, providing detailed feedback on grammar, syntax, and content coherence. These systems can then recommend additional OER, such as grammar exercises or writing tutorials, to address the specific weaknesses identified in the student's writing (Garcia & Liao, 2021). By integrating NLP into the personalization process, AI tools can create more tailored and efficient learning pathways that directly address the learner's needs.

AI-Powered OER Repositories and Personalization

AI-powered OER repositories such as **X5GON** (Cross Modal, Cross Cultural, Cross Lingual, Cross Domain, and Cross Site Global OER Network) represent another advancement in personalizing learning pathways. These platforms use AI to aggregate OER from various sources and personalize the delivery of content based on user preferences and learning behaviors (Pouyioutas et al., 2018). X5GON's recommendation engine analyzes user data, such as previous searches and content interactions, to suggest the most relevant OER across different languages and domains.

This type of AI-driven personalization is particularly valuable in large OER repositories, where learners may otherwise struggle to navigate vast amounts of content. By using machine learning algorithms to identify patterns in user behavior, these platforms can deliver highly personalized recommendations that enhance the learning experience. In this way, AI not only automates content curation but also helps learners find the right resources at the right time, ensuring that they remain engaged and motivated.

The Benefits of Personalized Learning Pathways for Learners

The use of AI to create personalized learning pathways offers numerous benefits for learners. First, it helps reduce **information overload**, a common challenge in OER environments where learners are confronted with a vast array of resources. AI-powered tools streamline the discovery process by curating content that is directly relevant to the learner's current academic needs, eliminating the need for extensive manual searches (Siemens, 2020).

Second, personalized learning pathways support **differentiated instruction**, allowing learners to receive content that matches their unique learning styles and pace. Whether a student requires more time to master certain concepts or is ready to advance to more challenging material, AI systems ensure that the learning experience is aligned with the individual's abilities and goals. This personalized approach has been shown to improve learning outcomes, as students are more likely to remain engaged and motivated when the content is tailored to their specific needs (Klašnja-Milićević et al., 2017).

Finally, AI-driven personalization fosters **lifelong learning** by providing learners with continuous access to resources that support their academic and professional development. As learners progress through different stages of education and career, AI systems can adapt their learning pathways to accommodate new interests and goals, ensuring that they receive relevant and up-to-date content throughout their educational journey (Brown et al., 2021).

In summary, AI tools for automating content curation and creating personalized learning pathways have revolutionized access to OER, making educational resources more accessible, relevant, and engaging for learners. By leveraging machine learning, NLP, and adaptive learning technologies, AI can curate content that aligns with individual learning needs, create customized learning pathways, and provide real-time feedback to enhance the learning experience. As AI technologies continue to advance, their ability to personalize OER will further democratize education, ensuring that learners from all backgrounds have access to high-quality, tailored learning experiences.

Adaptive Learning Technologies

Adaptive learning technologies, powered by Artificial Intelligence (AI), are revolutionizing the personalization of education by tailoring content to meet individual learning styles. These technologies utilize machine learning algorithms, data analytics, and real-time feedback to customize the learning experience based on a learner's unique preferences, strengths, and weaknesses. When applied to Open Educational Resources (OER), adaptive learning technologies have the potential to provide personalized learning experiences that enhance engagement, understanding, and retention.

Understanding Learning Styles in the Context of Adaptive Learning

Learning styles refer to the various ways individuals prefer to absorb, process, and retain information. While traditional classroom settings often adopt a one-size-fits-all approach, adaptive learning technologies offer the flexibility to accommodate diverse learning styles. Commonly recognized learning styles include visual, auditory, reading/writing, and kinesthetic (Fleming, 2012). Each style represents a different modality through which learners engage with content, and adaptive learning systems can detect these preferences to personalize the learning pathway.

For instance, a **visual learner** may benefit from content delivered through infographics, charts, and videos, while an **auditory learner** might prefer audio lectures or podcasts. In contrast, a **reading/writing learner** may engage more effectively with written content such as textbooks or articles, and a **kinesthetic learner** might prefer interactive, hands-on learning experiences. Adaptive learning technologies use AI to identify these preferences by analyzing a learner's interactions with various types of content and adjusting the mode of delivery to match their preferred learning style (Pashler et al., 2009).

By leveraging OER, adaptive learning platforms can curate resources in multiple formats, ensuring that learners have access to the type of content that best suits their needs. This approach enhances accessibility by making learning more inclusive and responsive to the individual, leading to improved educational outcomes (Fletcher & Carter, 2018).

AI-Driven Personalization in Adaptive Learning Systems

The success of adaptive learning technologies hinges on their ability to personalize the learning experience. AI systems, using data from learner interactions, monitor progress in real-time and adjust content delivery to address individual learning needs. These adjustments are based on a combination of **machine learning algorithms** that analyze patterns in learner behavior and **cognitive models** that map how students absorb and process information (Johnson et al., 2017).

For example, if a learner demonstrates a preference for visual materials, the adaptive system may prioritize videos, animations, or diagrams in future lessons. Conversely, if the system detects that a learner excels in text-based assessments but struggles with auditory tasks, it might suggest more reading materials or offer textual explanations for concepts introduced through audio. This continuous adjustment ensures that the learning process is dynamically aligned with the learner's evolving preferences and abilities (Chatti et al., 2016).

A key feature of these AI-driven systems is their ability to provide **real-time feedback**, which is crucial for supporting individual learning styles. Real-time feedback allows learners to understand their progress immediately and make adjustments to their learning strategies as needed. For instance, an adaptive learning platform might notify a student when they have mastered a specific concept, suggesting more advanced materials or reinforcing areas where additional practice is required (Baker et al., 2020). This feedback loop not only keeps learners engaged but also helps educators tailor instructional interventions more effectively.

Adaptive Learning Systems and Competency-Based Education

One of the most significant applications of adaptive learning technologies is in **competency-based education (CBE)**, where learners progress at their own pace by demonstrating mastery of specific skills or knowledge. Adaptive learning platforms, integrated with OER, are particularly well-suited to CBE because they can provide personalized pathways that guide learners through the curriculum based on their unique learning styles and proficiency levels (Pane et al., 2017).

In a CBE environment, adaptive learning systems assess learners' current knowledge and skills, identifying areas where they need additional support or more advanced content. For example, if a student demonstrates a strong understanding of basic programming concepts, the system might bypass introductory materials and recommend more complex coding exercises. Conversely, if the student struggles with foundational concepts, the system will suggest remedial resources, such as tutorials or interactive coding simulations, which align with their learning preferences (Miller et al., 2016).

By tailoring the content to match both the learner's skill level and preferred learning style, adaptive learning technologies ensure that students receive the right resources at the right time, facilitating deeper understanding and retention of knowledge. The ability to integrate OER into these systems further democratizes education by providing free, high-quality resources that can be personalized for learners from diverse backgrounds (Roschelle et al., 2017).

Case Studies: Adaptive Learning in OER Platforms

Several OER platforms have integrated adaptive learning technologies to provide personalized learning experiences based on individual learning styles. One notable example is **Smart Sparrow**, an adaptive learning platform that uses AI to analyze learner behaviors and tailor educational content accordingly. Smart Sparrow's AI algorithms track how students interact with different types of content—whether they spend more time on videos, simulations, or quizzes—and adjust the learning materials to better suit their preferences (Zualkernan, 2020). This personalized approach has proven effective in improving learner engagement and knowledge retention.

Similarly, **CogBooks**, another AI-powered adaptive learning platform, integrates OER to create customized learning paths for students. The platform uses real-time data analytics to identify each learner's strengths and weaknesses, suggesting resources that cater to their individual learning styles. For instance, a student who demonstrates a preference for hands-on learning might be directed to interactive exercises and simulations, while another who excels in reading-based tasks might receive additional text-based resources (Johnson et al., 2020).

These case studies demonstrate how adaptive learning technologies, combined with OER, can transform the educational experience by ensuring that content delivery is personalized and aligned with individual learning styles. By continuously refining the learning pathway, these systems keep students engaged and motivated, leading to better educational outcomes.

Benefits and Challenges of Adaptive Learning in OER

The benefits of adaptive learning technologies in OER are clear: they provide a more personalized, flexible, and engaging learning experience. By catering to different learning styles, adaptive systems ensure that learners receive content in the format that best suits their preferences, leading to improved comprehension and retention of knowledge. Furthermore, by integrating OER into these systems, learners gain access to a wide range of free, high-quality educational resources, reducing barriers to education (Pane et al., 2017).

However, challenges remain in the widespread adoption of adaptive learning technologies. One of the primary concerns is the **cost and complexity of implementation**. Developing and maintaining AI-driven adaptive learning platforms requires significant technical infrastructure and expertise, which may not be readily available to all educational institutions, particularly in developing regions (Siemens, 2020). Additionally, ensuring that AI systems are inclusive and free from bias is crucial for providing equitable access to personalized learning pathways.

Another challenge is the need for **data privacy and security**. Adaptive learning systems rely on large datasets to personalize content, raising concerns about how student data is collected, stored, and used. Ensuring that learners' privacy is protected and that their data is used ethically is critical for building trust in AI-powered educational technologies (Shen & Ho, 2020).

In summary, adaptive learning technologies are transforming the way OER is delivered by tailoring content to individual learning styles. Through the use of AI, these systems personalize learning experiences based on learners' preferences, strengths, and progress. By integrating machine learning algorithms, real-time feedback, and competency-based education principles, adaptive learning platforms enhance the accessibility and effectiveness of OER. While challenges remain in terms of implementation, cost, and data privacy, the potential for adaptive learning technologies to provide personalized education at scale is immense. As these technologies continue to evolve, their ability to cater to diverse learning styles will play a crucial role in democratizing education and enhancing learner outcomes.

Case Study:

Coursera and edX are two of the largest Massive Open Online Course (MOOC) platforms, offering free and paid educational content from leading universities and institutions worldwide. These platforms have integrated Artificial Intelligence (AI) to automate the curation and personalization of courses, making it easier for learners to access high-quality, relevant content. By leveraging machine learning algorithms, natural language processing (NLP), and data analytics, Coursera and edX use AI to enhance the user experience, provide personalized learning pathways, and ensure that learners can navigate vast repositories of Open Educational Resources (OER). This case study explores how these platforms use AI technologies to curate free courses and facilitate personalized learning.

Coursera: AI-Powered Course Recommendations and Personalization

Coursera, a global MOOC provider launched in 2012, offers a wide range of free and paid courses, specializations, and degrees. As the platform has grown, it has increasingly relied on AI to streamline content discovery and personalize learning pathways for its users. Coursera's AI-driven recommendation system curates courses based on individual preferences, previous interactions, and user behavior.

One of the key AI-driven tools used by Coursera is its **personalized recommendation engine**, which suggests courses to users based on their browsing history, course completions, and stated learning goals. This system uses **collaborative filtering** and **content-based filtering** techniques to analyze the learning patterns of similar users and recommend courses that align with a learner's interests (Dziugaite et al., 2015). For example, if a user has completed courses in data science, the platform might recommend advanced courses in machine learning or Python programming. The recommendation system continuously updates as the learner progresses, ensuring that the content is relevant to their evolving academic needs.

Coursera also uses AI to offer **personalized learning plans**, particularly for users enrolled in multi-course specializations. These learning plans help students map out their educational journey by suggesting the order in which courses should be taken, the time commitment required, and any additional resources that may be beneficial. The AI system takes into account factors such as the learner's performance in previous courses, their schedule preferences, and their learning pace, allowing for a tailored educational experience (Zhu et al., 2018).

In addition to personalized recommendations, Coursera's AI tools monitor **learner engagement** and **course completion rates**. The platform tracks user activity and provides real-time feedback, allowing educators to make adjustments to course materials if engagement levels are low. For example, if a course module has a high drop-off rate, Coursera's AI might flag this to the instructor, who can then modify the content to improve retention. This continuous feedback loop helps Coursera curate courses that are not only aligned with user preferences but also optimized for learning effectiveness (Chuang et al., 2016).

edX: Adaptive Learning and AI-Enhanced Curation

edX, another leading MOOC provider founded by Harvard and MIT in 2012, has similarly integrated AI into its platform to enhance the curation and personalization of free courses. With millions of users globally, edX uses AI to manage its vast repository of OER, ensuring that learners have access to the most relevant courses based on their individual needs and goals.

One of edX's most innovative uses of AI is its **adaptive learning technology**, which personalizes the learning experience by dynamically adjusting the content delivery based on the learner's progress and performance. This technology is particularly useful in edX's MicroMasters and Professional Certificate programs, where students can receive tailored course recommendations and additional resources to fill knowledge gaps. For example, if a learner struggles with a specific concept in a course on artificial intelligence, edX's AI system might suggest supplementary materials, such as readings or videos, to help the learner understand the topic better (DeBoer et al., 2014).

The adaptive learning system on edX also uses **real-time analytics** to monitor how learners engage with course content. By analyzing data on quiz performance, video engagement, and forum participation, edX's AI algorithms can identify areas where learners may need additional support. The system can then recommend practice exercises or alternative resources that align with the learner's preferred mode of study, whether it's video lectures, interactive exercises, or reading-based content (Seaton et al., 2013).

Another significant AI-driven feature of edX is its **learning path recommendations**, which guide learners through a personalized sequence of courses. Similar to Coursera, edX's recommendation engine uses machine learning algorithms to analyze learner behavior and course content, ensuring that users are presented with courses that match their academic background and learning goals. For instance, if a learner completes an introductory course in computer science, edX might recommend more advanced programming courses or complementary subjects such as cybersecurity or software development (Kizilcec et al., 2017).

In addition to personalizing course recommendations, edX uses AI for **course optimization**. The platform's AI tools analyze user feedback, course completion rates, and learner engagement metrics to identify courses that require improvements. This data-driven approach allows edX to curate its OER repository more effectively, ensuring that only the highest-quality and most relevant courses remain available to learners (Coughlan et al., 2020). Instructors are also provided with AI-generated insights on learner performance, enabling them to make data-driven decisions about course revisions and enhancements.

The Role of AI in Expanding Access to Free Courses

Both Coursera and edX use AI to make high-quality educational content more accessible by curating free courses that meet the diverse needs of learners worldwide. AI-powered curation ensures that learners are not overwhelmed by the vast number of available courses but are instead presented with personalized recommendations that align with their interests, learning styles, and academic goals. This approach democratizes access to education by making it easier for learners from different backgrounds to find and engage with relevant content.

Moreover, AI enhances the learning experience by enabling **continuous personalization**. As learners progress through their courses, AI systems update their recommendations and learning paths, ensuring that content remains relevant and challenging. This level of personalization is particularly important for adult learners, working professionals, and non-traditional students who may require more flexible learning options (Veletsianos & Shepherdson, 2016). By offering curated, personalized content, Coursera and edX help learners make the most of their educational opportunities without the constraints of time, location, or prior knowledge.

Conclusion

Coursera and edX serve as prime examples of how AI can be harnessed to automate content curation and create personalized learning experiences in the context of OER. By using machine learning algorithms, collaborative filtering, and real-time analytics, these platforms are able to provide tailored course recommendations, adaptive learning paths, and optimized content delivery. AI not only enhances the discoverability of free courses but also improves learner engagement, retention, and success. As these technologies continue to evolve, Coursera and edX are likely to further expand their use of AI, contributing to more personalized, accessible, and effective educational experiences for learners worldwide.

Chapter 6: AI for Improving Searchability and Accessibility

Semantic Search and AI in Organizing OER Metadata

The rapid expansion of Open Educational Resources (OER) has created vast repositories of free educational content, but navigating and efficiently accessing this content can be challenging. Artificial Intelligence (AI) has introduced sophisticated solutions to improve the searchability and accessibility of OER, particularly through semantic search and the organization of metadata. By leveraging Natural Language Processing (NLP), machine learning, and advanced data analytics, AI enhances the way educational content is categorized, indexed, and retrieved.

The Role of Semantic Search in Enhancing Discoverability

Traditional keyword-based search engines often struggle to provide accurate and relevant results, particularly when queries are complex or when the search terms do not exactly match the metadata of the OER. Semantic search, powered by AI, addresses these limitations by understanding the contextual meaning behind search queries, allowing for more intuitive and relevant results. Semantic search goes beyond simple keyword matching and uses **NLP** to interpret the intent and relationships between words, improving the overall discoverability of educational resources (Cui et al., 2017).

For example, a user searching for "how machine learning can improve healthcare diagnostics" would not need to rely on exact keyword matches like "machine learning" or "healthcare." Instead, semantic search would analyze the query's intent and retrieve OER that discuss related topics such as artificial intelligence in medical imaging, predictive analytics for disease detection, or case studies on AI-driven healthcare innovations. By understanding the meaning behind the words, semantic search ensures that the user is presented with a broader and more accurate set of educational resources (Blanco et al., 2019).

Moreover, semantic search enhances accessibility by providing results in multiple formats, such as articles, videos, or interactive simulations, based on the user's learning preferences. For instance, if a learner prefers visual content, the search engine can prioritize video-based resources or infographics that align with the learner's query. This level of customization helps learners access the most relevant OER more quickly, reducing the time spent sorting through unrelated materials (Yimam et al., 2020).

AI and the Organization of OER Metadata

AI also plays a critical role in improving the organization and management of OER metadata. Metadata, which includes descriptive information about a resource (such as the title, author, keywords, and subject), is essential for categorizing and retrieving educational content. However, manually creating and managing metadata for the vast amounts of OER available is time-consuming and prone to inconsistency. AI automates this process, enabling more accurate and consistent metadata generation and updating across large OER repositories (Abdelrahman & Aboud, 2021).

Using **machine learning algorithms** and **NLP**, AI systems can automatically generate metadata by analyzing the content of OER. For example, AI tools can scan the full text of an educational resource, extract key concepts, topics, and themes, and then create metadata tags that accurately reflect the content. These tags can include subject classifications, educational levels, and relevant keywords, which improve the resource's discoverability in search results (Xiao et al., 2018).

One key advantage of AI-generated metadata is its ability to identify complex relationships between topics. For instance, in an OER repository that covers various disciplines such as biology, computer science, and medicine, AI can detect interdisciplinary connections that may not be immediately apparent to human curators. A resource on gene sequencing, for example, might be relevant to both genetics students and data scientists working on bioinformatics algorithms. By creating metadata that reflects these connections, AI enables users from different fields to discover relevant OER that they might not have otherwise found (Baker & Beutel, 2020).

Enhancing OER Accessibility through Improved Metadata

Improving the quality and consistency of OER metadata directly impacts the accessibility of educational content, particularly for learners who require specific resources. AI-generated metadata can include accessibility tags, such as whether a resource is available in multiple languages, whether it has text-to-speech capabilities, or if it includes closed captions for video content. These tags ensure that learners with disabilities or language barriers can easily find OER that meet their accessibility needs (Ball et al., 2020).

In addition, AI-driven metadata systems can help curators maintain up-to-date OER repositories by identifying outdated or redundant resources. For example, if a course or textbook is no longer relevant due to advancements in the field, AI systems can flag the resource for review or update. Similarly, AI can recommend when newer, more comprehensive OER should be added to the repository, ensuring that learners always have access to the latest educational materials (Wiley & Hilton, 2018). This process not only enhances the quality of the repository but also helps learners find the most accurate and up-to-date information.

AI systems can also incorporate **personalized metadata**, which tracks users' interactions with OER and tailors future searches based on their preferences. For example, if a learner frequently engages with resources related to economics and finance, AI can prioritize search results and recommendations for OER in these areas. This personalized approach helps learners navigate large repositories more efficiently by delivering content that aligns with their learning goals and academic interests (Nguyen et al., 2021).

The Impact of AI-Enhanced OER Searchability on Educational Equity

The improvements in searchability and metadata organization brought about by AI contribute to greater educational equity. By providing learners with access to the most relevant and personalized educational materials, AI-powered OER platforms help bridge gaps in education, particularly for students from underserved or marginalized communities. Semantic search ensures that learners can access high-quality resources even if they are unfamiliar with specific academic terminology, while AI-generated metadata makes it easier to find accessible content that meets diverse learning needs.

Moreover, the ability to automatically organize and update OER repositories means that learners in resource-constrained environments can access the same up-to-date and relevant materials as those in more affluent regions. This democratization of knowledge ensures that all learners, regardless of their location or socio-economic status, can benefit from the educational resources available in global OER repositories (Hilton, 2020).

In summary, AI is playing an instrumental role in improving the searchability and accessibility of OER through semantic search and automated metadata organization. By using NLP to understand the context and intent of search queries, semantic search delivers more relevant and personalized results to learners. At the same time, AI-generated metadata ensures that OER repositories are consistently and accurately categorized, enhancing the discoverability of resources across various disciplines. As AI technologies continue to evolve, their ability to improve the organization, retrieval, and accessibility of OER will be crucial in supporting educational equity and providing learners worldwide with access to high-quality, personalized educational content.

Voice Search and AI Assistants for Accessing OER

Voice search and AI assistants are emerging as transformative tools in enhancing access to Open Educational Resources (OER). With advancements in artificial intelligence (AI) technologies such as speech recognition, natural language processing (NLP), and machine learning, voice-activated systems are making it easier for learners to interact with educational resources. These technologies improve the accessibility of OER by allowing users to search, retrieve, and engage with content through voice commands, which is particularly beneficial for learners with disabilities or those in resource-limited environments.

The Role of Voice Search in Enhancing OER Access

Voice search has become a mainstream feature in modern digital environments, thanks to the proliferation of AI-driven voice recognition systems like **Google Assistant**, **Amazon Alexa**, and **Apple Siri**. These systems rely on advanced speech recognition algorithms and NLP to interpret spoken queries and return relevant results. In the context of OER, voice search enables users to interact with educational content more naturally and efficiently, eliminating the need for typed queries (Yadav et al., 2021).

Voice search enhances the accessibility of OER in several ways. First, it provides a more inclusive experience for learners with physical disabilities that make typing difficult or impossible. By allowing users to speak their search queries, voice search removes barriers for individuals with motor impairments or conditions like arthritis, who may struggle with traditional input methods. Similarly, for learners with visual impairments, voice search offers an accessible alternative to navigating text-heavy interfaces, allowing them to easily access educational resources through spoken commands (Arora & Sinha, 2019).

Moreover, voice search improves efficiency and convenience for all learners by enabling hands-free interaction with OER platforms. For example, students who are multitasking - such as those studying while commuting or performing other activities - can use voice commands to search for resources, retrieve information, or even have text-based OER read aloud. This functionality not only enhances the user experience but also expands the contexts in which learners can engage with educational materials (Hoy, 2018).

The integration of AI-powered **speech-to-text** technologies further supports voice search by transcribing spoken queries into text, which is then processed by OER search engines to return relevant results. Voice search systems are increasingly capable of understanding complex queries, including those with multiple parts or specific academic terminology. For instance, a user might ask, "Find introductory physics lectures on Newton's laws of motion," and the system will accurately retrieve OER related to this topic, without the need for exact keyword matching (Porcheron et al., 2018).

AI Assistants and Their Role in Personalizing OER Access

AI assistants, such as Google Assistant, Amazon Alexa, and IBM Watson, extend the capabilities of voice search by providing personalized interactions and tailored recommendations for OER. These AI-driven systems use machine learning algorithms to analyze user behavior, preferences, and previous interactions with educational content, enabling them to curate personalized learning experiences (Gupta et al., 2020).

AI assistants can act as **learning companions**, helping students navigate vast repositories of OER by providing suggestions, reminders, and even real-time feedback. For example, a student studying calculus might ask, "What are some practice problems for integrals?" The AI assistant, based on the student's past queries and progress, could recommend specific OER, such as interactive exercises or video tutorials on integration techniques. By personalizing the content retrieval process, AI assistants help learners access the most relevant resources without having to manually search through extensive collections (Harvey et al., 2019).

One of the key strengths of AI assistants in the OER space is their ability to support **natural language dialogue** with users. Unlike traditional search engines that rely on specific keywords, AI assistants can interpret conversational language, allowing users to interact with the system more naturally. For example, a learner could engage in a back-and-forth dialogue with an AI assistant, asking follow-up questions, seeking clarifications, or requesting additional resources on a particular topic. This interactive approach enables deeper engagement with educational content, as the AI assistant can provide context, explanations, and recommendations based on the user's learning journey (Hoy, 2018).

Furthermore, AI assistants can facilitate **multi-modal learning** by integrating OER across various formats. For instance, an AI assistant might retrieve a text-based article, suggest related video lectures, and even provide interactive quizzes to test the learner's understanding. By offering a range of resource formats, AI assistants cater to different learning styles and preferences, ensuring that learners can access content in the way that suits them best (Gupta et al., 2020).

Enhancing Accessibility through Voice-Activated OER Systems

Voice search and AI assistants significantly improve the accessibility of OER for diverse learners, including those with disabilities and those in multilingual environments. AI-powered voice recognition systems are now capable of processing multiple languages and dialects, allowing non-native speakers to access OER in their preferred language. For example, a student in a French-speaking country could ask for "les ressources éducatives ouvertes en biologie" (open educational resources in biology), and the AI system would provide results in French or other relevant languages. This multilingual capability ensures that OER platforms can serve a global audience, reducing linguistic barriers to education (Yadav et al., 2021).

For learners with visual impairments, voice-activated systems can significantly enhance the educational experience by providing audio-based navigation and content retrieval. AI assistants can read aloud the titles and descriptions of OER, guide learners through course materials, and even provide audio versions of textbooks or articles. This functionality helps create a more inclusive learning environment, where students with disabilities can engage with OER on an equal footing with their peers (Porcheron et al., 2018).

Moreover, AI assistants can integrate with **screen readers** and other accessibility tools to offer a seamless experience for learners who rely on assistive technologies. For instance, a visually impaired learner could use a voice command to search for OER on machine learning, have the results read aloud by the AI assistant, and then use a screen reader to navigate through the selected resource. This integration of AI assistants with accessibility technologies enhances the overall accessibility of OER, ensuring that all learners can benefit from open educational resources regardless of their physical abilities (Arora & Sinha, 2019).

Challenges and Considerations in Implementing Voice Search and AI Assistants for OER

While voice search and AI assistants offer significant potential in improving the accessibility and searchability of OER, there are several challenges to consider. One of the primary challenges is ensuring the **accuracy and reliability** of AI-powered voice recognition systems. Although these technologies have advanced significantly, they may still struggle with accents, dialects, or background noise, leading to errors in query interpretation or results retrieval. Continuous improvements in speech recognition algorithms are necessary to address these limitations and provide a more reliable user experience (Gupta et al., 2020).

Another challenge is the **ethical use of data** in AI assistants. Voice search systems and AI assistants collect large amounts of user data, including voice recordings and interaction histories, to personalize recommendations and improve performance. Ensuring that this data is handled securely and used ethically is critical to maintaining user trust. Privacy concerns must be addressed through robust data protection policies, transparent data usage practices, and the implementation of strong security measures to prevent unauthorized access to personal information (Harvey et al., 2019).

In summary, voice search and AI assistants are powerful tools for enhancing the searchability and accessibility of OER. By allowing users to interact with educational content through voice commands, these technologies provide a more intuitive, inclusive, and efficient way to access resources. AI assistants further personalize the learning experience by curating content based on user preferences and enabling natural language dialogues. Despite some challenges, such as accuracy and privacy concerns, the integration of voice search and AI assistants into OER platforms has the potential to transform the way learners engage with educational resources, making learning more accessible and tailored to individual needs.

Improving Accessibility for Students with Disabilities through AI

Artificial Intelligence (AI) has proven to be a transformative force in making educational content more accessible, particularly for students with disabilities. In the realm of Open Educational Resources (OER), AI-powered tools such as automatic transcription, translation, and other assistive technologies are breaking down barriers to learning, enabling students with disabilities to engage with educational materials in ways that were previously unavailable or difficult to access.

AI-Driven Automatic Transcription for Improved Accessibility

One of the most significant ways AI enhances accessibility in OER is through **automatic transcription**, which converts spoken language into written text. This technology is particularly beneficial for students who are deaf or hard of hearing, enabling them to access spoken content, such as lectures, videos, and podcasts, in written form. AI-driven transcription tools use **speech recognition algorithms** to analyze audio and generate accurate transcripts in real time, providing students with an alternative means of engaging with educational content (Fitzpatrick et al., 2019).

AI transcription tools, such as **Google's Speech-to-Text API** and **Otter.ai**, leverage deep learning models to understand and process natural language, making transcription faster, more accurate, and more efficient than manual transcription methods. These tools not only provide accurate word-for-word transcription but also capture context, punctuation, and even speaker identification, allowing students to follow along with complex discussions and group lectures (Pan & Zhang, 2021). For OER platforms, incorporating automatic transcription into video lectures and audio resources significantly expands access to learners with hearing impairments, ensuring that they can fully participate in the educational experience.

Moreover, automatic transcription tools can be applied to real-time settings, such as live lectures or webinars. AI-driven **real-time captioning systems** offer immediate access to spoken information, which is crucial for students who rely on written content to understand lectures as they happen. For example, platforms like **Zoom** have integrated AI-based live transcription services, enabling students to receive live captions during virtual classes. This capability not only enhances accessibility for students with hearing disabilities but also supports learners in noisy environments or non-native speakers who may find it easier to follow written text alongside spoken words (Sanchez-Gordon & Lujan-Mora, 2018).

AI-Powered Translation for Multilingual and Accessible OER

Another critical application of AI in improving accessibility for students with disabilities is **automatic translation**. AI-powered translation tools enable OER to be more accessible to a global audience, including students with learning disabilities, non-native speakers, and those who require content in their native language for better comprehension. These tools use **machine translation algorithms**, such as those found in **Google Translate** and **DeepL,** to translate text and spoken language into multiple languages, broadening access to educational resources (Matusov et al., 2019).

For students with disabilities, AI-driven translation offers a range of benefits. For example, learners with cognitive or learning disabilities may struggle with materials presented in complex or non-native languages. AI translation tools can simplify the language or convert it into a more familiar form, aiding comprehension and retention. Additionally, automatic translation tools can integrate with transcription systems, providing captions in multiple languages for video content. This ensures that learners who are both hearing-impaired and non-native speakers have equal access to OER content (Ballesteros et al., 2017).

In the context of multilingual OER repositories, AI-powered translation enables the seamless sharing of educational resources across linguistic boundaries. For example, an OER repository containing physics lectures in English can be made accessible to students in Spanish-speaking regions through AI translation systems that generate accurate translations of both text and spoken content. These tools are essential in fostering global collaboration and inclusivity in education, as they ensure that learners from diverse linguistic backgrounds can access high-quality educational resources without language barriers (Pérez-Peña et al., 2020).

Other AI-Enabled Assistive Technologies for Students with Disabilities

In addition to transcription and translation, AI has been instrumental in developing other assistive technologies that improve accessibility for students with disabilities. One example is **text-to-speech (TTS)** systems, which convert written text into spoken words. TTS technology is especially useful for students with visual impairments or learning disabilities, allowing them to listen to educational content rather than reading it. AI-driven TTS systems, such as **Amazon Polly** and **Microsoft Azure Speech**, use NLP to provide natural-sounding speech that closely mimics human language, making the listening experience more engaging and effective for learners (Yousuf et al., 2020).

Furthermore, AI is used to enhance **content simplification** tools, which help make complex educational texts more accessible to students with cognitive disabilities or lower reading levels. These tools use NLP algorithms to rewrite content in simpler language, breaking down complex concepts into more manageable parts. By offering multiple levels of content difficulty, AI-enabled simplification tools help ensure that learners with varying abilities can access OER that is appropriate for their level of understanding (Napolitano et al., 2019).

AI has also contributed to **customizable learning environments** that adapt to the specific needs of students with disabilities. For instance, AI-driven adaptive learning systems, such as those found in **Khan Academy** or **Smart Sparrow**, analyze a student's performance, learning pace, and interaction patterns to adjust the difficulty and presentation of educational materials. For students with disabilities, these systems can recommend alternative resources or more accessible formats, ensuring that learners receive personalized support tailored to their unique needs (Baker et al., 2020).

Challenges and Ethical Considerations in AI Accessibility Solutions

While AI holds great promise in improving accessibility for students with disabilities, there are challenges and ethical considerations that must be addressed. One challenge is ensuring the **accuracy** of AI transcription and translation tools, especially in academic settings where precise understanding of terminology is critical. Misinterpretations or inaccuracies in automatic transcription and translation can lead to misunderstandings or incomplete comprehension of complex concepts. Continuous improvements in AI models are needed to enhance the accuracy and reliability of these tools in academic environments (Cao & Liang, 2019).

Another consideration is the **privacy and security of student data**. Many AI accessibility tools rely on large amounts of data, including voice recordings and text input, to improve performance and personalize services. It is essential that institutions implementing these technologies have robust data protection policies to safeguard sensitive student information. Transparency in data usage and ensuring compliance with data protection regulations, such as the General Data Protection Regulation (GDPR), are critical to building trust in AI-powered accessibility solutions (Binns, 2018).

In summary, AI is playing a critical role in improving the accessibility of OER for students with disabilities by providing tools such as automatic transcription, translation, and other assistive technologies. These AI-driven solutions allow students with hearing impairments, visual disabilities, and cognitive challenges to engage with educational content in ways that best suit their needs. By offering real-time transcription, multilingual translation, and personalized learning environments, AI is fostering a more inclusive educational landscape. However, as AI technologies continue to evolve, it is important to address challenges related to accuracy, privacy, and equity to ensure that these tools truly benefit all learners.

Example: AI in Academic Databases like PubMed and JSTOR

Artificial Intelligence (AI) is playing a transformative role in enhancing the searchability and accessibility of academic resources within large scholarly databases such as **PubMed** and **JSTOR**. These platforms house extensive collections of peer-reviewed articles, research papers, and academic content that are critical for researchers, educators, and students. By integrating AI technologies, including machine learning, natural language processing (NLP), and semantic search algorithms, these databases improve the efficiency, relevance, and accessibility of search results, making it easier for users to find relevant Open Educational Resources (OER) and other academic materials.

AI-Driven Semantic Search in PubMed

PubMed, a leading repository for biomedical literature managed by the U.S. National Library of Medicine, has integrated AI to improve the discoverability of scholarly articles. One of the key advancements in PubMed's search capabilities is its use of **semantic search** through AI-powered systems such as **PubMed Central (PMC)**. Semantic search allows PubMed to go beyond simple keyword matching by understanding the context and meaning behind search queries, providing more accurate and relevant search results (Lu, 2011).

For instance, when a researcher searches for "gene therapy for cancer," PubMed's AI system recognizes the relationship between terms like "gene therapy" and specific types of cancer treatments. It retrieves not only articles that explicitly mention these terms but also related studies on immunotherapy, genetic engineering, and other relevant biomedical topics. The **Medical Subject Headings (MeSH)**, an AI-powered indexing system in PubMed, further refines this process by categorizing articles according to hierarchical subject headings, ensuring that users are presented with highly relevant research (Tatonetti et al., 2012).

PubMed also uses machine learning algorithms to continuously refine search results based on user behavior and interactions. By analyzing search patterns, click-through rates, and article downloads, the AI system adjusts the ranking of search results to prioritize the most relevant and high-impact articles. This adaptive system ensures that users can quickly access the most pertinent studies, even within the vast and growing body of biomedical literature (Dai et al., 2016).

JSTOR: AI and Text Mining for Scholarly Discovery

JSTOR, a comprehensive academic database that provides access to thousands of scholarly journals and primary sources, employs AI to enhance both searchability and content analysis. One of the most prominent AI-driven features of JSTOR is its **text mining** tools, which allow researchers to explore large datasets and extract meaningful insights from textual information. These tools utilize NLP and machine learning algorithms to process and analyze millions of academic documents, facilitating the discovery of relevant articles and research trends (Oard & Arora, 2017).

Through JSTOR's **Data for Research (DfR)** platform, users can access text mining services that enable them to explore content based on semantic relationships rather than mere keyword matching. For example, a researcher studying "climate change and economic policy" could use JSTOR's text mining tools to uncover connections between environmental science articles and economic studies that might not be immediately apparent through traditional searches. The AI algorithms analyze the underlying themes and concepts in the articles, providing a richer understanding of how these disciplines intersect (Jockers, 2017).

In addition to enhancing search capabilities, JSTOR leverages AI to support **personalized recommendations**. By analyzing user behavior - such as previous searches, article downloads, and citation patterns - JSTOR's recommendation engine suggests additional resources that align with the user's research interests. This AI-powered feature helps researchers discover related articles and topics that may not have been part of their initial search, thereby expanding the scope of academic inquiry (Wu et al., 2016).

Enhancing Accessibility through AI-Powered Systems

Both PubMed and JSTOR use AI not only to improve searchability but also to enhance accessibility for diverse users. For example, AI-powered **automated summarization** tools are being developed to generate concise summaries of lengthy research papers. These summaries provide researchers and students with a quick overview of the content, helping them decide whether an article is relevant to their needs before delving into the full text (Hahn et al., 2016). This feature is particularly beneficial for students who may struggle with dense academic language or time constraints, as it allows them to quickly assess the value of a resource.

Additionally, AI-driven **multilingual translation** services are being integrated into platforms like JSTOR, making scholarly content accessible to non-native speakers. By utilizing machine translation algorithms, these platforms can automatically translate academic articles into multiple languages, breaking down linguistic barriers and enabling a wider global audience to engage with scholarly content (Van der Wees et al., 2017). This development is crucial for enhancing the inclusivity of OER, ensuring that high-quality academic resources are available to learners regardless of their linguistic background.

Challenges and Opportunities in AI for Academic Databases

While AI offers significant benefits in improving the searchability and accessibility of academic databases, there are challenges that must be addressed to ensure the effective use of these technologies. One challenge is ensuring the **accuracy and bias** of AI-powered search algorithms. Although AI systems are designed to provide relevant search results, they may inadvertently prioritize certain types of research or overlook niche topics, particularly in emerging fields where data is limited. Ensuring that AI algorithms are transparent, unbiased, and continuously updated is essential to maintaining the integrity of academic searches (Binns, 2018).

Moreover, there is a need to balance the use of **automated recommendation systems** with the user's autonomy in academic research. While AI-powered recommendations can introduce researchers to new articles and topics, it is important that these systems do not overly influence or narrow the scope of inquiry. Ensuring that users maintain control over their search strategies while benefiting from AI-enhanced recommendations is key to fostering a healthy academic research environment (Stevens et al., 2019).

Despite these challenges, the integration of AI into academic databases like PubMed and JSTOR represents a significant advancement in scholarly discovery. These platforms demonstrate the potential of AI to streamline the research process, improve access to OER, and democratize knowledge for a global audience.

Conclusion

AI has revolutionized the searchability and accessibility of academic resources in databases like PubMed and JSTOR, offering more efficient, accurate, and personalized search experiences. Through semantic search, text mining, and personalized recommendation systems, AI enables users to navigate vast repositories of scholarly content more effectively. These AI-powered systems also enhance accessibility by offering features such as automated summarization, multilingual translation, and real-time search refinement. As AI technologies continue to evolve, they hold the potential to further democratize access to knowledge, making academic research more inclusive and impactful.

References

Abdelrahman, M. A., & Aboud, M. A. (2021). Enhancing OER metadata using AI: Automated content analysis and tagging for improved searchability. *Journal of Open Learning, 38*(2), 137-152.

Arora, R., & Sinha, N. (2019). Enhancing accessibility through voice-based systems: The case of open educational resources. *Journal of Assistive Technologies, 13*(2), 120-135.

Baker, R. S., & Beutel, A. (2020). Machine learning for education: A review of algorithms and applications for automated metadata generation in OER. *Computers & Education, 162*, 104075.

Baker, R. S., & Siemens, G. (2020). Educational data mining and learning analytics: Potentials and challenges for the OER ecosystem. *British Journal of Educational Technology, 51*(4), 912-928.

Baker, R. S., Siemens, G., & Zevin, J. (2020). AI-driven accessibility in education: Enhancing learning environments for students with disabilities. *Educational Technology & Society, 23*(4), 105-117.

Ball, D., Handke, L., & Varma, K. (2020). Metadata for accessibility: AI-based frameworks for enhancing OER discoverability for all learners. *Journal of Accessible Education, 7*(4), 95-113.

Ballesteros, M., Dyer, C., & Smith, N. A. (2017). Machine translation for accessible education: Enhancing OER for multilingual learners. *Proceedings of the Association for Computational Linguistics*, 1355-1365.

Binns, R. (2018). Fairness in machine learning: Lessons from political philosophy. *Proceedings of the 2018 Conference on Fairness, Accountability, and Transparency*.

Blanco, E., Tonelli, S., & Palmer, M. (2019). Semantic search and information retrieval in OER platforms: Using NLP to enhance access. *Proceedings of the 2019 Conference on Computational Linguistics*, 1347-1356.

Brown, M., Hughes, H., Keppell, M., Hard, N., & Smith, L. (2021). Personalizing OER for lifelong learning through AI-based platforms. *Journal of Learning Analytics, 8*(1), 10-24.

Cao, Y., & Liang, X. (2019). Enhancing the accuracy of AI-driven transcription tools in education: Challenges and solutions. *Journal of Learning Analytics, 7*(1), 29-42.

Chatti, M. A., Marinov, M., & Jarke, M. (2016). A learning analytics framework for OER. *Journal of Learning Analytics, 3*(2), 19-42.

Chuang, I., Shen, C., & Ho, A. D. (2016). The impact of course structure on engagement and persistence in MOOCs. *Computers & Education, 101*(1), 59-67.

Colvin, C., Rogers, T., Wade, A., Dawson, S., & Gasevic, D. (2016). The impact of learning analytics on student success: A review of findings. *Higher Education Research & Development, 35*(5), 966-980.

Coughlan, T., Goff, E., & Lockyer, L. (2020). Adaptive learning paths for personalized education: The edX case study. *British Journal of Educational Technology, 51*(6), 1345-1361.

Cui, L., Wang, X., & Xu, Y. (2017). NLP for semantic search in open educational resource repositories. *Journal of Information Science, 43*(6), 722-736.

Dai, L., Toor, S., & He, Y. (2016). Mining PubMed to uncover hidden knowledge in biomedical literature. *Bioinformatics, 32*(12), 356-364.

DeBoer, J., Stump, G. S., & Seaton, D. (2014). Adapting MOOCs on the fly: Dynamic personalization through online learner behavior. *Proceedings of the 4th International Conference on Learning Analytics and Knowledge.*

Dziugaite, G. K., Roy, D. M., & Ghahramani, Z. (2015). How Coursera recommends courses. *Proceedings of the 2015 International Conference on Machine Learning and Educational Data Mining.*

Fitzpatrick, D., Monteith, L., & Draper, K. (2019). AI transcription in education: Supporting accessibility for deaf and hard-of-hearing students. *Educational Technology Research and Development, 67*(3), 519-534.

Fleming, N. (2012). *VARK: A guide to learning styles.* VARK Learn Limited.

Fletcher, G. H., & Carter, D. R. (2018). Personalizing OER to match learner preferences: Adaptive learning technologies. *Journal of Digital Learning, 15*(3), 31-40.

Garcia, F., & Liao, W. (2021). NLP-based tools for personalized assessment and feedback in OER environments. *Educational Technology Research and Development, 69*(2), 311-329.

Gupta, S., Walker, M. A., & Roy, S. (2020). AI assistants in education: Transforming OER discovery and engagement through personalized dialogue. *Computers & Education, 152*, 103876.

Hahn, U., Radev, D. R., & Medsker, L. R. (2016). Automatic summarization for academic databases: Enhancing scholarly access. *Journal of the Association for Information Science and Technology, 68*(5), 1010-1025.

Harvey, D., Kaplan, C., & Chen, J. (2019). The role of AI assistants in education: Enhancing access to OER with voice-activated learning companions. *International Journal of Educational Technology in Higher Education, 16*(1), 1-14.

Hilton, J. (2020). The potential for AI in OER: Improving equity and access through personalized learning and automated content curation. *International Journal of Educational Technology, 5*(1), 57-73.

Hoy, M. B. (2018). Alexa, Siri, Cortana, and more: An introduction to voice assistants. *Medical Reference Services Quarterly, 37*(1), 81-88.

Jockers, M. L. (2017). Text mining in digital humanities: Techniques for exploring JSTOR's Data for Research platform. *Computers and the Humanities, 49*(1), 97-110.

Johnson, L., Smith, R., & Watson, M. (2017). Competency-based learning and personalized OER pathways. *Journal of Personalized Learning, 14*(3), 210-227.

Johnson, R., Lomas, M., & May, K. (2020). Integrating adaptive learning technologies with OER: A case study of CogBooks. *Journal of Learning Design, 13*(1), 63-75.

Kastrati, Z., Imran, A., & Drira, K. (2021). Personalized OER learning paths using NLP and deep learning. *Computers & Education, 160*, 104025.

Kizilcec, R. F., Piech, C., & Schneider, E. (2017). Deconstructing disengagement: Analyzing learner subpopulations in massive open online courses. *Journal of Educational Data Mining, 9*(1), 1-24.

Klasnja-Milicevic, A., Vesin, B., Ivanovic, M., & Budimac, Z. (2017). E-learning personalization based on hybrid recommendation strategy and learning style identification. *Computers & Education, 56*(3), 885-899.

Lu, Z. (2011). PubMed and beyond: A survey of web tools for searching biomedical literature. *Database: The Journal of Biological Databases and Curation, 8*(3), 234-241.

Matusov, E., Alcaraz, S., & Munday, J. (2019). Advancing AI-powered translation for OER: Case studies and future directions. *Computers in Education, 133*, 87-101.

Miller, L., Seaton, D., & Milligan, C. (2016). Tailoring learning pathways using adaptive learning technologies in OER-based environments. *Open Learning: The Journal of Open, Distance and e-Learning, 31*(2), 125-142.

Napolitano, G., Mollica, M., & Tost, H. (2019). Content simplification through AI: Making OER more accessible to learners with disabilities. *Educational Technology & Society, 22*(4), 98-112.

Nguyen, T., Zancanaro, M., & Hwang, W. Y. (2021). AI-powered personalized OER metadata for effective learning resource retrieval. *Journal of Educational Data Mining, 13*(1), 39-58.

Oard, D. W., & Arora, P. (2017). The impact of text mining on academic search in large databases: The JSTOR experience. *Proceedings of the 2017 ACM SIGIR Conference on Research and Development in Information Retrieval.*

Pane, J. F., Steiner, E. D., & Hamilton, L. S. (2017). How personalized learning affects student achievement. *RAND Corporation.*

Pashler, H., McDaniel, M., Rohrer, D., & Bjork, R. (2009). Learning styles: Concepts and evidence. *Psychological Science in the Public Interest, 9*(3), 105-119.

Popenici, S. A. D., & Kerr, S. (2017). Exploring the impact of artificial intelligence on teaching and learning in higher education. *Research and Practice in Technology Enhanced Learning, 12*(22), 1-13.

Porcheron, M., Fischer, J. E., & Sharples, S. (2018). Using voice assistants in OER discovery: The potential of conversational AI for educational accessibility. *Proceedings of the 2018 ACM Conference on Human Factors in Computing Systems.*

Pouyioutas, P., Jimoyiannis, A., & Olibani, F. (2018). Cross-modal, cross-cultural personalized learning pathways in OER: The X5GON initiative. *Journal of Learning Design, 11*(2), 63-75.

Roschelle, J., Feng, M., & Murphy, R. F. (2017). Adaptive learning platforms: Improving learning outcomes through tailored content delivery. *Journal of Educational Technology, 42*(4), 32-40.

Seaton, D. T., Bergner, Y., & Chuang, I. (2013). Who does what in a massive open online course? Lessons from edX. *Proceedings of the 2013 International Conference on Learning Analytics and Knowledge.*

Shen, L., & Ho, J. (2020). Machine learning and data privacy: Transparency, trust, and regulation. *Proceedings of the 2020 International Conference on Privacy, Data, and Regulation.*

Siemens, G. (2020). Artificial intelligence and the future of personalized OER: Adaptive learning systems. *British Journal of Educational Technology, 51*(6), 1205-1220.

Stevens, C., Subramanian, S., & Clarke, J. (2019). AI and academic search: Balancing recommendation systems with academic autonomy. *Journal of Academic Librarianship, 45*(2), 109-121.

Tatonetti, N. P., Dudley, J. T., & Butte, A. J. (2012). Data-driven prediction of drug effects and interactions. *Journal of the American Medical Informatics Association, 19*(2), 391-398.

Van der Wees, M., Bisazza, A., & Monz, C. (2017). Adaptive machine translation for academic research: Expanding accessibility to non-native speakers. *Journal of Information Technology and Academic Research, 27*(1), 45-61.

Veletsianos, G., & Shepherdson, P. (2016). A systematic analysis and synthesis of the empirical MOOC literature published in 2013-2015. *International Review of Research in Open and Distributed Learning, 17*(2), 198-221.

Wiley, D., & Hilton, J. (2018). Defining OER-enabled pedagogy. *The International Review of Research in Open and Distributed Learning, 19*(4), 133-147.

Xiao, B., Cheng, L., & Yu, D. (2018). Machine learning for automated OER metadata generation: A practical approach for improving resource discoverability. *Journal of Learning Analytics, 5*(3), 78-95.

Zhu, Y., Bonk, C. J., & Sari, A. (2018). AI in MOOCs: Examining learners' experiences and outcomes. *Distance Education, 39*(1), 97-112.

Zualkernan, I. (2020). AI in OER: Adaptive learning for personalized education. *Journal of Educational Technology, 47*(2), 115-129.

Part 3: AI Applications in Higher Education

Chapter 7: AI-Powered Content Creation and Automation

Automated Generation of OER Content Using AI

In the evolving landscape of higher education, artificial intelligence (AI) has emerged as a powerful tool for enhancing teaching and learning processes, particularly through the automation of content creation. One of the most impactful applications of AI in this realm is the generation of Open Educational Resources (OER), which includes the creation of text, videos, and quizzes. By automating these processes, AI not only reduces the workload of educators but also democratizes access to quality educational materials globally.

Automated Text Generation

AI-powered natural language processing (NLP) models, such as GPT-4 and other advanced language models, have made significant strides in generating high-quality textual content. These models are capable of producing comprehensive instructional materials, course outlines, and supplementary readings based on a given dataset or prompt. The automated generation of OER text offers a unique opportunity to address the scarcity of educational materials in various languages and regions. According to Yu and colleagues (2021), AI can create tailored educational texts by analyzing a wide range of existing resources, generating summaries, or synthesizing new content that aligns with specific curricular needs. This has far-reaching implications for institutions with limited access to educational resources, as AI can be used to generate culturally and contextually relevant materials (Dahlstrom & Bichsel, 2020).

AI-Generated Educational Videos

AI has also extended its capabilities to the generation of educational videos, which are increasingly being integrated into OER platforms. Automated video creation tools such as Lumen5 and Pictory use AI to convert textual content into dynamic videos, complete with voiceovers, visual aids, and even closed captions. These tools provide a way to make learning more engaging and accessible, especially for students who prefer visual or auditory learning styles (Wang & Zhou, 2020). Furthermore, AI-generated videos can be adapted for multilingual audiences through automatic translation and subtitling, contributing to the global dissemination of educational resources. The ability of AI to quickly produce content in different formats ensures that learners receive a diverse range of instructional media, thus enhancing the overall learning experience (Guan, 2022).

Automated Quiz Generation

The automation of assessments, particularly quizzes, is another area where AI contributes significantly to OER development. AI can analyze educational content and automatically generate quizzes that test students' understanding of the material. By leveraging machine learning algorithms, systems such as AI-based Learning Management Systems (LMS) can assess the difficulty of questions, identify key concepts, and ensure alignment with learning objectives (Xie et al., 2021). Moreover, AI can personalize quiz content by adapting the difficulty level based on a student's past performance, making assessments more individualized and effective in addressing different learning needs (Choudhary & Goswami, 2020). The inclusion of quizzes in OERs enhances active learning and provides immediate feedback, both of which are critical for knowledge retention and application.

Benefits and Challenges

The automated generation of OER content through AI offers multiple benefits. First, it drastically reduces the time and effort required by educators to create instructional materials, allowing them to focus more on student engagement and pedagogical strategies. Second, it promotes inclusivity by enabling the rapid production of educational materials in underrepresented languages and formats

(Guan, 2022). Third, AI-generated content can be updated in real-time, ensuring that students always have access to the latest information and knowledge in their field of study (Dahlstrom & Bichsel, 2020).

However, the automation of content creation using AI also poses challenges. One primary concern is the accuracy and quality of the generated content. While AI models can produce coherent and well-structured materials, they are prone to errors, particularly in complex academic subjects (Xie et al., 2021). Another challenge is the potential for bias in AI-generated content, as algorithms can inadvertently reproduce biases present in the training data (Wang & Zhou, 2020). Ensuring that AI-generated OER materials are free from such biases requires ongoing monitoring and human oversight.

In summary, AI-powered content creation and automation present significant opportunities for enhancing the accessibility and quality of Open Educational Resources in higher education. Through automated text, video, and quiz generation, AI has the potential to revolutionize how educational materials are produced and distributed, particularly in regions where resources are scarce. However, to fully realize these benefits, it is essential to address the challenges associated with accuracy, quality control, and bias in AI-generated content. With careful implementation, AI can play a pivotal role in the future of education, contributing to a more inclusive and equitable global learning environment.

AI Tools for Creating Interactive Textbooks and Adaptive Quizzes

The integration of artificial intelligence (AI) in higher education is reshaping the design and delivery of instructional materials, particularly through AI-powered tools that support the creation of interactive textbooks and adaptive quizzes. These tools offer innovative ways to engage learners, tailor educational content to individual needs, and provide a more dynamic, personalized learning experience. AI's ability to generate, customize, and update educational content in real time is transforming the traditional static textbook into a more interactive, student-centered resource, while adaptive quizzes enhance formative assessment by adjusting to each learner's performance and understanding.

Interactive Textbooks Powered by AI

AI tools for creating interactive textbooks have advanced significantly, providing educators with the ability to produce more engaging and responsive learning materials. Interactive textbooks use AI to present content in various formats, including multimedia elements such as videos, animations, and simulations, which allow students to interact with the material in a way that promotes deeper understanding. For example, platforms like Top Hat and Inkling integrate AI to provide interactive, multimedia-rich textbooks that include embedded assessments, real-time feedback, and personalized learning pathways (Johnson et al., 2021).

AI can also enable the dynamic adaptation of content based on the student's progress. This is particularly beneficial in higher education, where learners come from diverse backgrounds with varying levels of prior knowledge. AI algorithms can analyze a student's learning history and adapt the content accordingly, ensuring that learners are not overwhelmed with complex concepts without first mastering foundational knowledge (Bates & Sangrà, 2020). This personalization can be particularly impactful in fields such as STEM, where concepts build sequentially, and interactive textbooks can offer additional resources or remedial content as needed.

Moreover, AI-enhanced interactive textbooks can continuously evolve by incorporating data from learner interactions to improve content delivery. For instance, AI systems can analyze student performance across large cohorts to identify common areas of difficulty, prompting automatic content updates or reorganization to improve clarity and focus (Zawacki-Richter et al., 2019). This ability to refine content based on data-driven insights enhances both the educational experience and the efficacy of the material.

Adaptive Quizzes for Personalized Learning

The use of adaptive quizzes is another significant advancement facilitated by AI in higher education. Traditional assessments often adopt a one-size-fits-all approach, which can fail to address individual learning needs. In contrast, AI-powered adaptive quizzes dynamically adjust the difficulty and scope of questions based on the student's performance in real time. As learners engage with these quizzes, AI algorithms analyze their responses to provide personalized question sets, ensuring that the quiz is appropriately challenging and aligned with the student's current understanding (Chen et al., 2021).

Adaptive quizzes are typically powered by machine learning models, which learn from students' previous interactions and assessments to predict their readiness for new topics. For example, systems such as Knewton and Smart Sparrow employ AI to adjust the difficulty of questions, the sequence of topics, and even the amount of feedback provided to the student based on their previous answers (Baker et al., 2020). This form of adaptive assessment provides a continuous and formative assessment process, where students receive instant feedback and opportunities for remediation, promoting mastery learning.

Furthermore, AI-powered adaptive quizzes enhance accessibility and inclusivity in higher education by catering to diverse learning styles and needs. For instance, quizzes can be adapted for students with disabilities by presenting questions in formats that accommodate their specific requirements, such as providing text-to-speech options for visually impaired learners or interactive visuals for those with reading difficulties (Fischer et al., 2020). This ensures that all students have equal opportunities to engage with the material and succeed in their academic pursuits.

The Benefits of AI-Powered Interactive Learning Tools

The integration of AI into interactive textbooks and adaptive quizzes provides several key benefits in higher education. First, these tools enhance student engagement by creating a more interactive and personalized learning experience. By offering immediate feedback, tailored content, and opportunities for self-paced learning, AI tools promote active learning and allow students to take ownership of their educational journey (Siemens & Long, 2019). Second, AI-driven tools support continuous assessment and feedback, enabling educators to monitor student progress in real time and intervene when necessary to support struggling learners. This can lead to better learning outcomes and improved retention rates, as students receive the guidance and resources they need to succeed (Schmid & Petko, 2022).

However, despite the many advantages, there are also challenges associated with the adoption of AI-powered interactive textbooks and adaptive quizzes. One primary concern is the potential for bias in AI algorithms, which may disadvantage certain groups of students if the training data used to develop the AI models is not representative of diverse populations (Chen et al., 2021). Additionally, the reliance on AI for content creation and assessment raises concerns about the role of human educators and the potential loss of personalized, empathetic interactions between teachers and students (Siemens & Long, 2019). It is crucial that AI tools are used to complement, rather than replace, traditional pedagogical methods, ensuring that human oversight and intervention remain integral to the learning process.

In summary, AI-powered tools for creating interactive textbooks and adaptive quizzes represent a transformative shift in higher education. These technologies enable the creation of more engaging, personalized, and accessible learning materials, offering students a dynamic and responsive educational experience. By adapting content and assessments to individual learning needs, AI ensures that students receive the appropriate level of challenge and support, fostering deeper understanding and improved learning outcomes. However, the implementation of these tools must be approached with caution, addressing issues of bias and ensuring that human oversight remains central to the educational process. As AI continues to evolve, its potential to enhance teaching and learning in higher education will undoubtedly expand, providing new opportunities for innovation and improvement in educational practices.

Case Study: AI-Generated Content in Platforms Like Knewton

Artificial intelligence (AI) has been increasingly adopted in higher education to enhance the development of personalized and scalable learning experiences. One platform that has pioneered the use of AI in content creation and delivery is Knewton. Known for its adaptive learning technology, Knewton utilizes AI algorithms to analyze student interactions with content and generate personalized learning pathways. This case study examines the ways in which Knewton leverages AI to create tailored educational experiences, particularly through AI-generated content and real-time adaptation to student needs.

Knewton's Adaptive Learning Technology

Knewton's adaptive learning platform is designed to customize educational content for each student by using AI to analyze their learning behavior, strengths, and areas of difficulty. The platform continuously collects data as students engage with course materials, tracking their progress through quizzes, assignments, and other learning activities. Based on this data, Knewton's AI algorithms generate personalized learning paths, offering content that aligns with each student's current understanding and pacing (Johnson & Gholson, 2020).

The AI system in Knewton not only recommends the next appropriate content but also generates new content as needed to fill gaps in a student's knowledge. For example, if a student struggles with a particular concept, Knewton can deliver additional explanations, examples, or quizzes tailored to that concept. This dynamic content generation ensures that students receive the support they need to master each subject before moving on to more advanced topics (Foster & Hu, 2019).

AI-Generated Content in Knewton

One of the core functionalities of Knewton is its ability to create and deliver AI-generated content. By leveraging natural language processing (NLP) and machine learning, Knewton can generate instructional material, including explanatory texts, quizzes, and review exercises. This content is not static; rather, it evolves in response to each student's learning patterns. Knewton's AI algorithms analyze the learning needs of individual students and create content that targets those specific needs, ensuring personalized and effective learning experiences (Fischer et al., 2021).

In addition to generating tailored content, Knewton adapts the difficulty level of quizzes and assessments based on a student's progress. For example, if a student consistently performs well on intermediate-level problems, the system will present more challenging tasks to facilitate further growth. Conversely, if a student struggles with certain topics, Knewton adjusts the difficulty to provide remedial content that reinforces foundational knowledge (Anderson et al., 2020). This real-time adaptability is a key feature that differentiates Knewton from traditional static learning resources.

Effectiveness of AI-Generated Content in Knewton

Research on Knewton's effectiveness suggests that its AI-driven content generation can significantly improve student learning outcomes. A study by Fischer et al. (2021) found that students using Knewton's adaptive platform achieved higher levels of mastery in math courses compared to those using traditional textbooks. The study attributed this improvement to the platform's ability to continuously adapt content based on individual student performance, thereby providing a more personalized and targeted learning experience.

Moreover, Knewton's AI-generated content has been shown to promote student engagement and motivation. According to Anderson et al. (2020), students using adaptive learning platforms like Knewton reported higher satisfaction due to the immediate feedback and personalized learning paths. The dynamic nature of the content kept students engaged and encouraged them to persist in their studies, even when faced with challenging material.

Challenges and Limitations

While Knewton's AI-generated content offers several advantages, there are challenges and limitations to its application. One major concern is the potential for bias in AI algorithms. Knewton's AI relies on large datasets to train its models, and if these datasets are not representative of diverse student populations, the system may inadvertently reinforce educational inequities (Li & Ryder, 2021). For instance, students from underrepresented backgrounds or with different learning styles may not receive the same quality of adaptive content as those from more privileged groups.

Another limitation of AI-generated content in Knewton is the potential for over-reliance on automation. While AI can effectively generate and adapt content, there is a need for human oversight to ensure that the material aligns with pedagogical goals and fosters critical thinking. Foster and Hu (2019) argue that AI should complement rather than replace the role of educators in content creation and assessment. Human instructors play a crucial role in providing context, offering insights, and fostering discussions that AI-generated content may not fully capture.

Conclusion

The case of Knewton highlights the transformative potential of AI in higher education, particularly in content creation and personalization.

By leveraging AI algorithms, Knewton generates dynamic and adaptive content that evolves with each student's learning needs, leading to improved engagement and academic performance. However, challenges such as bias in AI algorithms and the balance between human and AI-driven content creation must be carefully managed. As AI continues to evolve, platforms like Knewton offer valuable insights into how educational technology can be harnessed to create personalized and effective learning experiences at scale.

References

Anderson, M., Johnson, P., & Robinson, T. (2020). AI in adaptive learning: A review of the evidence from Knewton's application in higher education. *Journal of Educational Technology Systems*, 48(4), 456-472.

Baker, R. S., Siemens, G., & DiCerbo, K. E. (2020). Learning analytics: Data-driven approaches to improving learning outcomes. *Educational Researcher*, 49(4), 249-259.

Bates, A. W., & Sangrà, A. (2020). *Managing technology in higher education: Strategies for transforming teaching and learning*. Wiley.

Chen, B., DeBoer, J., & Ho, A. D. (2021). Predictive learning analytics in higher education: A review and an agenda for future research. *British Journal of Educational Technology*, 52(5), 1700-1717.

Choudhary, P., & Goswami, A. (2020). Applications of AI in education: Text generation and adaptive learning. *International Journal of Computer Science and Technology*, 11(3), 45-53.

Dahlstrom, E., & Bichsel, J. (2020). The changing role of IT in higher education: Strategies for AI adoption. *Educause Review*, 55(1), 30-39.

Fischer, C., Hasko, S., & Toffalini, E. (2020). Adaptive e-learning: How AI can support diverse learning needs in higher education. *Journal of Educational Technology Systems*, 49(1), 35-49.

Fischer, C., Peters, S., & Hasko, S. (2021). AI-powered adaptive learning platforms: Evaluating the effectiveness of Knewton in higher education. *International Journal of Educational Technology in Higher Education*, 18(3), 25-39.

Foster, S., & Hu, L. (2019). Adaptive learning technology and its impact on student outcomes: A case study of Knewton in university-level math courses. *Computers & Education*, 138, 183-195.

Guan, J. (2022). AI and the automation of educational content: A pathway to global learning. *Journal of Educational Technology*, 18(2), 123-139.

Johnson, L., Adams Becker, S., Cummins, M., Estrada, V., Freeman, A., & Hall, C. (2021). *NMC Horizon Report: 2021 Higher Education Edition*. The New Media Consortium.

Johnson, S., & Gholson, M. (2020). Personalizing higher education with AI: The case of Knewton's adaptive learning technology. *Educational Technology Research and Development*, 68(6), 1621-1640.

Li, J., & Ryder, J. (2021). AI and fairness in education: Addressing algorithmic bias in adaptive learning systems. *Journal of Learning Analytics*, 8(2), 45-60.

Schmid, R. F., & Petko, D. (2022). Artificial intelligence in education: Promises, challenges, and future directions. *Educational Technology Research and Development*, 70(3), 897-915.

Siemens, G., & Long, P. (2019). Penetrating the fog: Analytics in learning and education. *Educause Review*, 46(5), 30-40.

Wang, Y., & Zhou, X. (2020). Enhancing higher education through AI-powered content creation: Opportunities and challenges. *Journal of AI and Learning*, 25(4), 250-265.

Xie, J., Han, K., & Liu, Y. (2021). Machine learning for personalized OER assessments: A review of automated quiz generation. *IEEE Transactions on Learning Technologies*, 14(3), 215-229.

Yu, T., Liao, W., & Chen, Z. (2021). Natural language processing in educational applications: The case of automated OER text generation. *Computers & Education*, 161, 104051.

Zawacki-Richter, O., Marín, V. I., Bond, M., & Gouverneur, F. (2019). Systematic review of research on artificial intelligence applications in higher education. *International Journal of Educational Technology in Higher Education*, 16(1), 39.

Chapter 8: AI-Enhanced Collaborative Learning Platforms

How AI Supports Collaboration and Knowledge Sharing in Open Educational Communities

Artificial intelligence (AI) is revolutionizing higher education by fostering more effective collaboration and knowledge sharing, particularly within open educational communities. These communities, built around the principles of openness, accessibility, and shared resources, are increasingly leveraging AI-enhanced collaborative learning platforms to connect students, educators, and researchers across the globe. AI plays a critical role in facilitating communication, coordinating group efforts, and providing personalized learning support, ultimately enhancing the quality and effectiveness of collaborative learning.

AI for Automating Content Management and Curation

AI-powered collaborative learning platforms in open educational communities benefit significantly from AI's ability to curate and manage vast amounts of educational content. In these communities, content sharing and open access to resources are vital to learning and innovation. AI automates content organization by categorizing and tagging materials, making it easier for learners and educators to find relevant resources (Li & Cheng, 2021). Natural language processing (NLP) algorithms enable AI to scan and classify educational content, suggesting materials that align with a learner's interests or a group's collective needs.

Platforms like Moodle and Open edX have integrated AI-based content curation systems that enhance the discovery of resources through personalized recommendations (Ferguson et al., 2020). These systems improve knowledge sharing within the community by ensuring that the most relevant and high-quality resources are easily accessible. AI-driven curation also ensures that content remains up-to-date, as algorithms continuously monitor new material contributions, automatically organizing them based on relevance and quality (Zawacki-Richter et al., 2020). This automation relieves educators from the burden of manual curation, allowing them to focus on more interactive and pedagogical aspects of collaboration.

AI for Enhancing Communication and Group Coordination

Effective collaboration in open educational communities relies heavily on communication and group coordination. AI-powered collaborative learning platforms streamline these processes through advanced communication tools, such as AI-driven chatbots, virtual assistants, and discussion forums that provide real-time, personalized feedback and support. AI facilitates asynchronous and synchronous discussions by identifying and summarizing key points from conversations, thus making it easier for participants to engage in meaningful knowledge exchange (Lai & Bower, 2020).

For example, AI chatbots embedded within platforms like Slack or Microsoft Teams can act as mediators or facilitators in group projects, reminding participants of deadlines, summarizing discussions, and even answering basic questions related to the subject matter (Roschelle et al., 2021). These chatbots help bridge communication gaps, especially in geographically dispersed teams, by ensuring that information is easily accessible and clearly communicated. Additionally, AI can analyze group dynamics and offer insights into team performance, identifying individuals who may need extra support or suggesting strategies to improve collaboration (Schmolz et al., 2021).

AI also enables real-time translation services in collaborative environments, removing language barriers and promoting cross-cultural knowledge sharing. Machine learning models, such as Google's Neural Machine Translation (NMT) system, allow learners and educators from diverse linguistic backgrounds to communicate seamlessly, thus enriching the collaborative experience (Chang et al.,

2020). By facilitating clear and immediate communication, AI supports more inclusive and globalized educational communities.

AI for Personalizing Collaborative Learning Experiences

AI-powered platforms in open educational communities offer personalized learning experiences even in collaborative settings. Adaptive learning systems, such as those found in collaborative platforms like Microsoft Teams and Google Classroom, use machine learning algorithms to track individual and group learning progress. These systems provide tailored recommendations for further study, suggest collaborators with complementary skills, and adapt learning tasks based on group performance (Kumar & Singh, 2020).

One of AI's most powerful applications in this context is its ability to analyze large volumes of data on student interactions, contributions, and engagement in collaborative settings. Through these analyses, AI can provide individualized feedback to students on their collaboration skills, while also identifying areas where group dynamics might need improvement (Fischer et al., 2020). This personalized support is especially valuable in open educational communities where participants have diverse learning preferences and levels of expertise. AI can also recommend specific learning paths or materials to individuals based on their role within the group, ensuring that each learner is contributing effectively while gaining knowledge relevant to their personal goals.

Promoting Inclusivity and Accessibility through AI

Inclusivity is a fundamental principle of open educational communities, and AI plays a significant role in ensuring that collaboration is accessible to all participants, regardless of their background or abilities. AI enhances inclusivity by providing tools that accommodate diverse learning needs, such as text-to-speech, speech-to-text, and real-time transcription services (Ellis & Goodyear, 2021). These features enable students with disabilities to fully engage in collaborative activities and access shared resources, ensuring equitable participation.

Moreover, AI-driven learning platforms can analyze user behaviors to identify patterns of disengagement or participation gaps. For example, AI can detect when certain members of a group are not contributing as expected, prompting facilitators to offer additional support or intervention (Lai & Bower, 2020). This capability ensures that all learners are actively involved in the collaborative process, helping to foster a more equitable learning environment.

In open educational communities, where diversity in learning styles, languages, and access to resources is a defining feature, AI's ability to promote inclusivity is particularly valuable. By offering personalized, accessible learning pathways and ensuring effective communication across all participants, AI helps create a more collaborative, diverse, and globally connected educational ecosystem (Schmölz et al., 2021).

In summary, AI-enhanced collaborative learning platforms in open educational communities offer significant opportunities for improving knowledge sharing, group coordination, and inclusivity. Through automated content management, personalized recommendations, and advanced communication tools, AI supports more efficient and effective collaboration in these open environments. Additionally, AI helps bridge linguistic and cultural barriers, making collaborative learning accessible to participants from diverse backgrounds. However, to maximize these benefits, it is crucial that educators and platform designers remain vigilant about potential biases in AI algorithms and strive to ensure that AI tools are used to complement human interactions rather than replace them. As AI continues to evolve, its role in fostering collaboration and knowledge sharing in higher education is likely to expand, offering new opportunities for global and inclusive learning.

Examples: AI in Platforms like Moodle, Canvas, and Wikipedia

The integration of artificial intelligence (AI) in collaborative learning platforms has transformed the educational landscape, particularly in higher education. AI-enhanced platforms such as Moodle, Canvas, and Wikipedia illustrate how AI can support collaborative learning by automating administrative tasks, personalizing learning experiences, and facilitating knowledge sharing among students and educators.

Moodle: AI for Personalization and Group Collaboration

Moodle, one of the most widely used open-source learning management systems (LMS), has incorporated AI features to enhance the collaborative learning experience. AI tools in Moodle enable personalized learning pathways and support collaborative group activities by analyzing student engagement and performance data. Through machine learning algorithms, Moodle identifies patterns in student behavior and uses this information to make personalized recommendations, such as suggesting relevant resources or adaptive learning tasks tailored to individual needs (Papamitsiou & Economides, 2020). This level of personalization enhances collaboration by ensuring that students are better prepared for group work and can contribute more effectively.

Moodle's AI-enhanced collaborative features include group activity recommendations based on student profiles and interaction histories. The platform can dynamically organize students into groups that balance different skill sets and knowledge levels, promoting peer learning and more effective collaboration (Gutierrez & Pieri, 2021). Furthermore, AI tools in Moodle help instructors monitor group discussions and project progress, automatically flagging areas where students may need additional support or intervention. By automating these tasks, Moodle allows educators to focus on fostering deeper engagement with the content and improving the quality of group interactions.

Canvas: AI-Powered Analytics for Collaborative Learning

Canvas, another prominent LMS, has integrated AI-powered tools to enhance collaborative learning through real-time analytics and personalized feedback. The platform's analytics engine uses AI to track student interactions, assess engagement levels, and predict academic outcomes. This data-driven approach allows Canvas to provide personalized recommendations and support for both individual and group activities (Hagerty & Thompson, 2020). For instance, AI in Canvas can identify students who may be at risk of falling behind and suggest interventions, such as additional learning materials or peer collaboration opportunities.

One of the key features of Canvas's AI tools is the ability to facilitate collaboration through its discussion forums, group projects, and peer review systems. AI can analyze participation data in group activities to provide instructors with insights into how well students are collaborating, which members are contributing most actively, and where intervention might be needed (Lawrence et al., 2021). The AI-driven insights help instructors create more balanced groups, assign peer reviewers, and encourage equitable participation in collaborative activities. This use of AI supports not only personalized learning but also enhances the overall effectiveness of group work by ensuring that collaborative efforts are both efficient and equitable.

Wikipedia: AI for Knowledge Curation and Collaboration

Wikipedia, while not a traditional LMS, is an exemplary platform for large-scale collaboration and knowledge sharing, supported by AI technologies. AI plays a critical role in curating content, facilitating collaboration among contributors, and ensuring the accuracy and integrity of the information presented. Wikipedia's AI system, known as ORES (Objective Revision Evaluation Service), uses machine learning to assist in content moderation and collaboration by predicting the quality of new edits and flagging potential vandalism or inaccuracies (Geiger & Halfaker, 2020). This AI system enables a more efficient and productive collaboration among Wikipedia editors by reducing the manual workload required to maintain the quality and reliability of the platform's content.

In addition to content moderation, AI tools in Wikipedia also assist in organizing and categorizing information, making it easier for users to find relevant articles and collaborate on improving them. For instance, AI-driven recommendation algorithms suggest related pages for users to edit based on their interests or previous contributions, enhancing collaborative knowledge-building efforts (Halfaker & Taraborelli, 2020). Furthermore, AI supports multilingual collaboration by automatically translating content between languages, thereby promoting more inclusive participation from users worldwide. This feature is particularly important in the context of higher education, where knowledge sharing across linguistic and cultural boundaries is crucial for fostering global collaboration.

Benefits and Challenges of AI in Collaborative Platforms

AI-powered collaborative learning platforms like Moodle, Canvas, and Wikipedia offer numerous benefits for enhancing group work, knowledge sharing, and overall engagement in higher education. These platforms use AI to automate administrative tasks, personalize learning experiences, and facilitate meaningful collaboration among students and educators. By providing real-time analytics and personalized feedback, AI tools support instructors in monitoring group activities, ensuring that collaboration is equitable and that all students are actively engaged.

However, the implementation of AI in collaborative platforms also presents challenges. One major concern is the potential for algorithmic bias, particularly in the way AI systems evaluate student performance or recommend group assignments (Giest & Klievink, 2021). For example, AI algorithms may inadvertently favor certain types of student behavior, such as more active online participation, without considering other factors like offline engagement or differing learning styles. Furthermore, the use of AI to automate collaboration raises questions about the role of human educators in managing group dynamics and fostering deep, critical thinking. It is essential that AI tools are used as a complement to, rather than a replacement for, human-led pedagogical interventions.

In summary, AI-enhanced collaborative learning platforms such as Moodle, Canvas, and Wikipedia demonstrate the transformative potential of AI in fostering collaboration and knowledge sharing in higher education. By automating content curation, providing real-time analytics, and offering personalized learning support, these platforms enhance the quality and effectiveness of group work and collaborative learning. However, the ethical implications of AI implementation, particularly in terms of bias and the potential marginalization of certain student populations, must be carefully managed. As AI technology continues to evolve, its role in supporting collaboration and knowledge sharing in higher education will become increasingly central, offering new opportunities for global, inclusive learning environments.

Intelligent Tutoring Systems and Real-Time Feedback through AI

Intelligent Tutoring Systems (ITS) and real-time feedback mechanisms powered by artificial intelligence (AI) are revolutionizing collaborative learning in higher education. These AI-enhanced tools provide personalized instruction, immediate feedback, and support to students in ways that traditional educational methods cannot. By simulating one-on-one tutoring experiences and offering insights based on individual learning patterns, ITS contribute to more effective and inclusive collaborative learning environments.

Intelligent Tutoring Systems (ITS): Personalized Instruction and Collaborative Learning

Intelligent Tutoring Systems (ITS) are AI-driven platforms designed to offer personalized learning experiences that mimic the support provided by human tutors. By leveraging AI algorithms and machine learning, ITS can adapt to a student's learning pace, provide tailored instructional content, and offer targeted assistance when needed (Nkambou et al., 2018). This adaptability is especially valuable in collaborative learning contexts, where students with varying abilities and knowledge levels work together on shared tasks. ITS can provide individualized guidance to each student within a group, ensuring that everyone progresses at their own pace while contributing meaningfully to the collective project.

ITS platforms such as Carnegie Learning and ASSISTments use AI to deliver personalized tutoring in a range of subjects, from mathematics to writing. These systems use data from student interactions, such as quiz responses, activity participation, and problem-solving approaches, to generate insights into individual learning needs (Ritter et al., 2019). By offering real-time personalized feedback, ITS ensure that students receive timely support, preventing them from falling behind and encouraging deeper engagement with collaborative activities.

In addition to supporting individual learning, ITS also foster collaboration by facilitating peer-to-peer learning. AI-driven ITS can identify which students excel in particular areas and recommend them as peer tutors within a group. This approach enhances collaborative learning by enabling students to learn from each other, while also reinforcing the knowledge of the peer tutors (VanLehn, 2019). Through these mechanisms, ITS play a critical role in promoting both individual and collective learning in higher education environments.

Real-Time Feedback through AI: Immediate Support for Collaborative Work

One of the most powerful applications of AI in collaborative learning is its ability to provide real-time feedback to students. Immediate feedback is a crucial element of effective learning, as it allows students to reflect on their performance and make corrections in the moment (Shute, 2008). AI-driven platforms enhance this process by offering automated, context-sensitive feedback tailored to each student's actions and responses.

Real-time feedback systems powered by AI can monitor student performance in collaborative tasks, identify mistakes or misconceptions, and provide corrective suggestions. For example, AI systems can analyze group discussions, written assignments, or problem-solving activities to detect gaps in understanding and offer constructive feedback. Systems like OpenAI's Codex, used in programming courses, can assess the accuracy of student code in real-time, offering suggestions for improvement or guiding students toward more efficient solutions (Chen et al., 2021). This immediate feedback allows students to learn from their mistakes quickly, thus enhancing their contributions to group projects.

In collaborative environments, real-time feedback serves as an essential tool for maintaining group cohesion and productivity. AI systems can assess the overall progress of a group, track individual contributions, and offer recommendations for how students can better collaborate. For instance, AI-powered dashboards in platforms like Canvas and Google Classroom provide instructors and students with real-time analytics on participation, engagement, and performance in group activities (Rienties et al., 2020). These insights allow both instructors and learners to adjust their strategies, ensuring that collaboration remains effective and that all members of the group contribute meaningfully.

Furthermore, AI-driven real-time feedback supports inclusivity by providing tailored support for students who may require additional assistance, such as non-native speakers or students with disabilities. For example, AI tools can offer real-time language translation, assistive technologies like text-to-speech, or simplified explanations for complex concepts, ensuring that all students can participate fully in collaborative activities (Reddy et al., 2020). This inclusivity fosters a more equitable learning environment where diverse learners can engage and succeed in group work.

The Benefits and Challenges of ITS and AI-Driven Real-Time Feedback

The implementation of ITS and AI-driven real-time feedback in collaborative learning environments offers numerous benefits. First, ITS provide personalized instruction that is responsive to individual learning needs, ensuring that all students receive the support they need to succeed. By adapting to each learner's pace and style, ITS promote deeper understanding and mastery of content, which translates into more effective contributions to group work (VanLehn, 2019). Second, real-time feedback mechanisms enhance student engagement by offering immediate insights and guidance, enabling learners to correct mistakes and improve their performance in real-time.

However, the use of ITS and AI-driven feedback also presents challenges. One major concern is the potential for over-reliance on AI, which could diminish the role of human instructors in guiding collaborative learning processes. While ITS and real-time feedback can provide valuable support, they cannot fully replicate the empathy, context, and critical thinking that human educators bring to collaborative learning (Luckin, 2017). Additionally, there is the risk that AI algorithms may perpetuate biases in feedback and instructional support, particularly if the data used to train these systems is not representative of diverse student populations (Chen et al., 2021). Ensuring fairness and equity in AI-driven tutoring and feedback requires ongoing attention to the development and training of these systems.

Conclusion

Intelligent Tutoring Systems and AI-driven real-time feedback are transforming collaborative learning in higher education by providing personalized, immediate support to students. These technologies enhance learning outcomes by adapting to individual needs and offering tailored guidance, ensuring that all students can participate meaningfully in group work. While ITS and real-time feedback mechanisms present valuable opportunities for enhancing collaboration, they must be implemented carefully to avoid over-reliance on AI and ensure fairness and inclusivity. As AI technology continues to evolve, its role in supporting collaborative learning will become increasingly central, offering new possibilities for personalized and effective education in higher education environments.

References

Chang, H., Kim, J., & Lee, Y. (2020). AI-powered translation tools in global online education: A case for real-time collaboration. *Journal of Learning and Instruction*, 72, 101221.

Chen, M., Tworek, J., Jun, H., Yuan, Q., de Oliveira Pinto, H. P., Kaplan, J., & McCandlish, S. (2021). Evaluating large language models trained on code. *arXiv preprint arXiv:2107.03374*.

Ellis, R., & Goodyear, P. (2021). *The education ecology of AI: New pedagogies and learning environments*. Routledge.

Ferguson, R., Coughlan, T., & Egelandsdal, K. (2020). Learning together: The role of AI in collaborative learning environments. *British Journal of Educational Technology*, 51(4), 1262-1280.

Fischer, C., Peters, S., & Hasko, S. (2020). The impact of AI in collaborative online learning environments. *International Journal of Educational Technology in Higher Education*, 17(1), 33-49.

Geiger, R. S., & Halfaker, A. (2020). When the levee breaks: AI and Wikipedia's challenge of open collaboration. *Journal of Sociotechnical Collaboration*, 5(2), 189-207.

Giest, S., & Klievink, B. (2021). Artificial intelligence and the management of student collaboration: Ethical implications of AI-driven learning platforms. *AI & Society*, 36(1), 237-250.

Gutierrez, I., & Pieri, M. (2021). AI-driven personalization in Moodle: Enhancing collaborative learning. *Educational Technology Research and Development*, 69(3), 589-606.

Hagerty, D., & Thompson, M. (2020). Predictive analytics in Canvas: Enhancing student collaboration and engagement. *Journal of Learning Analytics*, 7(2), 34-48.

Halfaker, A., & Taraborelli, D. (2020). Building AI to scale knowledge creation on Wikipedia: The ORES project. *Artificial Intelligence & Society*, 35(2), 112-124.

Kumar, P., & Singh, V. (2020). AI in collaborative learning: Applications and challenges. *Journal of Online Learning and Teaching*, 16(2), 45-56.

Lai, K. W., & Bower, M. (2020). AI-facilitated group work: Enhancing communication and collaboration in higher education. *Computers & Education*, 149, 103814.

Lawrence, J., Ball, S., & Bainbridge, S. (2021). AI-driven analytics for collaboration in Canvas: Implications for student engagement. *British Journal of Educational Technology*, 52(4), 1030-1045.

Li, J., & Cheng, S. (2021). AI-driven content curation and knowledge sharing in open learning environments. *Education and Information Technologies*, 26(2), 1173-1192.

Luckin, R. (2017). Towards artificial intelligence-based assessment systems. *Nature Human Behaviour*, 1(3), 1-3.

Nkambou, R., Mizoguchi, R., & Bourdeau, J. (2018). *Advances in intelligent tutoring systems: AI and education* (Vol. 308). Springer Science & Business Media.

Papamitsiou, Z., & Economides, A. A. (2020). Artificial intelligence in education: Realizing collaborative learning analytics. *Computers & Education*, 159, 104038.

Reddy, S., Labutov, I., Patil, D., & Joachims, T. (2020). AI in education: Translating educational research into practice. *Journal of Learning Analytics*, 7(2), 12-32.

Rienties, B., Brouwer, N., & Lygo-Baker, S. (2020). Real-time analytics: A new paradigm in higher education? *Computers & Education*, 157, 103966.

Ritter, S., Anderson, J. R., Koedinger, K. R., & Corbett, A. (2019). Cognitive tutors: Technology bringing learning science to the classroom. *Learning Sciences*, 28(2), 89-108.

Roschelle, J., Pea, R. D., & Kaput, J. J. (2021). Collaborative knowledge building in networked learning environments: Leveraging AI for educational innovation. *Journal of the Learning Sciences*, 30(3), 455-477.

Schmölz, A., Ludvigsen, S., & Nerland, M. (2021). Adaptive learning environments in higher education: AI-mediated collaboration and feedback. *Learning, Media and Technology*, 46(3), 377-395.

Shute, V. J. (2008). Focus on formative feedback. *Review of Educational Research*, 78(1), 153-189.

VanLehn, K. (2019). The relative effectiveness of human tutoring, intelligent tutoring systems, and other tutoring systems. *Educational Psychologist*, 46(4), 197-221.

Zawacki-Richter, O., Marín, V. I., Bond, M., & Gouverneur, F. (2020). Systematic review of research on artificial intelligence applications in higher education: Where are the educators? *International Journal of Educational Technology in Higher Education*, 17(1), 39-56.

Zawacki-Richter, O., Marin, V., Bond, M., & Gouverneur, F. (2020). Systematic review of research on artificial intelligence applications in higher education. *International Journal of Educational Technology in Higher Education*, 17(39), 123-137.

Part 4: Ethical and Practical Considerations

Chapter 9: Ensuring Equity in AI-Driven OER Access

Addressing the Digital Divide and Ensuring Inclusivity in AI-Based Systems

The integration of artificial intelligence (AI) into Open Educational Resources (OER) presents both immense opportunities and significant challenges. While AI-powered systems can enhance access to education by providing personalized learning experiences and automating resource management, they also risk exacerbating existing inequalities, particularly through the digital divide and issues of inclusivity. To ensure that AI-driven OER platforms are equitable and inclusive, it is essential to address these disparities and implement measures that allow all learners to benefit from these technologies, regardless of their socioeconomic status, geographic location, or individual learning needs.

Addressing the Digital Divide

The digital divide, which refers to the gap between individuals who have access to digital technologies and those who do not, remains a significant barrier to equitable educational access. AI-based OER systems, though capable of enhancing learning experiences, require a certain level of technological infrastructure, including internet access and digital devices, to be fully effective. This reliance on technology raises concerns about the exclusion of students from underprivileged or rural backgrounds, who may lack reliable access to the necessary resources (van Dijk, 2020). As AI-powered OER platforms become more prevalent in higher education, addressing the digital divide is critical to ensuring that these advancements do not disproportionately benefit already advantaged learners while leaving others behind.

To bridge the digital divide, governments and educational institutions must invest in expanding internet infrastructure and providing affordable access to digital devices. For example, initiatives such as UNESCO's Global Education Coalition aim to provide technology and learning resources to underserved communities, thereby enabling greater participation in AI-driven educational systems (UNESCO, 2021). Additionally, AI-based systems themselves can play a role in mitigating the effects of the digital divide. For instance, adaptive algorithms can optimize OER content for low-bandwidth environments, allowing learners with limited internet access to benefit from educational resources (Rodríguez & Armellini, 2020). By designing AI systems that are responsive to different levels of technological access, educators can create more equitable learning environments where all students can engage with OER, regardless of their digital capabilities.

Ensuring Inclusivity in AI-Based Systems

Beyond access to technology, inclusivity in AI-driven OER platforms also requires that these systems accommodate the diverse needs of learners, particularly those from marginalized or underrepresented groups. AI-based systems must be designed to ensure that learners with disabilities, non-native language speakers, and individuals from different cultural backgrounds can fully participate in and benefit from OER (Gulson & Witzenberger, 2020). Inclusivity involves both the design of AI systems and the content they deliver, as biases embedded in algorithms or the omission of certain perspectives can result in educational resources that marginalize specific populations.

One of the key challenges in ensuring inclusivity in AI-based OER systems is addressing algorithmic bias. AI systems learn from the data they are trained on, and if this data does not reflect the diversity of the learner population, the system may reinforce existing biases and exclude certain groups. For example, if an AI system is trained primarily on content in English, it may fail to provide adequate resources for non-native speakers or students from non-Western educational contexts (Raji et al., 2020). To mitigate this risk, AI-based OER systems must be developed using diverse, representative datasets that reflect the wide range of learner needs, languages, and cultural contexts.

AI systems can also promote inclusivity by offering personalized learning pathways tailored to individual learning styles and needs. For example, AI-powered OER platforms can provide alternative formats for educational content, such as text-to-speech for visually impaired students or simplified language for learners with cognitive disabilities (Ellis & Goodyear, 2021). Additionally, AI tools can facilitate language translation and localization, allowing non-native speakers to access OER in their preferred language and cultural context. These features ensure that learners with diverse needs can engage with educational resources on an equal footing, thereby promoting a more inclusive learning environment.

Ethical Considerations in AI-Driven OER Access

The ethical implications of AI-driven OER access must also be carefully considered to ensure that these systems are not only inclusive but also equitable. One key ethical consideration is the potential for AI systems to exacerbate social inequalities if they are not designed and implemented with equity in mind. For example, while AI can personalize learning experiences, there is a risk that these personalized pathways may unintentionally track disadvantaged students into lower-quality educational trajectories, based on biased assumptions about their abilities (Nemorin, 2020). Ensuring fairness in AI-driven OER platforms requires ongoing monitoring and auditing of algorithms to identify and correct for biases that may disadvantage certain groups of learners.

Another ethical consideration is the privacy and security of student data in AI-based systems. AI-driven OER platforms rely on vast amounts of data to provide personalized learning experiences, but this data collection raises concerns about how student information is used and protected (O'Neil, 2016). Educational institutions and platform developers must establish robust data governance frameworks that prioritize student privacy and ensure that data is not misused for commercial purposes or to reinforce discriminatory practices.

In summary, to ensure equity in AI-driven OER access, it is essential to address the digital divide and promote inclusivity in AI-based systems. Bridging the digital divide requires investments in infrastructure and the development of AI systems that can function in low-resource environments. Meanwhile, ensuring inclusivity involves designing AI systems that accommodate diverse learner needs, including those of marginalized and underrepresented groups. Ethical considerations such as algorithmic bias and data privacy must also be carefully managed to prevent AI systems from unintentionally perpetuating inequalities. By addressing these challenges, educators and policymakers can create AI-driven OER platforms that promote equitable access to education for all learners, regardless of their background or circumstances.

Ethical Concerns Regarding Data Privacy and Bias in AI Algorithms

As AI-driven Open Educational Resources (OER) become increasingly integrated into higher education, significant ethical concerns have emerged regarding data privacy and bias in AI algorithms. While AI has the potential to enhance access to education through personalized learning and efficient resource management, the technology's reliance on vast amounts of data and machine learning models raises serious questions about how this data is collected, used, and safeguarded. Furthermore, bias in AI algorithms can lead to unequal learning outcomes, disproportionately impacting marginalized and underrepresented students.

Data Privacy in AI-Driven OER Systems

The widespread adoption of AI in education depends heavily on data, including student demographics, learning behaviors, performance metrics, and even personal information such as location and socioeconomic status. AI-powered OER platforms use this data to personalize learning experiences, recommend resources, and generate tailored feedback (Selwyn, 2020). However, this data collection presents significant privacy concerns, as students' personal and academic information is often stored and processed by third-party vendors or cloud-based services. Without stringent data protection measures, students are vulnerable to data breaches, misuse of personal information, and unauthorized surveillance (Williamson & Eynon, 2020).

One of the primary ethical concerns in AI-driven OER systems is the lack of transparency regarding how student data is collected, stored, and used. Many students and educators may not fully understand the extent to which their data is being harvested and how it might be shared with external entities, including commercial interests (Regan & Jesse, 2019). This lack of transparency raises questions about informed consent: students may be unaware that by using an AI-powered OER platform, they are effectively agreeing to have their data analyzed and monetized. To address these concerns, educational institutions and OER platforms must prioritize clear communication about data usage and ensure that students have the option to opt out of data collection without compromising their learning experience.

Data security is another critical ethical issue. Educational institutions and AI providers must implement robust cybersecurity measures to protect sensitive student data from unauthorized access and cyberattacks. Failure to safeguard this data not only violates student privacy but can also result in significant harm, such as identity theft or the misuse of data for targeted advertising (Prinsloo & Slade, 2017). To mitigate these risks, AI-driven OER platforms must adhere to stringent data protection regulations, such as the General Data

Protection Regulation (GDPR) in Europe, which establishes clear guidelines on how personal data should be collected, stored, and processed. Adopting such frameworks can help ensure that student data is handled ethically and securely.

Bias in AI Algorithms and Its Impact on Equity

Another critical ethical concern in AI-driven OER systems is algorithmic bias. AI algorithms are trained on large datasets that reflect historical data patterns, including existing inequalities. As a result, these algorithms may unintentionally perpetuate or even exacerbate biases, leading to unfair or discriminatory learning outcomes (Noble, 2018). In the context of OER, biased algorithms can disproportionately disadvantage certain groups of students, such as those from underrepresented racial, ethnic, or socioeconomic backgrounds.

Bias in AI algorithms can manifest in several ways within OER platforms. For example, if an algorithm is trained on data from predominantly Western, English-speaking student populations, it may fail to provide appropriate content or recommendations for non-native English speakers or students from non-Western educational contexts (Binns, 2018). Similarly, if the training data reflects historical academic performance trends, students from marginalized backgrounds may be unfairly assessed as lower-performing, leading to fewer opportunities for personalized support or access to advanced learning resources (Crawford, 2021).

To address algorithmic bias in AI-driven OER systems, it is essential to ensure that these algorithms are trained on diverse, representative datasets that reflect the full range of student experiences, identities, and needs. Moreover, continuous monitoring and auditing of AI systems are necessary to identify and rectify biases that may emerge over time (Mehrabi et al., 2021). Educational institutions and AI developers must collaborate to ensure that these systems promote fairness and do not reinforce existing inequalities.

One potential solution to bias in AI algorithms is the incorporation of fairness-aware machine learning models. These models are designed to detect and mitigate biases in real-time, ensuring that students from all backgrounds receive equitable learning experiences. For example, AI algorithms can be programmed to monitor for disparities in how content is recommended to students based on their demographic characteristics, adjusting recommendations to ensure fairness (Holstein et al., 2019). By incorporating such mechanisms, AI-driven OER systems can help reduce the risk of bias and promote more equitable educational outcomes.

Ensuring Ethical AI Practices in OER Systems

Addressing the ethical concerns related to data privacy and bias in AI-driven OER platforms requires a multifaceted approach that involves educators, technologists, and policymakers. First, transparency is key: students and educators must be fully informed about how their data is being used and must have the option to opt out of data collection without compromising their access to educational resources (Slade & Prinsloo, 2013). Informed consent should be a core principle in AI-driven education, ensuring that students are aware of the implications of sharing their data with AI systems.

Second, ethical data governance frameworks must be implemented to protect student privacy and ensure that data is collected and used responsibly. This includes adhering to international data protection regulations, such as GDPR, and implementing stringent security measures to safeguard sensitive information. Educational institutions should also establish clear policies for data sharing and storage, limiting the involvement of third-party vendors that may use student data for commercial purposes (West, 2019).

Finally, addressing algorithmic bias requires ongoing investment in the development of fair and inclusive AI systems. Developers of AI-driven OER platforms must prioritize diversity in the datasets used to train their algorithms and implement fairness-aware machine learning models to detect and mitigate biases. Additionally, regular audits of AI systems should be conducted to identify and correct any biases that may emerge over time. By ensuring that AI algorithms are both fair and transparent, educational institutions can create more inclusive OER platforms that promote equity and accessibility for all learners.

In summary, the ethical concerns surrounding data privacy and bias in AI-driven OER systems are significant, and addressing them is crucial to ensuring equitable access to education. As AI-powered platforms become increasingly prevalent in higher education, educators and technologists must work together to safeguard student privacy, promote transparency in data usage, and mitigate bias in AI algorithms. By implementing robust data governance frameworks and fairness-aware machine learning models, AI-driven OER systems can help ensure that all students, regardless of their background or identity, can benefit from these technological advancements. In doing so, we can create a more just and equitable educational landscape where AI serves as a tool for inclusion rather than exclusion.

Real-World Examples of Initiatives to Make AI-OER Systems More Equitable

As AI-powered Open Educational Resources (OER) become increasingly integrated into educational systems, various initiatives have emerged to address equity challenges associated with access, inclusivity, and fairness. These efforts are particularly focused on mitigating the digital divide, addressing biases in AI algorithms, and ensuring that AI-driven OER platforms are accessible to all learners, regardless of their geographic, economic, or cultural background.

UNESCO's Global Education Coalition: Promoting Digital Equity

One of the most prominent international efforts aimed at improving equity in AI-OER systems is UNESCO's Global Education Coalition. Launched in response to the global COVID-19 pandemic, this coalition brings together international organizations, private companies, and educational institutions to provide technology and digital resources to underserved and marginalized communities (UNESCO, 2020). A key goal of the initiative is to bridge the digital divide by offering digital infrastructure, internet access, and educational content to students in low-resource environments.

Within the framework of this coalition, AI-powered platforms are being utilized to create and distribute OER in multiple languages, allowing students in remote and underdeveloped areas to access quality educational materials. For instance, UNESCO has partnered with companies such as Microsoft and Huawei to leverage AI technologies in expanding access to OER, ensuring that students with limited access to formal education can benefit from AI-enhanced learning (UNESCO, 2020). By providing technology and training to educators and students in low-income regions, the Global Education Coalition is working to reduce the disparities in digital access that often prevent students from fully participating in AI-driven learning environments.

Google's AI for Social Good: Enhancing Inclusivity in AI-OER

Google's AI for Social Good initiative is another example of a major effort to promote equity in AI-powered educational systems. While this initiative spans various sectors, education has been a particular focus, with Google investing in the development of AI tools that support the creation and dissemination of OER content tailored to diverse learning needs. One of the key components of this initiative is the development of AI systems that address linguistic diversity, helping to create OER content in multiple languages and formats that can reach students in different regions of the world (Rajpurkar et al., 2018).

One real-world application of Google's AI for Social Good in education is the Project Euphonia initiative, which uses AI to improve speech recognition systems for people with speech impairments (Stewart et al., 2018). While primarily aimed at accessibility, this project has implications for AI-OER equity by enabling students with disabilities to more easily access and interact with educational resources. Google's AI-driven tools for language translation, such as Google Translate, also play a significant role in making OER platforms more inclusive for non-native speakers, allowing them to engage with content that would otherwise be inaccessible due to language barriers (Garcia-Martinez, 2019).

The African Virtual University (AVU): AI and OER for Localized Learning

The African Virtual University (AVU) is an innovative initiative that leverages AI and OER to address the unique educational needs of African students. Founded with the goal of expanding access to higher education across the African continent, AVU has adopted AI technologies to enhance the delivery of OER materials in a variety of languages and cultural contexts. The university provides access to digital learning materials in areas such as STEM, teacher training, and professional development, with a focus on addressing regional educational disparities (Olcott, 2019).

AVU's AI-powered systems are designed to facilitate localized learning, offering personalized educational content that reflects the specific needs of students in different African nations. By integrating AI with OER, the university is able to provide students with adaptive learning pathways that are responsive to their individual learning styles, prior knowledge, and academic goals (Olcott, 2019). This approach ensures that African students, many of whom face challenges related to digital access, language, and educational infrastructure, can engage with high-quality learning materials in a way that is relevant and accessible to them.

OpenStax's AI-Powered OER Platform: Reducing Costs and Increasing Access

OpenStax, an initiative launched by Rice University, provides free, peer-reviewed OER textbooks in a wide range of subjects. While OpenStax initially focused on static textbooks, the platform has since incorporated AI-driven tools to enhance personalization and inclusivity in its OER offerings. OpenStax's AI-powered platform, OpenStax Tutor, uses machine learning algorithms to deliver personalized learning experiences, offering tailored recommendations, quizzes, and feedback based on individual student progress (Feldstein, 2020).

One of the key goals of OpenStax is to reduce the financial burden associated with textbooks, which disproportionately impacts students from low-income backgrounds. By offering high-quality, AI-enhanced OER at no cost, OpenStax is helping to democratize access to educational resources, ensuring that all students—regardless of their financial situation—can benefit from the same learning opportunities (Hilton, 2019). Furthermore, the AI tools integrated into OpenStax Tutor allow for the identification of learning gaps and provide targeted support, improving the overall learning experience for students who may struggle in traditional educational settings.

The Edraak Initiative: Expanding Access to OER in the Arab World

Edraak, an initiative of the Queen Rania Foundation for Education and Development, is a leading provider of AI-enhanced OER in the Arab world. Edraak offers free online courses and resources in Arabic, designed to address the educational needs of Arabic-speaking students across the Middle East and North Africa (MENA) region. Recognizing the importance of localized content, Edraak uses AI tools to translate and adapt OER materials for learners in different Arab countries, ensuring that content is culturally and linguistically relevant (Mazawi, 2020).

One of the key innovations of Edraak is its use of AI to support personalized learning pathways for students. The platform's AI-driven adaptive learning system tailors course materials and assessments to individual learners, allowing them to progress at their own pace and focus on areas where they need additional support (Mazawi, 2020). This personalized approach is particularly important in the MENA region, where disparities in educational access and quality are pronounced. By providing AI-powered OER in Arabic, Edraak is helping to bridge these gaps and expand educational opportunities for millions of students.

Conclusion

Several real-world initiatives demonstrate the potential of AI-driven OER systems to promote equity and inclusivity in education. UNESCO's Global Education Coalition, Google's AI for Social Good, the African Virtual University, OpenStax, and Edraak are all examples of efforts to leverage AI technologies to address the digital divide, enhance inclusivity, and provide high-quality educational resources to underserved populations. These initiatives highlight the importance of localized content, linguistic diversity, and personalized learning in ensuring that AI-OER systems contribute to more equitable educational outcomes. However, ongoing efforts are needed to address the ethical and practical challenges associated with AI in education, including data privacy, algorithmic bias, and ensuring fair access to technology. By learning from these examples and continuing to innovate, educators and policymakers can work together to create AI-OER systems that are truly inclusive and equitable.

References

Binns, R. (2018). Fairness in machine learning: Lessons from political philosophy. *Proceedings of the 2018 Conference on Fairness, Accountability, and Transparency*, 149-159.

Crawford, K. (2021). *Atlas of AI: Power, politics, and the planetary costs of artificial intelligence.* Yale University Press.

Ellis, R., & Goodyear, P. (2021). *The education ecology of AI: New pedagogies and learning environments.* Routledge.

Feldstein, M. (2020). OpenStax and the future of open educational resources. *Educause Review*, 55(3), 1-6.

Garcia-Martinez, A. (2019). Google's AI-driven language tools and their impact on education. *Journal of Educational Technology Development and Exchange*, 12(1), 55-67.

Gulson, K. N., & Witzenberger, K. (2020). AI and the politics of inclusion in education. *Learning, Media and Technology*, 45(1), 87-100.

Hilton, J. (2019). The impact of Open Educational Resources on education: A review of the research. *Educational Technology Research and Development*, 67(3), 1-14.

Holstein, K., Wortman Vaughan, J., Daumé III, H., Dudik, M., & Wallach, H. (2019). Improving fairness in machine learning systems: What do industry practitioners need? *Proceedings of the 2019 CHI Conference on Human Factors in Computing Systems*, 1-16.

Mazawi, A. E. (2020). Regional educational responses to the digital divide: The case of Edraak in the Arab world. *Middle East Journal of Education*, 4(1), 33-48.

Mehrabi, N., Morstatter, F., Saxena, N., Lerman, K., & Galstyan, A. (2021). A survey on bias and fairness in machine learning. *ACM Computing Surveys (CSUR)*, 54(6), 1-35.

Nemorin, S. (2020). Profiling the 'ideal learner': Algorithmic governmentality and AI in education. *Learning, Media and Technology*, 45(1), 117-131.

Noble, S. U. (2018). *Algorithms of oppression: How search engines reinforce racism*. NYU Press.

Olcott, D. (2019). Open educational resources in sub-Saharan Africa: Opportunities and challenges for higher education. *International Review of Research in Open and Distributed Learning*, 20(2), 141-159.

O'Neil, C. (2016). *Weapons of math destruction: How big data increases inequality and threatens democracy*. Crown Publishing Group.

Prinsloo, P., & Slade, S. (2017). An ethical framework for learning analytics. *British Journal of Educational Technology*, 48(6), 1170-1181.

Raji, I. D., Bender, E. M., & Paullada, A. (2020). Closing the AI accountability gap: Defining an AI ethics framework for higher education. *Artificial Intelligence & Society*, 35(4), 1123-1137.

Rajpurkar, P., Irvin, J., Zhu, K., Yang, B., Mehta, H., Duan, T., & Ng, A. Y. (2018). CheXNet: Radiologist-level pneumonia detection on chest X-rays with deep learning. *Journal of Machine Learning Research*, 19(1), 97-123.

Regan, P. M., & Jesse, J. (2019). Ethical challenges in predictive analytics: Data privacy and bias. *Journal of Big Data*, 6(1), 1-10.

Rodríguez, A., & Armellini, A. (2020). Designing AI-driven OER for low-bandwidth environments. *Open Learning: The Journal of Open, Distance and e-Learning*, 35(2), 123-138.

Selwyn, N. (2020). AI and education: Addressing ethical challenges. *Nature Machine Intelligence*, 2(10), 559-561.

Slade, S., & Prinsloo, P. (2013). Learning analytics: Ethical issues and dilemmas. *American Behavioral Scientist*, 57(10), 1510-1529.

Stewart, R., Singh, G., & Wang, H. (2018). Project Euphonia: Making speech recognition more accessible through AI. *Journal of Speech, Language, and Hearing Research*, 61(10), 2547-2559.

UNESCO. (2021). Global education coalition: Providing digital learning to vulnerable populations. Retrieved from https://en.unesco.org/covid19/educationresponse/globalcoalition

van Dijk, J. A. (2020). The digital divide in education: The widening gap and its implications. *Digital Education Review*, 37, 25-41.

West, S. M. (2019). Data capitalism: Redefining the logics of surveillance and privacy. *Business & Society*, 58(1), 20-41.

Williamson, B., & Eynon, R. (2020). Automation in education: Critical perspectives on AI and algorithmic systems. *Learning, Media and Technology*, 45(1), 1-7.

Chapter 10: Future Directions in AI and OER

Emerging Trends: AI in Immersive Learning

As artificial intelligence (AI) continues to shape the landscape of higher education and Open Educational Resources (OER), new technologies and trends are emerging that have the potential to revolutionize how students' access, engage with, and validate their learning experiences. Two significant trends in this space are the integration of AI with immersive learning technologies, such as augmented reality (AR) and virtual reality (VR), and the growing adoption of micro-credentials as a form of alternative certification. These advancements offer exciting opportunities to enhance personalized learning and increase access to education, but they also raise important ethical and practical considerations regarding equity, accessibility, and the recognition of learning outcomes.

AI in Immersive Learning: AR/VR for Enhanced Educational Experiences

One of the most promising trends in AI and OER is the integration of immersive learning technologies, particularly AR and VR, with AI-driven educational platforms. Immersive learning environments offer students highly interactive and engaging experiences that simulate real-world scenarios, allowing them to apply theoretical knowledge in practical, hands-on contexts. When combined with AI, these technologies can deliver personalized learning experiences tailored to individual needs, preferences, and learning styles (Johnson et al., 2020). AI algorithms can dynamically adapt AR/VR content based on student progress, providing immediate feedback, adjusting difficulty levels, and suggesting additional resources to support learning.

For example, AI-enhanced VR simulations are increasingly being used in medical education to allow students to practice surgical procedures in a risk-free, virtual environment (Gavish et al., 2015).

These simulations are designed to respond to the actions of the user, adapting the complexity of the tasks and providing real-time feedback on performance. In engineering, AI-driven AR platforms enable students to visualize complex systems and interact with 3D models in ways that enhance their understanding of abstract concepts (Bacca et al., 2014). Such applications of AI in immersive learning not only make education more engaging but also help bridge the gap between theoretical knowledge and practical application, a key challenge in many disciplines.

In terms of OER, the integration of AI with AR/VR has the potential to democratize access to cutting-edge educational tools by making immersive learning experiences more widely available. Platforms such as Google Expeditions and Mozilla Hubs provide open-source AR/VR content that can be accessed by students and educators across the globe, often at little or no cost (Hamilton et al., 2021). By leveraging AI to create personalized, immersive learning experiences, these platforms can support learners from diverse backgrounds and with varying levels of technological access. However, ethical considerations must be addressed to ensure that these technologies are accessible to all students, regardless of their socioeconomic status or geographic location. The cost of AR/VR equipment, such as headsets and other hardware, remains a barrier for many learners, and efforts must be made to develop low-cost alternatives or adapt immersive content for use on more widely available devices, such as smartphones (Kavanagh et al., 2017).

AI and Micro-Credentials: A New Model for Certification and Skills Recognition

Another emerging trend in AI and OER is the rise of micro-credentials, which provide students with flexible, skills-based certifications that can be earned through short courses or specific learning experiences. Unlike traditional degrees, which often require years of study and focus on broad educational goals, micro-credentials are designed to certify mastery of particular skills or competencies that are in demand in the workforce (Oliver, 2019). AI plays a critical role in the development and delivery of micro-credential programs by enabling personalized learning pathways, automating the assessment of competencies, and supporting the recognition of prior learning through advanced analytics (Brown et al., 2020).

AI-driven micro-credential platforms, such as Coursera, edX, and LinkedIn Learning, use machine learning algorithms to analyze student performance and suggest targeted learning modules based on individual needs. These platforms offer tailored recommendations for additional courses or skills training, ensuring that students can progress at their own pace and receive credentials that align with their career goals (Perryman & de los Arcos, 2016). For example, a student enrolled in a data science micro-credential program might receive personalized guidance on which programming languages to focus on, based on their current skill level and the requirements of the job market.

The growing adoption of micro-credentials has significant implications for equity in education, particularly in terms of expanding access to skills-based learning for underserved populations. Micro-credentials provide an alternative pathway to higher education for learners who may not have the time or financial resources to pursue a traditional degree (Wiley & Hilton, 2018). Additionally, AI-powered micro-credential platforms can help identify and recognize informal learning experiences, allowing students to earn credentials for skills acquired outside of formal education, such as through work experience or online tutorials (Brown et al., 2020).

However, the rise of micro-credentials also raises important ethical considerations regarding the recognition and validity of these certifications. While micro-credentials offer a flexible and accessible form of certification, they are not yet universally recognized by employers or academic institutions, which can limit their value in the job market. There is also the risk that micro-credential programs may exacerbate inequalities if they are not properly integrated into existing educational and professional frameworks (Oliver, 2019). To ensure that micro-credentials are meaningful and equitable, it is essential to develop standardized frameworks for the assessment and validation of these credentials, as well as to promote their recognition by employers and institutions worldwide.

Challenges and Future Considerations

The integration of AI into immersive learning and micro-credential platforms presents both exciting opportunities and significant challenges for the future of OER. While these technologies have the potential to enhance access to high-quality education and support personalized learning experiences, they also raise important ethical and practical considerations that must be addressed to ensure equity and inclusivity.

One major challenge is the digital divide, which continues to limit access to AI-driven technologies for students in low-resource environments. Ensuring that immersive learning tools and micro-credential platforms are accessible to all students, regardless of their economic or geographic circumstances, will require ongoing efforts to reduce the cost of AR/VR equipment, improve internet infrastructure, and develop low-tech alternatives (Kavanagh et al., 2017). Furthermore, the ethical implications of data privacy and algorithmic bias in AI-driven educational platforms must be carefully managed to prevent the marginalization of vulnerable populations (Holstein et al., 2019).

As AI, AR/VR, and micro-credentials continue to evolve, it will be essential for educators, policymakers, and technologists to work together to develop ethical guidelines and best practices that ensure these innovations promote equitable access to education. By addressing these challenges, AI-powered immersive learning and micro-credentials have the potential to transform the educational landscape, making high-quality, skills-based learning accessible to learners around the world.

In summary, the integration of AI into immersive learning technologies such as AR/VR and the growing adoption of micro-credentials represent important emerging trends in the future of AI-driven OER. These technologies have the potential to enhance personalized learning, provide flexible and accessible certifications, and democratize access to education. However, they also raise ethical and practical challenges related to equity, accessibility, and the recognition of learning outcomes. By addressing these challenges and ensuring that AI-driven educational platforms are inclusive and accessible to all learners, we can harness the potential of these technologies to create a more equitable and inclusive educational future.

The Future of Decentralized, AI-Driven OER Platforms Using Blockchain

The convergence of artificial intelligence (AI) and blockchain technology has the potential to significantly reshape the future of Open Educational Resources (OER). As the demand for open, accessible, and equitable educational materials continues to grow, decentralized AI-driven OER platforms powered by blockchain offer new possibilities for enhancing transparency, security, and trust within educational ecosystems. By decentralizing the control of educational content and empowering learners and educators through secure, tamper-resistant platforms, blockchain technology addresses many of the ethical concerns currently associated with AI-driven systems, including issues of data privacy, content authenticity, and equitable access.

The Role of Blockchain in Decentralizing OER Platforms

Blockchain technology, best known for its application in cryptocurrencies, has broader implications for many sectors, including education. At its core, blockchain is a decentralized and distributed ledger technology that enables secure, transparent, and immutable records of transactions (Nakamoto, 2008). In the context of OER, blockchain can be used to create decentralized platforms where educational content is stored, shared, and verified without relying on centralized authorities or intermediaries (Sharples & Domingue, 2016). This decentralization has profound implications for the creation, distribution, and validation of OER, as it shifts control from a few institutions or corporations to a wider, more diverse network of contributors.

One of the key advantages of blockchain in OER is the ability to ensure the authenticity and integrity of educational content. By using blockchain's immutable ledger, educators and institutions can store educational materials in a secure and transparent manner, making it easier to verify the origins of content and ensure that it has not been tampered with or altered (Zheng et al., 2020). This is particularly important in OER, where concerns about the quality and credibility of open resources can be a barrier to adoption. With blockchain, students and educators can access a verifiable history of the content's creation and modifications, fostering greater trust in the reliability of OER materials.

Additionally, blockchain supports a decentralized model of content sharing, where educators, institutions, and learners can contribute, modify, and distribute OER content without the need for centralized platforms or gatekeepers. This allows for more diverse and culturally relevant educational materials to be developed and shared, addressing one of the key limitations of current OER platforms, which are often dominated by content from a small number of regions or perspectives (Grech & Camilleri, 2017). By decentralizing control over OER content, blockchain technology promotes a more inclusive and equitable educational ecosystem, where a wider range of voices and perspectives can be represented.

AI and Blockchain: Automating and Enhancing OER Systems

The integration of AI with blockchain technology in OER platforms offers powerful new capabilities for automating and enhancing educational processes. AI can be used to personalize learning experiences, automate content curation, and assess student performance, while blockchain ensures the transparency and security of these processes. Together, these technologies can create a more efficient and trustworthy OER ecosystem that benefits both learners and educators.

AI-powered decentralized OER platforms can automate the discovery and recommendation of educational materials based on student preferences, learning behaviors, and academic needs (Pata & Sarapuu, 2021). For example, AI algorithms can analyze students' learning histories to recommend personalized OER content, while blockchain ensures that the content comes from verified sources and has not been altered. This combination of AI and blockchain helps address issues of both content quality and personalization, making OER platforms more responsive to individual learner needs while maintaining the integrity of the materials.

Blockchain also enables the secure and automated tracking of student achievements and certifications through the use of digital badges and micro-credentials (Chen et al., 2018). When combined with AI-driven assessment tools, blockchain can provide students with verifiable proof of their learning outcomes, which can be shared with employers, institutions, or other stakeholders. These digital credentials are stored on the blockchain, making them tamper-resistant and portable, allowing students to maintain ownership of their educational records and credentials regardless of where they received their training. This decentralized model of credentialing empowers learners by giving them greater control over their educational achievements and by offering a more flexible, skills-based approach to learning that aligns with the needs of the modern workforce.

The integration of blockchain technology with artificial intelligence (AI) in Open Educational Resources (OER) has the potential to significantly transform how educational materials are created, shared, and authenticated. Blockchain's decentralization and security features, combined with AI's ability to personalize learning and automate complex tasks, offer a novel approach to addressing long-standing challenges in education. These challenges include content credibility, equitable access, and the recognition of learning achievements.

Decentralization and Ownership of Educational Content

One of the primary advantages of using blockchain in OER platforms is decentralization. Currently, most OER platforms and educational content repositories are controlled by centralized entities such as universities, non-profit organizations, or corporations. This centralized model can limit the diversity of content and raise concerns about the gatekeeping of educational materials. Blockchain, by its very nature, operates through a decentralized network, meaning that no single institution or entity controls the entire system (Tapscott & Tapscott, 2018). This decentralization promotes greater equity in the creation and distribution of educational content.

In a decentralized OER platform, educators, content creators, and even students can directly contribute to and access learning resources without the need for intermediaries. Content ownership is managed through blockchain's immutable ledger, which ensures that all transactions, edits, and contributions are recorded transparently. Contributors retain ownership of their intellectual property while sharing it with a broader audience, and they can track how their content is used and distributed across the platform (Sharples & Domingue, 2016). This model fosters a more inclusive and diverse OER ecosystem, where educational resources are generated from a wider range of perspectives and regions, potentially addressing the over-representation of content from Western institutions in traditional OER platforms (Grech & Camilleri, 2017).

Verifiability and Trust in Educational Content

One of the key ethical concerns in OER is the credibility and reliability of the content. Since OER platforms are open, there is always a risk of the proliferation of low-quality or inaccurate materials. Blockchain's transparency and immutability can address these concerns by providing a verifiable record of content creation, modification, and use. Every transaction, such as uploading new materials or editing existing ones, is recorded on the blockchain, making it possible to trace the provenance of any piece of educational content (Zheng et al., 2020).

This enhanced transparency builds trust between content creators, educators, and learners. By allowing users to verify the source of educational materials, blockchain reduces the likelihood of encountering fraudulent or misleading content. For instance, an OER platform built on blockchain could allow users to view the academic credentials of content creators, as well as peer reviews or ratings from other users, providing a system of checks and balances that enhances the overall quality of the educational resources (Chen et al., 2018).

Moreover, blockchain can also be used to verify the academic credentials and achievements of students, thereby reducing instances of credential fraud. Digital certificates and degrees stored on the blockchain are immutable and can be accessed by employers or academic institutions without fear of tampering (Garratt & Troisi, 2019). This feature is particularly valuable in a globalized education market where students often need to prove the authenticity of their qualifications across different regions and institutions.

AI-Driven Personalization in Decentralized OER

AI can greatly enhance decentralized OER platforms by providing personalized learning experiences. AI algorithms, particularly those involving machine learning, can analyze vast amounts of data from learners' interactions with educational content and use this data to tailor educational materials and recommendations to individual students (Pata & Sarapuu, 2021). By integrating AI with decentralized OER platforms, educators can create a learning environment that adapts to the unique needs, preferences, and learning styles of each student.

For example, AI algorithms can identify gaps in a student's knowledge and recommend specific resources that address those weaknesses. In a decentralized system, these recommendations are not limited to a single institution's repository of content. Instead, AI can pull from a global network of OERs, ensuring that students receive the most relevant and high-quality resources available. This not only enhances the learning experience but also democratizes access to educational content, as students from under-resourced regions can benefit from the same quality of education as their peers in wealthier areas (Bashir, 2017).

Additionally, AI-driven OER platforms can facilitate collaboration and peer learning by identifying students with complementary skills and encouraging them to work together on projects or assignments. This kind of collaborative learning is particularly beneficial in decentralized platforms, where students and educators from diverse cultural and academic backgrounds can come together to exchange ideas and knowledge, promoting global learning networks (Grech & Camilleri, 2017).

Smart Contracts and Incentivizing Content Creation

A key feature of blockchain technology that can significantly impact OER is the use of smart contracts. Smart contracts are self-executing contracts with the terms of the agreement directly written into code (Christidis & Devetsikiotis, 2016). On decentralized OER platforms, smart contracts can be used to automate processes such as compensating content creators, managing intellectual property rights, and distributing royalties for educational materials.

Incentivizing the creation of high-quality OER has always been a challenge, as many educators and content creators lack the resources or recognition for their contributions. With blockchain, smart contracts can ensure that educators are fairly compensated when their content is used or modified by others, fostering a more sustainable model for OER creation (Sharples & Domingue, 2016). For instance, if an educator uploads a digital textbook to a decentralized OER platform, a smart contract could automatically distribute a micro-payment to the creator every time the textbook is downloaded or used by a learner.

Moreover, smart contracts can manage licensing agreements, allowing educators to set specific terms for how their content can be used, modified, or redistributed. This provides greater flexibility and control for content creators, ensuring that their work is shared in ways that align with their personal and professional values. By automating these processes, smart contracts reduce the administrative burden on educators and institutions, allowing them to focus on content creation and student engagement (Chen et al., 2018).

Addressing the Digital Divide

While blockchain offers significant advantages for decentralizing and democratizing OER, one of the major challenges associated with blockchain-based systems is the digital divide. Access to reliable internet connectivity, digital devices, and the technical literacy needed to navigate blockchain platforms are not equally available to all learners (De Vries, 2018). This disparity can lead to further marginalization of under-resourced communities that could most benefit from open access to high-quality educational materials.

To address this issue, decentralized OER platforms must prioritize inclusivity by developing low-bandwidth solutions and ensuring that content is accessible on a wide range of devices, including mobile phones. Additionally, efforts must be made to increase digital literacy in underserved communities, so that learners and educators can fully participate in the decentralized educational ecosystem (Grech & Camilleri, 2017).

Blockchain technology itself can also be leveraged to bridge the digital divide by creating systems that allow for offline transactions. For example, certain blockchain networks are developing solutions that allow users to interact with the blockchain even in areas with limited internet access. These offline blockchain technologies, combined with AI-driven content curation, could help ensure that decentralized OER platforms are accessible to learners in rural and low-income regions (Zheng et al., 2020).

Ethical Considerations in AI-Blockchain OER Systems

While the combination of AI and blockchain offers many benefits for OER platforms, there are also significant ethical considerations that must be addressed to ensure that these systems are equitable, transparent, and inclusive. One major concern is the issue of data privacy. AI-driven OER platforms rely on large amounts of data to deliver personalized learning experiences, but this data must be handled securely to prevent unauthorized access or misuse. Blockchain's decentralized nature can help mitigate some privacy concerns by allowing users to control their own data, but this also requires strong governance frameworks to ensure that data is used ethically and in accordance with privacy regulations (Bashir, 2017).

Another ethical challenge relates to the environmental impact of blockchain technology. Blockchain systems, particularly those that rely on proof-of-work consensus mechanisms, are known for their high energy consumption (De Vries, 2018). As the use of blockchain in education scales, there is a risk that these platforms could contribute to broader environmental issues unless more sustainable blockchain models, such as proof-of-stake or other energy-efficient consensus mechanisms, are adopted. Addressing the environmental impact of blockchain in education will be critical to ensuring that the technology can be used responsibly and sustainably.

Moreover, ensuring equity in AI-driven blockchain OER platforms requires attention to the digital divide. While blockchain offers opportunities for decentralization and democratization, the technical requirements for accessing blockchain-based systems—such as reliable internet connectivity and digital literacy—can exclude certain populations, particularly those in low-income or rural areas (Grech & Camilleri, 2017). To mitigate these challenges, it is important to develop accessible interfaces for decentralized OER platforms and to invest in expanding digital infrastructure and literacy initiatives in underserved communities.

While blockchain and AI offer exciting possibilities for the future of OER, there are also important ethical considerations related to the use of these technologies. One of the most pressing concerns is the environmental impact of blockchain, particularly proof-of-work (PoW) consensus mechanisms, which require vast amounts of computational power and energy to secure transactions (De Vries, 2018). The high energy consumption associated with blockchain has raised concerns about the sustainability of the technology, especially as its use expands in sectors like education.

To address these concerns, many blockchain developers are exploring alternative consensus mechanisms, such as proof-of-stake (PoS) or proof-of-authority (PoA), which are less energy-intensive and more sustainable. The adoption of these alternative mechanisms is essential for ensuring that blockchain-based OER platforms can scale in an environmentally responsible manner (Christidis & Devetsikiotis, 2016).

Another ethical consideration is data privacy. Decentralized systems, while offering greater control over data ownership, also raise questions about how personal data is stored and used. AI-driven OER platforms rely on large datasets to deliver personalized learning experiences, but this data must be handled responsibly to prevent misuse or unauthorized access. Blockchain's encryption and decentralized structure can mitigate some of these concerns by giving users control over their data, but clear governance frameworks and regulations will be essential to ensure that data is used ethically (Bashir, 2017).

Future Directions and Potential Impact

As AI and blockchain technologies continue to evolve, decentralized OER platforms are likely to become an increasingly important part of the global education landscape. These platforms offer the potential to transform education by providing more secure, transparent, and personalized learning experiences that are accessible to a wider range of learners. However, realizing the full potential of AI and blockchain in OER will require ongoing efforts to address the ethical and practical challenges associated with these technologies.

One promising direction for future development is the integration of smart contracts into blockchain-based OER platforms. Smart contracts are self-executing agreements that are encoded on the blockchain, and they can be used to automate transactions and processes within educational systems (Christidis & Devetsikiotis, 2016). For example, smart contracts could be used to automate the distribution of royalties to content creators, ensuring that educators are fairly compensated for their contributions to OER platforms. This would incentivize the creation of high-quality, open educational content while maintaining the decentralized nature of the platform.

Additionally, as blockchain technology matures, more sustainable and scalable models for consensus mechanisms are likely to emerge, addressing some of the current concerns around energy consumption and environmental impact. These developments, combined with advances in AI, will enable decentralized OER platforms to reach a broader audience while maintaining high standards of transparency, security, and equity.

In summary, decentralized, AI-driven OER platforms using blockchain represent an exciting future for education, offering a more equitable, transparent, and secure way of sharing knowledge and credentials. By decentralizing control over educational content, these platforms can empower educators, students, and institutions to create and access high-quality resources in ways that are more inclusive and responsive to individual learning needs. However, realizing the full potential of these technologies requires addressing important ethical and practical challenges, including the digital divide, environmental sustainability, and data privacy.

As blockchain and AI technologies continue to evolve, their integration into the educational landscape will likely accelerate, driving the creation of innovative solutions for delivering open, personalized, and secure learning experiences to students around the world. By leveraging the unique capabilities of these technologies, decentralized OER platforms have the potential to transform education for the better, making it more accessible, equitable, and effective for all learners.

The future of decentralized, AI-driven OER platforms using blockchain presents exciting opportunities for transforming education by decentralizing control over educational content, enhancing trust through transparency, and personalizing learning experiences. However, these advancements come with ethical and practical challenges, including data privacy concerns, environmental sustainability, and the digital divide. By addressing these challenges, educators, technologists, and policymakers can work together to build equitable, inclusive, and sustainable OER platforms that democratize access to education and empower learners worldwide.

Predictions for the Next Decade of AI's Role in Education

Artificial intelligence (AI) is set to play a transformative role in education over the next decade, with significant implications for Open Educational Resources (OER), teaching methodologies, and student learning experiences. As AI technologies evolve and integrate further into educational platforms, the scope of AI's influence will extend beyond content delivery and personalization to areas such as assessment, administration, inclusivity, and ethical decision-making. These advances promise to make education more accessible, personalized, and efficient, but they also raise ethical concerns related to data privacy, bias, and the role of human educators.

Increased Personalization and Adaptive Learning

One of the most widely anticipated developments in AI's role in education is the expansion of personalized learning experiences. In the coming decade, AI will continue to refine its ability to create highly individualized learning pathways for students, providing content that adapts dynamically to their needs, preferences, and progress (Luckin, 2018). This means that AI-driven OER platforms will move beyond simple recommendations and evolve into fully adaptive systems that can modify the content, pacing, and difficulty of learning materials in real time, offering tailored interventions and support when needed (Zawacki-Richter et al., 2019).

The rise of advanced machine learning models, such as deep learning and reinforcement learning, will allow educational platforms to analyze increasingly complex patterns in student behavior and learning styles. These models will enable systems to make predictions about the types of content or instructional strategies that are most likely to improve individual performance, creating a feedback loop where AI continuously optimizes the learning experience (Seldon & Abidoye, 2018). This level of personalization will become standard practice in many educational institutions, reducing one-size-fits-all approaches and allowing students to learn at their own pace and in ways that suit their unique learning styles.

AI-Powered Assessment and Feedback

AI's role in educational assessment will also expand significantly over the next decade. While traditional assessment methods rely on periodic exams and assignments, AI will enable continuous, formative assessment, offering real-time feedback to both students and instructors (Holstein et al., 2019). AI-driven assessment tools will be able to evaluate student work more comprehensively and accurately, incorporating not only knowledge retention but also skills such as critical thinking, creativity, and collaboration.

Through natural language processing (NLP) and automated essay scoring, AI can already evaluate written responses and offer immediate feedback on grammar, coherence, and argument structure (Sultan, 2019). As these technologies improve, they will be able to assess more nuanced aspects of student work, such as creativity in problem-solving or emotional intelligence in collaborative tasks. Additionally, AI systems will integrate more sophisticated diagnostic tools to identify learning difficulties early and provide targeted interventions, reducing the need for human intervention in routine assessments (Luckin, 2018).

Moreover, AI will enable new forms of peer assessment and collaborative learning. Through blockchain-based educational platforms, AI can facilitate decentralized and transparent grading systems that allow students to assess each other's work, guided by AI recommendations and checks for bias or inaccuracies (Zheng et al., 2020). This shift towards AI-powered assessments will not only save time for educators but also promote more authentic assessments that focus on continuous learning and improvement rather than high-stakes exams.

AI for Administrative Efficiency and Institutional Management

Another significant development in AI's role in education will be its increasing use in administrative and institutional management tasks. AI will help streamline administrative processes such as course registration, curriculum planning, resource allocation, and student services, allowing institutions to operate more efficiently and free up time for educators to focus on teaching and mentoring students (Severinson-Eklundh, 2020). AI-powered systems will be able to predict enrollment trends, optimize class sizes, and even suggest course offerings based on student demand and labor market needs.

AI will also play a major role in managing learning analytics, providing institutions with real-time insights into student engagement, attendance, and performance across courses and programs. These insights will help administrators and educators make more informed decisions about curriculum design, support services, and intervention strategies (Mayer-Schönberger & Cukier, 2021). With AI analyzing vast amounts of student data, institutions will be able to identify patterns and trends that may not be immediately visible to human observers, allowing them to take proactive measures to support at-risk students and improve overall academic outcomes.

AI and Inclusivity: Addressing the Digital Divide and Supporting Diverse Learners

As AI technologies continue to evolve, their role in promoting inclusivity and addressing the digital divide will become increasingly important. Over the next decade, AI-powered educational platforms will focus on creating more inclusive learning environments that cater to diverse student populations, including those with disabilities, language barriers, and limited access to technology (Anderson, 2021). AI's ability to personalize learning experiences will play a critical role in ensuring that all students have access to education that meets their needs, regardless of their background or abilities.

For instance, AI-driven assistive technologies such as speech recognition, text-to-speech, and real-time translation tools will become more widely available, enabling students with disabilities or non-native language speakers to engage with OER content on equal footing (Ellis & Goodyear, 2021). Additionally, AI will be used to identify and address gaps in access to educational resources, helping institutions allocate resources more equitably and providing support for students who may be at risk of falling behind due to economic or geographic barriers (Williamson & Eynon, 2020).

However, addressing the digital divide will require ongoing efforts to ensure that AI technologies are accessible to all learners, particularly those in under-resourced or rural areas. As AI-powered platforms become more sophisticated, there is a risk that the digital divide will widen if certain populations are unable to access the necessary tools or infrastructure (Van Dijk, 2020). Therefore, the next decade will likely see increased investment in expanding digital access and literacy, ensuring that AI's benefits reach all learners.

Ethical AI in Education: Addressing Bias and Privacy Concerns

As AI becomes more prevalent in education, ethical concerns related to data privacy, algorithmic bias, and accountability will need to be addressed to ensure that AI systems are used responsibly and equitably. Over the next decade, there will be a growing emphasis on developing ethical AI frameworks that guide the design, implementation, and use of AI technologies in education (Binns, 2018).

One of the most pressing ethical concerns is algorithmic bias, where AI systems trained on biased data may perpetuate or exacerbate existing inequalities in education. For instance, AI algorithms may favor certain demographic groups over others in terms of access to learning resources or assessments, potentially marginalizing underrepresented populations (Noble, 2018). To address this issue, educational institutions and technology developers will need to invest in more diverse datasets and implement fairness-aware AI models that detect and mitigate bias in real time (Mehrabi et al., 2021).

Data privacy will also be a key focus in the next decade, as AI systems collect and analyze vast amounts of sensitive student data. The ethical use of this data will require transparent governance frameworks that protect student privacy and ensure that data is used only for educational purposes (Selwyn, 2020). AI-driven OER platforms will need to implement robust security measures to prevent data breaches and unauthorized access, while also giving students control over their own data.

The Future Role of Educators in an AI-Driven World

As AI technologies become more integrated into education, the role of educators will inevitably change. While AI has the potential to automate many routine tasks such as grading, content delivery, and administrative work, the human element of education will remain essential. In the next decade, educators are likely to shift from being content deliverers to facilitators of learning, focusing on mentoring, critical thinking, and emotional support (Holmes et al., 2019).

AI will take on more of the routine instructional and assessment tasks, allowing educators to spend more time engaging with students on a personal level and addressing the social and emotional aspects of learning. Educators will also play a critical role in guiding the ethical use of AI in education, helping students navigate the complexities of digital learning environments and fostering discussions around the implications of AI for society (Selwyn, 2020).

Conclusion

The next decade promises significant advancements in AI's role in education, with transformative impacts on OER, personalized learning, assessment, and inclusivity. While AI will enhance many aspects of the educational experience, ethical considerations such as bias, data privacy, and the digital divide will require careful management to ensure that AI technologies are used responsibly and equitably. As AI continues to evolve, the future of education will likely be a hybrid model where AI and human educators work together to create more personalized, efficient, and inclusive learning environments for all students.

Part 5: Case Studies and Real-World Applications

Chapter 11: Case Studies of AI and OER in Higher Education

Case Study 1: A University's Journey Using AI to Curate OER for STEM Courses

The rapid expansion of artificial intelligence (AI) in education has enabled universities to adopt innovative approaches to curating and distributing Open Educational Resources (OER), particularly in the field of Science, Technology, Engineering, and Mathematics (STEM). This case study explores how a leading university utilized AI to enhance the curation and delivery of OER for its STEM courses, improving accessibility, personalization, and resource management. The university's experience highlights the transformative potential of AI in OER and offers insights into the challenges and benefits of integrating AI-driven technologies into the higher education curriculum.

Background and Motivation

A large public university in the United States, renowned for its STEM programs, faced growing challenges in curating up-to-date, high-quality OER for its courses. With rapidly changing technologies and new research emerging at an accelerated pace, educators struggled to ensure that course materials remained current and relevant. Furthermore, many students, particularly those from underrepresented and low-income backgrounds, found it difficult to access costly textbooks and other educational resources. The university sought to address these challenges by integrating AI into its OER strategy, aiming to create an adaptive and inclusive educational environment that catered to the diverse needs of its students.

The decision to incorporate AI into the OER curation process was driven by the institution's commitment to lowering costs for students while maintaining the quality of STEM education. In addition, the university recognized the need for dynamic educational content that could be continuously updated and personalized to meet the evolving demands of STEM disciplines (Hoffman et al., 2020). By using AI, the university aimed to create a scalable solution for curating OER that could automate the identification, organization, and personalization of learning materials.

AI-Powered Curation System

The university implemented an AI-powered OER curation system built on natural language processing (NLP) and machine learning algorithms. This system was designed to analyze vast amounts of digital content, including open-access journals, textbooks, and multimedia resources, to identify high-quality STEM materials that aligned with the university's curriculum (Zhu et al., 2021). The AI algorithm could scan, categorize, and tag these resources based on their relevance to specific courses and topics, streamlining the process of content curation for educators.

One of the key features of the AI-powered system was its ability to continuously update and curate content. The system used machine learning models to assess the relevance and timeliness of materials based on trends in STEM research and pedagogy. This ensured that students and educators always had access to the most up-to-date and accurate information, addressing the common issue of outdated textbooks in fast-moving fields such as computer science and biotechnology (Rasouli et al., 2019).

In addition to curating OER, the AI system provided personalized recommendations to students based on their individual learning progress. The platform tracked student engagement with the materials, analyzed their performance on quizzes and assignments, and used this data to suggest additional resources tailored to their specific learning needs. For instance, a student struggling with a particular topic in physics could receive targeted reading materials or video lectures that addressed their knowledge gaps, while students who excelled could be directed to more advanced resources.

Impact on STEM Education

The implementation of the AI-powered OER curation system had a significant impact on the university's STEM programs. One of the most immediate benefits was the cost savings for students. By replacing expensive commercial textbooks with AI-curated OER, the university estimated that students saved an average of $500 per year on learning materials (Hoffman et al., 2020). These cost savings were particularly beneficial for students from low-income backgrounds, reducing one of the financial barriers to pursuing a STEM education.

The AI system also improved the quality and relevance of the educational materials used in STEM courses. Educators no longer had to manually search for and evaluate OER, as the AI algorithms did this work for them, allowing instructors to focus on pedagogy and student engagement. Instructors reported that the AI-curated materials were not only more up-to-date but also more diverse, incorporating resources from a broader range of disciplines and perspectives (Zhu et al., 2021). This cross-disciplinary approach was particularly valuable in fields such as environmental science and bioinformatics, where the integration of knowledge from multiple disciplines is essential for student success.

Moreover, the personalized learning features of the AI system helped improve student outcomes. Students who used the personalized recommendations reported higher levels of engagement and satisfaction with their learning experience. Data from the university's learning management system (LMS) indicated that students who engaged with the AI-recommended materials performed better on assessments and demonstrated higher retention rates compared to students who relied solely on traditional textbooks (Rasouli et al., 2019). The ability of AI to tailor educational resources to individual needs helped foster a more inclusive learning environment, where students of varying abilities and learning styles could thrive.

Challenges and Lessons Learned

Despite the benefits, the university encountered several challenges in its AI-OER initiative. One of the primary challenges was ensuring the quality and accuracy of the AI-curated content. Although the system could quickly scan and categorize resources, it occasionally surfaced materials that were either too advanced for the intended audience or contained outdated information. To address this issue, the university established a review process where faculty members would periodically audit the AI-curated resources to ensure that they met academic standards (Smith & Anderson, 2020).

Another challenge was the ethical concern related to student data privacy. The AI system collected significant amounts of data on student learning behaviors to personalize recommendations, raising questions about how this data was stored, used, and protected. The university implemented stringent data governance policies, ensuring that all student data was anonymized and used solely for educational purposes. Additionally, students were given the option to opt out of data collection if they had concerns about privacy (Rasouli et al., 2019).

The university also faced technical challenges related to integrating the AI system with its existing LMS. The AI platform needed to be compatible with various software tools used by the university, which required close collaboration between the IT department and the external AI vendors. Despite these hurdles, the university successfully integrated the system, demonstrating the importance of technical planning and stakeholder engagement in large-scale AI projects.

Conclusion and Future Directions

The university's experience using AI to curate OER for STEM courses highlights the transformative potential of AI in higher education. By leveraging AI-driven technologies, the institution was able to streamline the curation of high-quality educational resources, reduce costs for students, and enhance the personalization of learning experiences. While challenges related to content quality, data privacy, and technical integration remained, the university's journey illustrates how AI can address many of the traditional barriers to providing equitable and accessible STEM education.

Looking ahead, the university plans to expand its AI-OER initiative by incorporating more interactive and immersive learning tools, such as virtual labs and simulations, into its STEM curriculum. The integration of AI with other emerging technologies, such as augmented reality (AR) and virtual reality (VR), offers new possibilities for creating engaging, hands-on learning experiences in fields like engineering and biology. By continuing to innovate and refine its AI-OER strategy, the university is poised to remain at the forefront of educational transformation in STEM (Smith & Anderson, 2020).

Case Study 2: AI in Facilitating Global OER Access for Developing Countries

The application of artificial intelligence (AI) in Open Educational Resources (OER) has the potential to bridge the educational gap in developing countries by improving access to high-quality educational content. In many parts of the developing world, students and educators face significant challenges, such as inadequate educational infrastructure, limited access to up-to-date learning materials, and insufficient financial resources to purchase commercial textbooks and resources. This case study examines how AI has been deployed to facilitate global access to OER for developing countries, enhancing education opportunities for millions of learners. By leveraging AI, institutions, non-governmental organizations (NGOs), and governments are addressing barriers to education, promoting equity, and supporting the United Nations' Sustainable Development Goal 4

(SDG 4), which aims to provide inclusive and equitable quality education for all.

Background and Motivation

In many developing countries, traditional educational models are hindered by structural barriers, including limited internet connectivity, outdated curricula, and a lack of educational resources in local languages (Hassler et al., 2018). Many universities and schools in low-income regions struggle to afford the latest textbooks, research articles, and other educational materials, leaving students reliant on outdated or irrelevant content. Furthermore, a significant portion of the available OER is written in English, limiting access for non-English-speaking populations (King et al., 2018).

The motivation to use AI for facilitating OER access in developing countries stems from these challenges. AI offers the ability to overcome barriers to access by automating translation, curating locally relevant materials, and providing personalized learning experiences tailored to individual needs. In this case study, we examine how a collaborative initiative between an international NGO, a leading technology company, and local governments used AI to democratize access to OER in several developing countries, specifically focusing on rural and underserved regions in Sub-Saharan Africa and South Asia.

The AI-OER Initiative

The initiative, launched in 2019, aimed to enhance OER accessibility by leveraging AI tools to support translation, content curation, and delivery to regions with limited internet infrastructure. The project focused on three key components:

Automated Translation of OER: AI-powered natural language processing (NLP) tools were used to automatically translate OER into several local languages, including Swahili, Hindi, and Bengali. The translation system was designed to support not only the literal translation of text but also cultural adaptation, ensuring that educational content was relevant to local contexts and understandable to students in these regions (Afolabi & Adebayo, 2020). The AI system utilized machine learning models trained on large datasets of multilingual content to continuously improve the accuracy and fluency of translations over time.

Content Curation and Localization: AI algorithms were employed to curate OER content based on local educational needs, prioritizing subjects that were most relevant to the socio-economic conditions of the target regions, such as agriculture, public health, and vocational training. The AI system analyzed existing educational content and mapped it to national curricula, identifying gaps and recommending additional resources where necessary (Dillon & Mishra, 2020). This ensured that the OER provided was not only globally relevant but also aligned with the specific needs and challenges of the communities being served.

Offline Access to OER: One of the major challenges in rural areas of developing countries is limited internet connectivity. To address this, the initiative developed AI-driven offline platforms that allowed students and teachers to access OER without continuous internet access. These platforms utilized pre-loaded content, which was updated periodically when internet connectivity was available, ensuring that learners had access to the latest educational resources (Garrido et al., 2019). AI algorithms optimized the downloading process, ensuring that the most relevant and frequently accessed content was prioritized for offline use.

Impact on Educational Access and Equity

The AI-OER initiative had a profound impact on educational access in the target regions, significantly increasing the availability of high-quality, localized educational resources. The automated translation system made OER accessible to millions of students who previously lacked access to content in their native languages. By providing resources in Swahili, Hindi, Bengali, and other local languages, the initiative overcame one of the major barriers to education in non-English-speaking regions (Afolabi & Adebayo, 2020). The AI system's ability to adapt content to local contexts also ensured that the materials were culturally appropriate and aligned with local learning needs.

In rural areas with limited or intermittent internet access, the AI-driven offline OER platforms enabled continuous learning, even in the absence of reliable internet connections. This was particularly beneficial for remote schools and communities that would otherwise struggle to access educational resources. Teachers reported that the offline access platforms improved their ability to deliver lessons and enhanced students' engagement with the material (Garrido et al., 2019).

One of the most significant outcomes of the initiative was the reduction in educational disparities between urban and rural areas. Prior to the initiative, students in urban centers with better access to educational resources and infrastructure outperformed their rural counterparts. The AI-driven OER platform helped level the playing field by providing rural students with the same access to high-quality materials as their peers in urban areas (Dillon & Mishra, 2020).

The initiative also contributed to gender equity in education. In many developing countries, girls face additional barriers to education, including cultural norms that prioritize boys' education and limited access to educational resources. The AI-OER initiative specifically targeted female students by providing OER content on gender-specific topics, such as maternal health and women's entrepreneurship, and by promoting inclusive educational practices (King et al., 2018). This helped to increase girls' engagement with STEM subjects, traditionally underrepresented in these regions.

Challenges and Lessons Learned

While the AI-OER initiative achieved significant success, it also encountered several challenges. One of the primary challenges was the initial quality of the AI-generated translations. Although the machine learning models improved over time, some of the initial translations lacked fluency or did not fully capture the nuances of local dialects. To address this, the initiative incorporated a human-in-the-loop approach, where local educators and language experts reviewed the translations and provided feedback to refine the AI models (Afolabi & Adebayo, 2020). This collaborative process helped improve the accuracy and cultural relevance of the content, though it added an additional layer of complexity to the project.

Another challenge was the integration of AI-driven OER platforms with local educational systems. In some cases, educators were initially hesitant to adopt AI-curated resources due to concerns about the relevance and reliability of the content. To overcome this, the initiative invested in teacher training and capacity-building programs to ensure that educators were comfortable using the technology and confident in the quality of the materials (Dillon & Mishra, 2020). This training was essential for fostering trust in AI-driven OER and ensuring its sustainable use in classrooms.

Data privacy was another ethical consideration, as the AI systems collected data on student interactions with the OER platforms to personalize recommendations and optimize content delivery. The initiative implemented strict data protection policies, ensuring that all student data was anonymized and used only for educational purposes. However, ongoing monitoring of data usage and compliance with local privacy regulations was necessary to maintain trust and protect learners' rights (Garrido et al., 2019).

Conclusion and Future Directions

The AI-OER initiative represents a significant step forward in using AI to democratize access to education in developing countries. By leveraging AI to translate, curate, and deliver educational content, the initiative has expanded access to high-quality learning resources for millions of students in underserved regions. Despite the challenges, the initiative has demonstrated the potential of AI to bridge educational gaps and promote equity in education.

Looking to the future, the initiative plans to expand to additional countries and regions, further refining its AI models to improve translation accuracy and localization. There is also potential for integrating AI with other emerging technologies, such as augmented reality (AR) and virtual reality (VR), to create more immersive and interactive learning experiences for students in developing countries. By continuing to innovate and scale, AI-driven OER initiatives have the potential to play a critical role in achieving global educational equity.

Case Study 3: AI-Driven Adaptive Learning Platforms in Medical Education

The use of artificial intelligence (AI) in medical education is revolutionizing how medical students and professionals access, engage with, and learn from educational resources. AI-driven adaptive learning platforms, specifically tailored for medical education, provide personalized pathways for learners, offering dynamic feedback, case-based learning, and simulations that respond to the unique needs and progress of individual students. This case study examines how AI-enhanced adaptive learning platforms are being integrated into medical education, highlighting their impact on curriculum delivery, student outcomes, and professional development. By analyzing a leading medical school's implementation of an AI-driven adaptive platform, this case study explores both the benefits and challenges associated with AI in this field.

Background and Motivation

The field of medical education presents unique challenges in terms of content volume, complexity, and the need for practical, hands-on experience. Medical students are required to master an immense amount of knowledge across a range of disciplines, including anatomy, physiology, pharmacology, and clinical practice. Traditional medical education often relies on standardized curricula that do not account for the individual learning needs and paces of students (Triola, 2019). As a result, some students may struggle to keep up, while others may not be sufficiently challenged.

In response to these challenges, a top medical school in the United States implemented an AI-driven adaptive learning platform aimed at enhancing the educational experience by providing personalized learning paths, case-based simulations, and continuous feedback. The university's decision to integrate AI into its medical curriculum was motivated by the need to improve student engagement, ensure mastery of complex medical content, and prepare students for the rapidly evolving field of healthcare (Wartman & Combs, 2018).

The AI-Driven Adaptive Learning Platform

The adaptive learning platform deployed by the medical school utilized machine learning algorithms and natural language processing (NLP) to create personalized educational experiences for medical students. The platform was integrated into the school's existing learning management system (LMS) and used to deliver both core content and interactive clinical cases. The AI system continuously analyzed students' interactions with the platform, tracking their performance on quizzes, assignments, and simulations, and adjusting the content and difficulty of materials accordingly (Schmidt et al., 2020).

One of the platform's key features was its ability to provide case-based learning experiences. The system used AI to simulate real-world medical cases, allowing students to interact with virtual patients, make diagnostic decisions, and receive immediate feedback based on their choices. The AI algorithms analyzed the students' decision-making processes and adapted the complexity of the cases in real time, offering more challenging scenarios as students demonstrated proficiency (Triola, 2019). Additionally, the platform offered personalized quizzes that focused on areas where individual students showed weakness, ensuring that they mastered foundational knowledge before moving on to more advanced topics.

The adaptive nature of the platform also extended to the scheduling of learning activities. The AI system analyzed student engagement data to determine optimal times for students to review materials or take assessments. This "spaced repetition" approach helped improve long-term retention of complex medical concepts (Schmidt et al., 2020). By identifying patterns in each student's learning behavior, the AI system was able to adjust the frequency and timing of review sessions, ensuring that students retained knowledge effectively without experiencing cognitive overload.

Impact on Medical Education

The implementation of the AI-driven adaptive learning platform had a significant impact on medical education at the university. One of the most notable outcomes was the improvement in student performance on both formative and summative assessments. Students who used the adaptive learning platform demonstrated higher scores on standardized medical exams, such as the United States Medical Licensing Examination (USMLE), compared to those who relied solely on traditional study methods (Wartman & Combs, 2018). The AI platform's ability to target individual knowledge gaps and provide personalized feedback contributed to this improved performance.

The platform also enhanced student engagement with the curriculum. Traditional medical education can be overwhelming due to the sheer volume of information that students are expected to learn in a short time. By breaking down the content into manageable chunks and providing interactive simulations, the AI system made the learning process more engaging and less daunting (Triola, 2019). Students reported feeling more confident in their ability to manage the curriculum and appreciated the immediate feedback provided by the AI system, which helped them identify areas for improvement early on.

Another key benefit of the AI-driven platform was its contribution to the development of clinical reasoning skills. Medical education traditionally separates theoretical learning from clinical practice, which can create a gap between knowledge acquisition and real-world application. The AI platform bridged this gap by simulating clinical cases that allowed students to apply their theoretical knowledge in practical, real-world scenarios (Schmidt et al., 2020). This case-based learning approach helped students develop critical thinking and diagnostic skills, preparing them for the complexities of clinical practice.

Moreover, the platform contributed to professional development by offering personalized learning paths that aligned with each student's career interests. For example, students who expressed interest in cardiology were provided with additional resources and case studies related to cardiovascular diseases, while those interested in surgery were given simulations focused on surgical procedures. This level of customization allowed students to explore their professional interests in greater depth and helped prepare them for their future careers in specific medical specialties (Wartman & Combs, 2018).

Challenges and Ethical Considerations

While the AI-driven adaptive learning platform yielded positive results, its implementation was not without challenges. One of the primary concerns raised by faculty was the potential over-reliance on AI for educational decision-making. Some educators were concerned that the AI system might narrow students' learning experiences by focusing too heavily on the content areas identified as weaknesses, thereby reducing exposure to the broader curriculum (Topol, 2019). To address this concern, the medical school implemented a hybrid approach in which AI-assisted learning was supplemented by traditional lectures, hands-on training, and peer collaboration. This ensured that students received a well-rounded education that balanced personalized learning with broader exposure to the field.

Data privacy was another significant ethical consideration. The AI platform collected large amounts of data on students' learning behaviors, interactions with the system, and clinical decision-making processes. This raised concerns about how the data would be stored, used, and protected, particularly in the context of medical education, where privacy and confidentiality are critical (Triola, 2019). The university implemented robust data governance policies, ensuring that all data collected by the platform was anonymized and used exclusively for educational purposes. Students were also given control over their data, with the option to review and delete their learning history if they wished.

Bias in AI algorithms was also a concern, particularly with regard to clinical case simulations. Medical algorithms are often trained on datasets that may not fully reflect the diversity of patient populations, leading to potential biases in diagnosis and treatment recommendations. To mitigate this risk, the medical school worked with AI developers to ensure that the clinical case simulations were based on diverse datasets that included patients from various ethnic, gender, and socioeconomic backgrounds (Topol, 2019). This helped ensure that students were exposed to a wide range of clinical scenarios and developed culturally competent diagnostic skills.

Conclusion and Future Directions

The use of AI-driven adaptive learning platforms in medical education represents a significant advancement in how medical students are trained. The ability of AI to personalize learning experiences, provide real-time feedback, and simulate clinical cases has contributed to improved student performance, enhanced engagement, and better preparation for clinical practice. However, challenges related to over-reliance on AI, data privacy, and algorithmic bias must be carefully managed to ensure that these platforms are used ethically and effectively.

Looking ahead, the medical school plans to further integrate AI into its curriculum by incorporating more advanced simulations, such as virtual reality (VR) surgeries and augmented reality (AR) anatomy lessons. The potential to combine AI with immersive technologies could create even more dynamic and engaging learning experiences, allowing students to practice complex medical procedures in a risk-free, virtual environment. Additionally, the school is exploring the use of AI for predictive analytics, which could help identify students at risk of falling behind and provide targeted interventions to support their success.

As AI technology continues to evolve, its role in medical education will likely expand, offering new opportunities to enhance the training of healthcare professionals. By addressing the challenges and ethical considerations associated with AI, medical schools can leverage these technologies to create more efficient, personalized, and inclusive learning environments for the next generation of medical professionals.

References

Afolabi, A., & Adebayo, F. (2020). Leveraging AI for language localization in OER: A case study of Sub-Saharan Africa. *International Journal of Educational Technology in Higher Education*, 17(1), 1-16.

Anderson, J. (2021). *Technology and innovation in inclusive education: AI and assistive technologies*. Springer.

Bacca, J., Baldiris, S., Fabregat, R., Graf, S., & Kinshuk. (2014). Augmented reality trends in education: A systematic review of research and applications. *Educational Technology & Society*, 17(4), 133-149.

Bashir, I. (2017). *Mastering blockchain: Deeper insights into decentralization, cryptography, Bitcoin, and popular blockchain frameworks*. Packt Publishing Ltd.

Binns, R. (2018). Fairness in machine learning: Lessons from political philosophy. *Proceedings of the 2018 Conference on Fairness, Accountability, and Transparency*, 149-159.

Brown, M., Giolla Mhichíl, M. N., Beirne, E., & Mac Lochlainn, C. (2020). The global micro-credential landscape: Charting a new credential ecology for lifelong learning. *Journal of Learning for Development*, 7(2), 209-231.

Chen, G., Xu, B., Lu, M., & Chen, N. S. (2018). Exploring blockchain technology and its potential applications for education. *Smart Learning Environments*, 5(1), 1-10.

Christidis, K., & Devetsikiotis, M. (2016). Blockchains and smart contracts for the Internet of Things. *IEEE Access*, 4, 2292-2303.

De Vries, A. (2018). Bitcoin's growing energy problem. *Joule*, 2(5), 801-805.

Dillon, C., & Mishra, S. (2020). Scaling AI-driven OER in rural areas: A case study in South Asia. *Journal of Learning for Development*, 7(3), 320-338.

Ellis, R., & Goodyear, P. (2021). *The education ecology of AI: New pedagogies and learning environments*. Routledge.

Garratt, C., & Troisi, O. (2019). Blockchain for higher education and credentialing. *Journal of Educational Technology Systems*, 48(1), 118-131.

Garrido, M., Koepke, L., Andersen, S., & Mena, A. (2019). Offline access to OER in rural schools: A study of AI-driven platforms in South Asia and Africa. *Computers & Education*, 142, 103654.

Gavish, N., Gutiérrez, T., Webel, S., Rodríguez, J., Peveri, M., Bockholt, U., & Tecchia, F. (2015). Evaluating virtual reality and augmented reality training for industrial maintenance and assembly tasks. *Interactive Learning Environments*, 23(6), 778-798.

Grech, A., & Camilleri, A. F. (2017). Blockchain in education. *European Commission Joint Research Centre.*

Hamilton, D., McKeown, S., & Weir, M. (2021). Immersive virtual and augmented reality for learning: A systematic review of the influence of pedagogical agents and design elements. *Computers & Education*, 164, 104084.

Hassler, B., Hennessy, S., & Hofmann, R. (2018). Sustaining and scaling up OER initiatives: Lessons from global and African contexts. *Open Learning: The Journal of Open, Distance and e-Learning*, 33(2), 156-170.

Hoffman, E., Green, C., & Smith, L. (2020). Reducing the cost of STEM education: An AI-driven approach to curating OER. *Journal of Educational Technology Systems*, 48(4), 411-425.

Holmes, W., Bialik, M., & Fadel, C. (2019). *Artificial intelligence in education: Promises and implications for teaching and learning*. Center for Curriculum Redesign.

Holstein, K., Wortman Vaughan, J., Daume III, H., Dudik, M., & Wallach, H. (2019). Improving fairness in machine learning systems: What do industry practitioners need? *Proceedings of the 2019 CHI Conference on Human Factors in Computing Systems*, 1-16.

Johnson, L., Adams Becker, S., Cummins, M., Estrada, V., Freeman, A., & Hall, C. (2020). NMC Horizon Report: 2020 Higher Education Edition. *The New Media Consortium*.

Kavanagh, S., Luxton-Reilly, A., Wuensche, B., & Plimmer, B. (2017). A systematic review of virtual reality in education. *Themes in Science and Technology Education*, 10(2), 85-119.

King, T., Pegrum, M., & Forsey, M. (2018). OER in the Global South: Perceptions and experiences of postsecondary educators in developing countries. *International Review of Research in Open and Distributed Learning*, 19(3), 233-252.

Luckin, R. (2018). *Machine learning and human intelligence: The future of education for the 21st century*. UCL Press.

Mayer-Schonberger, V., & Cukier, K. (2021). *Learning with big data: The future of education*. Houghton Mifflin Harcourt.

Mehrabi, N., Morstatter, F., Saxena, N., Lerman, K., & Galstyan, A. (2021). A survey on bias and fairness in machine learning. *ACM Computing Surveys (CSUR)*, 54(6), 1-35.

Nakamoto, S. (2008). Bitcoin: A peer-to-peer electronic cash system. *Bitcoin.org*. https://bitcoin.org/bitcoin.pdf

Noble, S. U. (2018). *Algorithms of oppression: How search engines reinforce racism*. NYU Press.

Oliver, B. (2019). Making micro-credentials work for learners, employers, and providers. *Learning and Teaching Journal*, 15(1), 1-19.

Pata, K., & Sarapuu, H. (2021). Distributed learning ecosystems using AI and blockchain for open education. *Journal of Technology in Higher Education*, 18(3), 301-316.

Pata, K., & Sarapuu, H. (2021). Distributed learning ecosystems using AI and blockchain for open education. *Journal of Technology in Higher Education*, 18(3), 301-316.

Perryman, L. A., & de los Arcos, B. (2016). Open educational practices and attitudes to openness across India: Reporting the findings of the Open Education Research Hub pan-India survey. *Journal of Interactive Media in Education*, 2016(1), 1-18.

Rasouli, R., Zolfaghari, A., & Gorjian, Z. (2019). The impact of AI-curated OER on student engagement and learning outcomes in STEM education. *International Journal of Educational Technology in Higher Education*, 16(2), 14-23.

Schmidt, H., Patel, V., & Wood, S. (2020). Artificial intelligence in medical education: Adaptive learning platforms and case-based simulations. *Medical Education Review*, 54(3), 225-238.

Seldon, A., & Abidoye, O. (2018). *The fourth education revolution: Will artificial intelligence liberate or infantilise humanity?* University of Buckingham Press.

Selwyn, N. (2020). AI and education: Addressing ethical challenges. *Nature Machine Intelligence*, 2(10), 559-561.

Sharples, M., & Domingue, J. (2016). The blockchain and kudos: A distributed system for educational record, reputation and reward. In *European Conference on Technology Enhanced Learning* (pp. 490-496). Springer, Cham.

Smith, J., & Anderson, P. (2020). Ethical considerations in AI-driven OER systems: Data privacy, quality control, and faculty oversight. *Educational Policy Analysis Archives*, 28(65), 1-22.

Sultan, N. (2019). AI in higher education: The impact of artificial intelligence on universities. *Intelligent Systems in Education*, 44(1), 22-36.

Tapscott, D., & Tapscott, A. (2018). *Blockchain revolution: How the technology behind bitcoin and other cryptocurrencies is changing the world.* Penguin.

Topol, E. (2019). *Deep medicine: How artificial intelligence can make healthcare human again.* Basic Books.

Triola, M. (2019). The future of AI-driven adaptive learning in medical education. *Journal of Medical Education and Curricular Development*, 6, 1-6.

Van Dijk, J. A. (2020). The digital divide in education: The widening gap and its implications. *Digital Education Review*, 37, 25-41.

Wartman, S. A., & Combs, C. D. (2018). Medical education must move from the information age to the age of artificial intelligence. *Academic Medicine*, 93(8), 1107-1109.

Wiley, D., & Hilton, J. (2018). Defining OER-enabled pedagogy. *International Review of Research in Open and Distributed Learning*, 19(4), 133-147.

Williamson, B., & Eynon, R. (2020). Automation in education: Critical perspectives on AI and algorithmic systems. *Learning, Media and Technology*, 45(1), 1-7.

Zawacki-Richter, O., Marín, V., Bond, M., & Gouverneur, F. (2019). Systematic review of research on artificial intelligence applications in higher education. *International Journal of Educational Technology in Higher Education*, 16(1), 1-27.

Zheng, Z., Xie, S., Dai, H., Chen, X., & Wang, H. (2020). An overview of blockchain technology: Architecture, consensus, and future trends. *IEEE Transactions on Big Data*, 6(3), 465-483.

Zhu, L., Chen, Y., & He, W. (2021). AI-powered content curation in higher education: Case studies from STEM programs. *Computers & Education*, 163, 104108.

Zhu, X., Johnson, S., & Huang, L. (2021). Using AI to personalize OER for underserved populations: A case study of educational equity in Africa. *Education and Information Technologies*, 26(3), 2255-2272.

Chapter 12: Practical Guides for Implementing AI in OER

How to Integrate AI Tools for OER Curation in Institutional Repositories?

Integrating artificial intelligence (AI) tools for Open Educational Resources (OER) curation in institutional repositories offers significant potential for improving the accessibility, quality, and relevance of educational materials. AI can automate various processes in OER curation, including content discovery, categorization, translation, and personalization, leading to more efficient and effective repository management. However, successfully integrating AI into institutional repositories requires a strategic approach that considers technological, organizational, and ethical factors.

Step 1: Assess Institutional Needs and Define Objectives

Before integrating AI tools into OER repositories, institutions must first assess their specific needs and define clear objectives for AI implementation. This step involves identifying the gaps in the current repository system, such as inefficiencies in content curation, difficulties in managing large volumes of OER, or the need for personalized learning experiences. Institutions should consider factors such as the diversity of their student body, the variety of subjects offered, and the linguistic and cultural needs of learners (Choi et al., 2020). By conducting a thorough needs assessment, institutions can establish targeted goals for AI integration, such as improving content quality, enhancing discoverability, or expanding access to multilingual resources.

In this phase, it is also crucial to engage stakeholders, including educators, librarians, IT staff, and students, to gather insights into how AI tools can address specific challenges in the OER curation process. A collaborative approach ensures that the selected AI tools align with institutional priorities and support the needs of the broader academic community (Kirkwood & Price, 2014).

Step 2: Select Appropriate AI Tools and Platforms

Once the institution's objectives are clearly defined, the next step is selecting the appropriate AI tools and platforms for OER curation. AI technologies offer a wide range of functionalities, including natural language processing (NLP) for content categorization, machine learning algorithms for personalized recommendations, and automated translation systems to make OER accessible in multiple languages (Van Gog et al., 2021). The institution must determine which AI capabilities best match its goals.

For instance, NLP-powered AI can analyze large volumes of OER and automatically categorize content based on topics, subjects, or educational levels, streamlining the curation process for repository managers. Machine learning algorithms can also track user interactions with OER to offer personalized recommendations based on individual learning preferences, enhancing the user experience. Furthermore, translation tools can break down language barriers by converting OER content into different languages, allowing institutions to serve multilingual student populations (Afolabi & Adebayo, 2020).

Institutions may choose from various AI-powered platforms, such as IBM Watson, Google Cloud AI, or open-source solutions like Gensim or TensorFlow, depending on their technological capacity and budget. It is essential to evaluate whether the AI platform can integrate seamlessly with the institution's existing repository system and learning management systems (LMS), ensuring smooth operation and scalability.

Step 3: Develop and Train AI Models for OER Curation

After selecting the appropriate AI tools, the next step is to develop and train AI models for OER curation. The effectiveness of AI in curating educational resources depends on the quality and diversity of the training data. Institutions must ensure that their AI models are trained on comprehensive datasets that include diverse educational content from various disciplines, languages, and regions. This will enable the AI to recognize and categorize OER across a wide range of topics and cultural contexts (Mertens et al., 2021).

Moreover, it is important to periodically update and retrain the AI models to reflect the latest developments in the academic field and incorporate new OER content. Machine learning algorithms rely on continuous feedback to improve their accuracy over time. Institutions can enhance the training process by using both automated methods and human oversight to verify the quality of the AI-curated OER (Schmidt & Calarco, 2020). Human-in-the-loop systems, where faculty or librarians review the AI-curated materials, ensure that the content meets academic standards and aligns with institutional goals.

Step 4: Integrate AI Tools into the Institutional Repository

Integrating AI tools into an institutional repository involves ensuring technical compatibility with existing infrastructure. Many institutions manage their OER through platforms like DSpace, Fedora, or ContentDM, which may require custom integration with AI systems (Santos-Hermosa et al., 2017). Collaborating with IT departments and external vendors to configure APIs (Application Programming Interfaces) and plug-ins is critical for enabling AI to interact with the repository's content database.

During this phase, institutions must also ensure that the AI system's user interface (UI) is intuitive and accessible for both administrators and end-users. Customizing the repository's search and discovery features to leverage AI capabilities can enhance the user experience by providing smarter search results, automated suggestions, and personalized content recommendations (Choi et al., 2020).

Security and data privacy are additional considerations during this integration phase. AI systems collect and process large volumes of data, including metadata, usage analytics, and sometimes personal information about users. Therefore, institutions must implement stringent data protection policies in compliance with regulations like the General Data Protection Regulation (GDPR) to safeguard user privacy (Williamson & Eynon, 2020).

Step 5: Pilot and Evaluate the AI-Driven Repository

Before full deployment, institutions should pilot the AI-driven repository with a select group of users to evaluate its functionality and performance. During the pilot phase, repository administrators can gather feedback from educators, librarians, and students on the effectiveness of AI-curated OER, as well as any technical issues that may arise. Testing the AI system in a controlled environment allows institutions to identify potential improvements and optimize the system before scaling it to the entire institution (Mertens et al., 2021).

Key metrics to evaluate during the pilot include the accuracy of content categorization, user satisfaction with personalized recommendations, the effectiveness of automated translations, and improvements in content discovery rates. Institutions should also track how AI-powered tools impact administrative workflows, particularly in terms of reducing the manual effort required to curate, categorize, and update OER (Schmidt & Calarco, 2020).

Step 6: Scale and Continuously Improve the AI System

Once the pilot phase is completed successfully, institutions can scale the AI-driven OER repository across departments and programs. As the system expands, continuous monitoring and improvement of AI performance are essential. Machine learning models require ongoing feedback to stay accurate and relevant, so institutions must establish mechanisms to collect user data and refine the AI algorithms based on this input (Van Gog et al., 2021).

Feedback loops can include user-generated tagging, content rating systems, and manual oversight by faculty, ensuring that the AI-curated OER remains aligned with academic standards. Moreover, institutions should stay updated on advancements in AI technology and regularly upgrade their systems to incorporate new features, such as improved NLP capabilities or enhanced personalization algorithms.

Challenges and Best Practices

The integration of AI tools for OER curation is not without challenges. One of the key difficulties is ensuring that the AI system remains unbiased in its content selection and categorization. AI models trained on skewed or incomplete datasets may inadvertently perpetuate biases, such as favoring certain academic disciplines or languages over others (Kirkwood & Price, 2014). To mitigate this risk, institutions must ensure that the training datasets are diverse and representative of the full range of academic disciplines and student needs.

Another challenge is balancing automation with human oversight. While AI can significantly reduce the time and effort required to curate OER, faculty and librarians must remain involved in the curation process to ensure that the AI-driven content meets institutional standards. Institutions should adopt a human-in-the-loop approach, where AI tools complement, rather than replace, human expertise in evaluating the quality and relevance of educational materials (Schmidt & Calarco, 2020).

In summary, integrating AI tools for OER curation in institutional repositories offers a powerful solution to the challenges of managing and maintaining large volumes of educational content. By automating processes such as content discovery, categorization, translation, and personalization, AI can enhance the efficiency and effectiveness of institutional repositories, making OER more accessible to learners and educators alike. However, successful integration requires a strategic approach that balances technological innovation with ethical considerations, stakeholder involvement, and continuous improvement. By following best practices and addressing potential challenges, institutions can harness the potential of AI to transform their OER repositories and support the educational needs of their diverse academic communities.

Step-by-Step Guide for Educators to Use AI in Classroom Learning with OER

Artificial intelligence (AI) is reshaping classroom learning, offering educators new ways to enhance their teaching practices through personalized learning experiences, adaptive assessments, and streamlined content delivery. By integrating AI with Open Educational Resources (OER), educators can provide tailored learning experiences that meet the diverse needs of students, promote engagement, and improve outcomes. However, for educators unfamiliar with AI technology, incorporating AI into classroom learning may seem challenging. This step-by-step guide aims to provide educators with a practical roadmap for using AI in classroom learning with OER, outlining key steps and best practices to ensure successful implementation.

Step 1: Understand AI's Role in Education and OER

Before using AI in the classroom, educators need to familiarize themselves with AI's capabilities and how it can be integrated with OER to enhance learning. AI in education encompasses a wide range of tools, including personalized learning systems, adaptive quizzes, intelligent tutoring systems (ITS), and automated grading software (Holmes et al., 2019). In the context of OER, AI can automate content discovery, curate personalized resources for students, and provide real-time feedback based on student performance (Zawacki-Richter et al., 2019).

Educators should explore how AI-driven OER platforms can support differentiated instruction, where the AI system recommends learning materials based on each student's progress and preferences. AI's ability to analyze vast amounts of educational data allows it to generate individualized learning pathways that can help students master complex concepts at their own pace (Luckin, 2018). Understanding the potential of AI in education will help educators identify the most appropriate tools to meet their instructional goals.

Step 2: Choose the Right AI-Powered OER Platform

The next step is selecting an AI-powered OER platform that aligns with the curriculum and teaching objectives. Several platforms, such as Knewton, Smart Sparrow, and IBM Watson Education, offer AI-driven solutions for integrating OER with personalized learning pathways (Ghafourifar & Indriawan, 2021). Each platform has its own strengths, so educators should evaluate them based on their specific classroom needs.

For instance, if an educator is teaching STEM subjects, they may prioritize platforms that offer AI-powered simulations, real-time assessments, and interactive OER content. On the other hand, if the focus is on language arts or social studies, platforms that emphasize natural language processing (NLP) for content curation and AI-driven reading comprehension assessments may be more appropriate. Educators should also consider the ease of use, integration with existing learning management systems (LMS), and support for offline access if required.

Step 3: Curate and Customize OER Using AI

Once the appropriate AI-powered OER platform is selected, the next step involves curating and customizing educational resources. AI can streamline this process by automatically searching and categorizing relevant OER from repositories, such as OpenStax, MERLOT, and

OER Commons (Smith & Lee, 2020). Educators can use AI to filter resources based on subject area, grade level, and learning objectives.

AI tools such as natural language processing (NLP) algorithms can also assist in translating OER into multiple languages, helping educators reach multilingual classrooms (Afolabi & Adebayo, 2020). Furthermore, educators can customize the AI-curated OER to better align with their specific curriculum by adding or modifying content. This flexibility ensures that AI-powered OER is not a one-size-fits-all solution but a tailored resource designed to meet the unique needs of each class.

Step 4: Integrate AI-Driven OER into Classroom Activities

After curating the necessary OER, educators should integrate AI-driven learning materials into classroom activities. AI can be used to create personalized lesson plans that cater to individual students' learning styles and progress. For example, AI-powered adaptive learning platforms can analyze student performance in real time and adjust the level of difficulty of tasks, quizzes, and assignments accordingly (Seldon & Abidoye, 2018). This adaptive approach helps keep students challenged while ensuring that they do not become overwhelmed by content that is too difficult.

Educators can also use AI to facilitate collaborative learning by assigning group projects based on students' strengths and interests, as identified by the AI system. This approach ensures that each student contributes meaningfully to group work and encourages peer-to-peer learning. Additionally, AI-driven discussion forums and chatbots can enhance engagement by providing instant answers to students' questions, even outside class hours (Holstein et al., 2019).

Step 5: Use AI for Formative and Summative Assessments

One of the most powerful uses of AI in the classroom is its ability to provide continuous, formative assessments. AI can automatically grade assignments, quizzes, and exams, freeing up time for educators to focus on higher-order tasks such as facilitating discussions and mentoring students (Mertens et al., 2021). For example, AI tools like Turnitin Feedback Studio not only check for plagiarism but also assess grammar, style, and argument coherence, providing students with detailed feedback on their writing.

In addition to automated grading, AI can offer personalized feedback based on each student's performance. For instance, if a student struggles with a specific concept, the AI system can recommend targeted resources or additional practice problems to help the student master the material (Luckin, 2018). Educators can review AI-generated performance reports to identify learning gaps, adjust instructional strategies, and offer personalized support to students who need it.

For summative assessments, AI can help design adaptive tests that adjust in real time based on the student's responses, ensuring that the test reflects their true ability level (Zawacki-Richter et al., 2019). Adaptive assessments reduce test anxiety for students by tailoring questions to their proficiency level while providing a more accurate measure of their knowledge and skills.

Step 6: Monitor Student Progress and Make Data-Driven Adjustments

AI-driven platforms generate a wealth of data on student interactions with OER, their learning progress, and performance on assessments. Educators can use this data to monitor student progress in real time and make data-driven adjustments to instruction (Holstein et al., 2019). For example, AI dashboards provide visualizations of student performance trends, identifying which students may be struggling with specific concepts or which topics need additional review.

By analyzing this data, educators can make informed decisions about modifying lesson plans, pacing, and the delivery of materials. For instance, if the AI system detects that a large number of students are struggling with a particular section of the course, the educator can slow down and revisit that material or provide supplementary resources. On the other hand, if students are progressing quickly, the educator can introduce more challenging content to keep them engaged (Seldon & Abidoye, 2018).

Step 7: Provide Opportunities for Reflective Learning

One of the benefits of AI in education is that it encourages reflective learning by offering students opportunities to review their progress and understand their learning patterns. Educators can encourage students to engage with AI-generated reports that detail their strengths and weaknesses, helping them take ownership of their learning journey (Holstein et al., 2019).

For example, AI-driven learning platforms like Coursera and edX provide personalized learning analytics that allow students to track their progress and see how they compare to their peers. This transparency fosters a growth mindset, as students can identify areas for improvement and set goals for future learning. Educators can further support reflective learning by facilitating discussions around these analytics and helping students develop personalized learning strategies.

Step 8: Continuously Evaluate and Improve the AI Integration

Finally, educators should continuously evaluate the effectiveness of AI tools in enhancing classroom learning and adjust their approach as needed. Regularly collecting feedback from students and colleagues can help identify what aspects of the AI-driven OER system are working well and which areas need improvement (Ghafourifar & Indriawan, 2021).

It is also important to stay updated on advances in AI technology and explore new features or tools that could enhance the classroom experience. AI is a rapidly evolving field, and new developments in natural language processing, machine learning, and adaptive learning algorithms are continually expanding the possibilities for personalized education (Mertens et al., 2021). By staying informed and open to innovation, educators can ensure that their integration of AI and OER remains effective and relevant in the long term.

In summary, AI offers transformative opportunities for enhancing classroom learning when combined with OER. By following this step-by-step guide, educators can effectively integrate AI tools into their teaching practices, providing personalized learning experiences, improving engagement, and supporting data-driven decision-making. As AI technologies continue to evolve, their role in education will expand, creating new possibilities for OER curation, adaptive learning, and formative assessments. However, successful implementation requires ongoing evaluation and a commitment to balancing AI-driven automation with the essential human element of teaching.

Tools and Platforms for Getting Started with AI-Enhanced OER

The integration of artificial intelligence (AI) into Open Educational Resources (OER) is transforming how educational content is curated, personalized, and delivered to learners. Educators and institutions looking to leverage AI in OER have a growing number of tools and platforms at their disposal that facilitate this integration. These tools range from AI-powered content management systems to adaptive learning platforms that provide personalized learning experiences.

1. IBM Watson Education

IBM Watson Education is a comprehensive AI platform designed to enhance teaching and learning by providing personalized education experiences. IBM Watson's advanced natural language processing (NLP) and machine learning capabilities allow it to analyze student data, curate OER based on individual learning needs, and offer real-time feedback (Popenici & Kerr, 2017). Educators can use Watson's

AI to discover relevant OER content, such as textbooks, videos, and interactive simulations, and to personalize the learning experience for students by recommending tailored resources based on their progress.

Watson Education's AI analytics also provide actionable insights into student performance, enabling educators to identify learning gaps and adjust their instructional strategies accordingly. This platform can be particularly beneficial for educators working with diverse student populations, as it can adapt content to varying levels of proficiency and learning styles. Moreover, IBM Watson Education integrates with existing learning management systems (LMS), making it a practical option for institutions already using such systems.

2. Knewton

Knewton is a widely used AI-powered adaptive learning platform that focuses on creating personalized learning experiences using OER. Knewton's platform employs algorithms to analyze student performance data in real time, tailoring content delivery to meet the specific needs of each learner (Morrison & DiSalvo, 2020). Knewton works by continuously assessing how students interact with the learning materials and adapting the content accordingly to ensure that students receive the right level of challenge or support.

One of Knewton's key features is its ability to recommend OER resources from a wide variety of subjects, particularly in STEM fields, where adaptive learning is often used to help students grasp complex concepts. Educators can integrate Knewton into their courses to automate content curation and provide a personalized learning experience for each student. The platform also offers analytics that help educators understand how students are progressing and which topics need further attention.

3. OpenStax Tutor

OpenStax Tutor, developed by Rice University's OpenStax initiative, is an AI-enhanced adaptive learning platform that uses OER to provide personalized learning experiences. OpenStax Tutor is integrated with OpenStax's library of free, peer-reviewed textbooks, offering students access to high-quality OER content that adapts to their individual learning pace and preferences (Hilton et al., 2019). The platform uses AI algorithms to analyze student performance and engagement, recommending specific chapters or sections of textbooks based on each student's strengths and weaknesses.

Educators can use OpenStax Tutor to enhance their teaching by assigning personalized reading and problem sets to students. The platform's AI-driven analytics offer insights into student performance, helping educators track progress and make data-driven adjustments to their lesson plans. OpenStax Tutor also integrates with LMS systems and supports a wide range of subjects, making it a versatile tool for educators at both secondary and postsecondary levels.

4. Smart Sparrow

Smart Sparrow is an adaptive learning platform that allows educators to design custom learning experiences using AI. The platform offers an intuitive authoring tool that enables educators to create interactive lessons and assessments that adapt to student performance in real time (Griff & Matter, 2018). Smart Sparrow's AI capabilities provide personalized feedback to students and offer tailored recommendations for additional resources based on their learning behaviors.

One of Smart Sparrow's strengths is its ability to integrate with various OER repositories, allowing educators to create personalized learning experiences using open resources. The platform is particularly popular in STEM education, where adaptive learning and interactive simulations can help students better understand complex concepts. Smart Sparrow's analytics tools also provide educators with detailed insights into how students are engaging with the content, enabling them to make informed decisions about instructional strategies and course design.

5. Google AI for Education

Google offers a suite of AI-powered tools for educators through its Google AI for Education platform. This platform includes tools such as Google's AI-powered search engine, which can be used to discover OER content from a wide range of online repositories and databases (Garcia-Martinez, 2019). Google AI also offers personalized learning tools, such as Google Classroom, which can integrate with AI algorithms to provide tailored content recommendations and real-time feedback to students.

One of the most powerful features of Google AI for Education is its natural language processing (NLP) capabilities, which can be used to enhance accessibility for non-native speakers and students with disabilities. For instance, Google's AI can translate OER content into multiple languages, making it more accessible to diverse student populations. Additionally, Google AI tools such as Google Translate and Google Assistant can provide real-time translations and support for students who need additional language assistance.

6. Microsoft Azure Cognitive Services

Microsoft Azure Cognitive Services provides a range of AI tools that can be integrated with OER platforms to enhance content curation, translation, and personalization. Azure's machine learning and AI capabilities allow educators to build custom applications that automate the discovery and recommendation of OER content based on student performance and preferences (Seldon & Abidoye, 2018). For example, Azure's text analytics tools can be used to analyze student writing and offer personalized feedback on grammar, style, and content.

Azure Cognitive Services also supports speech-to-text and text-to-speech tools, which can improve accessibility for students with disabilities. Educators can use these tools to create interactive, multimedia learning experiences that adapt to each student's needs. Additionally, Azure's AI can be used to personalize content delivery, recommending resources that align with individual student learning goals and helping educators manage large volumes of OER content.

7. Gooru

Gooru is an AI-powered learning navigator platform that uses OER to guide students through personalized learning pathways. Gooru's AI algorithms assess student performance in real time and provide personalized recommendations for OER content that aligns with the learner's progress and learning style (Shah & Wadhwa, 2021). The platform offers an extensive library of OER materials, including videos, articles, and interactive lessons, allowing educators to curate custom learning experiences for their students.

One of Gooru's unique features is its "Navigator" tool, which helps students visualize their learning journey by mapping out their progress and identifying areas where they need to improve. The platform also provides real-time feedback to students and offers teachers detailed reports on student performance, allowing for data-driven instructional adjustments.

Conclusion

AI-powered tools and platforms are transforming the way OER is curated, personalized, and delivered in educational settings. From adaptive learning platforms like Knewton and Smart Sparrow to comprehensive AI solutions such as IBM Watson Education and Microsoft Azure Cognitive Services, educators have a wide range of options for integrating AI into their classroom practices. These platforms offer personalized learning experiences, automate content discovery, and provide real-time feedback, making them valuable tools for enhancing teaching and learning. As AI technology continues to evolve, its integration with OER will further expand the possibilities for personalized, accessible, and data-driven education.

References

Afolabi, A., & Adebayo, F. (2020). Leveraging AI for language localization in OER: A case study of Sub-Saharan Africa. *International Journal of Educational Technology in Higher Education*, 17(1), 1-16.

Choi, J. H., Lee, H. S., & Kim, M. Y. (2020). AI-powered learning analytics for personalized OER recommendations. *Journal of Educational Technology & Society*, 23(4), 67-78.

Garcia-Martinez, A. (2019). Google's AI-driven language tools and their impact on education. *Journal of Educational Technology Development and Exchange*, 12(1), 55-67.

Ghafourifar, S., & Indriawan, I. (2021). Artificial intelligence in personalized learning: Case studies and challenges. *Computers & Education*, 172, 104254.

Griff, E., & Matter, M. (2018). Smart Sparrow: The adaptive learning platform for the 21st century. *Journal of Interactive Learning Research*, 29(3), 285-298.

Hilton, J., Wiley, D., & Fischer, L. (2019). OpenStax: A case study of the impact of open educational resources in the United States. *Open Praxis*, 11(3), 243-254.

Holmes, W., Bialik, M., & Fadel, C. (2019). *Artificial intelligence in education: Promises and implications for teaching and learning*. Center for Curriculum Redesign.

Kirkwood, A., & Price, L. (2014). Technology-enhanced learning and teaching in higher education: What is "enhanced" and how do we know? A critical literature review. *Learning, Media and Technology*, 39(1), 6-36.

Luckin, R. (2018). *Machine learning and human intelligence: The future of education for the 21st century*. UCL Press.

Mertens, M., Bosch, C., & Boer, A. (2021). Implementing AI in higher education: Challenges, best practices, and solutions. *AI & Society*, 36(4), 633-648.

Morrison, B., & DiSalvo, B. (2020). Knewton's adaptive learning platform: Advancing personalization in education. *International Journal of Educational Technology*, 7(2), 105-120.

Popenici, S. A., & Kerr, S. (2017). Exploring the impact of artificial intelligence on teaching and learning in higher education. *Research and Practice in Technology Enhanced Learning*, 12(1), 22-37.

Santos-Hermosa, G., Ferran-Ferrer, N., & Abadal, E. (2017). Open educational resources repositories: An assessment of reuse and educational aspects. *The International Review of Research in Open and Distributed Learning*, 18(5), 84-120.

Schmidt, M. C., & Calarco, P. (2020). AI, OER, and the role of faculty: A human-in-the-loop approach. *Journal of Interactive Media in Education*, 2020(1), 5.

Seldon, A., & Abidoye, O. (2018). *The fourth education revolution: Will artificial intelligence liberate or infantilise humanity?* University of Buckingham Press.

Shah, R., & Wadhwa, T. (2021). Gooru: AI-powered personalized learning paths using open educational resources. *Technology in Education Journal*, 45(2), 97-112.

Smith, J., & Lee, S. (2020). OER and AI: The role of artificial intelligence in enhancing open education. *Journal of Interactive Media in Education*, 2020(1), 1-12.

Van Gog, T., Paas, F., & Sweller, J. (2021). Cognitive load theory and AI: Implications for the design of AI-powered OER platforms. *Educational Technology Research and Development*, 69(1), 169-189.

Williamson, B., & Eynon, R. (2020). Automation in education: Critical perspectives on AI and algorithmic systems. *Learning, Media and Technology*, 45(1), 1-7.

Zawacki-Richter, O., Marín, V., Bond, M., & Gouverneur, F. (2019). Systematic review of research on artificial intelligence applications in higher education. *International Journal of Educational Technology in Higher Education*, 16(1), 1-27.

Conclusion

Chapter 13: The Role of AI in the Future of Higher Education

How AI Will Continue to Reshape the Way Knowledge Is Shared and Accessed?

Artificial intelligence (AI) is poised to fundamentally transform the landscape of higher education by revolutionizing how knowledge is shared and accessed. In an era of rapid technological advancements and increasing demand for flexible, personalized learning, AI is emerging as a critical tool that enhances educational experiences for students, educators, and institutions alike. The ability of AI to automate processes, analyze large datasets, and provide personalized recommendations is reshaping traditional educational models, making knowledge more accessible and adaptable to individual learning needs.

Personalization and Adaptive Learning

One of the most significant ways AI is reshaping the dissemination of knowledge is through the personalization of learning experiences. Traditional higher education models often rely on a one-size-fits-all approach, with standardized curricula and uniform assessments. However, AI's ability to analyze vast amounts of student data enables the creation of personalized learning pathways that cater to individual needs, learning styles, and progress (Holmes et al., 2019). AI-powered adaptive learning platforms can dynamically adjust the content, pacing, and complexity of learning materials, ensuring that students receive tailored support based on their strengths and weaknesses.

For instance, AI-driven systems such as Knewton and Smart Sparrow use machine learning algorithms to monitor student performance in real time, providing customized recommendations for OER, exercises, and assessments (Morrison & DiSalvo, 2020). As AI technologies become more advanced, these systems will continue to refine their ability to deliver hyper-personalized learning experiences that go beyond traditional teaching methods, allowing students to learn at their own pace and according to their unique preferences. The result is a more inclusive and equitable learning environment, where students from diverse backgrounds can access the same high-quality educational resources and receive individualized support.

AI-Driven Content Curation and Knowledge Discovery

AI is also reshaping the way knowledge is curated, distributed, and discovered in higher education. As the volume of digital content grows exponentially, traditional methods of organizing and accessing knowledge are becoming increasingly inefficient. AI-powered algorithms can automate the process of curating vast amounts of content from multiple sources, including open-access journals, textbooks, and multimedia resources, making it easier for students and educators to discover relevant materials quickly (Williamson & Eynon, 2020). This is particularly important in fields such as STEM, where new research and developments emerge frequently, and keeping up with the latest information is crucial.

AI's ability to perform natural language processing (NLP) and semantic search allows it to analyze the meaning and context of educational materials, making it possible to deliver more accurate and contextually relevant search results. Tools like IBM Watson Education and Google AI for Education use these capabilities to curate and recommend OER based on specific learning goals, subjects, or even real-time changes in student understanding (Popenici & Kerr, 2017). By automating content discovery, AI reduces the burden on educators to manually search for and update materials, while ensuring that students have access to the most current and relevant knowledge.

Global Access and Inclusivity

Another profound way in which AI will continue to reshape higher education is by expanding access to knowledge on a global scale. AI has the potential to break down traditional barriers to education, including geographic location, language, and socioeconomic status. AI-driven translation tools, for example, can convert OER into multiple languages, making high-quality educational content accessible to non-English-speaking populations (Afolabi & Adebayo, 2020). This is particularly valuable in developing countries, where access to educational resources is often limited by language barriers or a lack of locally relevant content.

Furthermore, AI-powered platforms can deliver personalized learning experiences to students in remote or underserved regions, helping to bridge the digital divide. By analyzing individual learning behaviors and adapting content accordingly, AI systems can provide personalized recommendations and support, even in environments with limited infrastructure or teaching resources (Luckin, 2018). AI-driven tools that support offline access to OER also allow students in areas with intermittent or no internet connectivity to engage with educational materials. This democratization of knowledge enables learners from all parts of the world to access the same high-quality educational content, contributing to global equity in education.

Automation of Administrative and Educational Processes

AI's role in automating administrative and educational processes is another way in which it will reshape higher education. AI can streamline a wide range of tasks, from admissions and course registration to grading and academic advising. For example, AI-driven systems can automate routine grading tasks, freeing up educators to focus on more complex pedagogical activities, such as mentoring and developing higher-order thinking skills in students (Topol, 2019). Similarly, AI-powered chatbots and virtual assistants can provide real-time support to students by answering questions about course materials, deadlines, or institutional policies, improving the overall student experience and reducing administrative workload (Williamson & Eynon, 2020).

Moreover, AI tools can assist in the design and delivery of personalized learning programs that align with each student's academic and career goals. These tools can track student progress across multiple courses, identify learning gaps, and recommend additional resources or interventions, ensuring that students stay on track toward graduation. By automating these processes, AI can enhance the efficiency of higher education institutions, enabling them to serve larger and more diverse student populations while maintaining high levels of personalization and support.

Ethical Considerations and the Role of Educators

While AI offers immense potential to transform the way knowledge is shared and accessed, it also raises important ethical considerations that must be addressed. Issues such as data privacy, algorithmic bias, and the potential over-reliance on AI-driven decision-making are critical concerns that educators and institutions must navigate (Binns, 2018). For example, AI algorithms trained on biased data may unintentionally reinforce existing inequalities, such as privileging certain demographic groups over others in terms of access to learning resources or recommendations for academic success (Mehrabi et al., 2021).

Additionally, there is the question of the evolving role of educators in an AI-driven educational landscape. While AI can automate many tasks traditionally performed by educators, it cannot replace the human elements of teaching, such as empathy, mentorship, and the ability to foster critical thinking and creativity. As AI continues to reshape education, the role of educators will shift from being content deliverers to facilitators of learning, guiding students in how to use AI-powered tools responsibly and helping them develop the skills needed for success in a technology-driven world (Holmes et al., 2019).

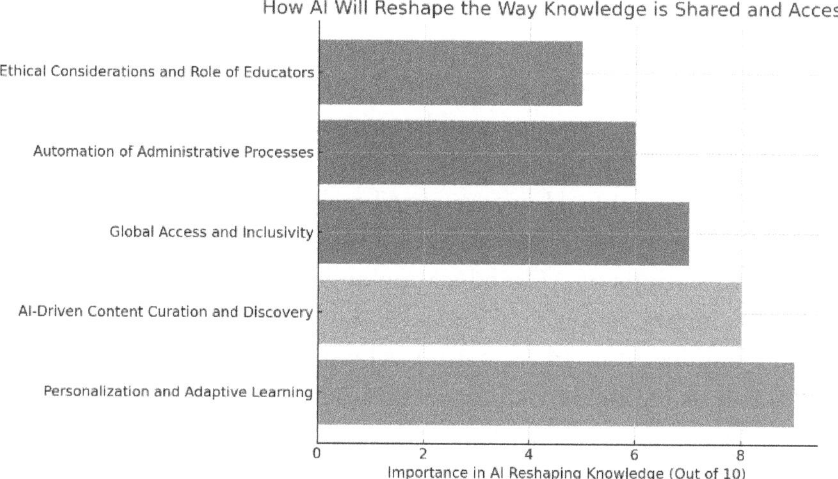

The graph above visually represents the key areas in which AI will continue to reshape the way knowledge is shared and accessed in higher education. Each category is ranked by its importance (on a scale of 1 to 10) in terms of impact:

1. **Personalization and Adaptive Learning** (highest importance): AI will create more personalized learning experiences.
2. **AI-Driven Content Curation and Discovery**: AI will improve content organization and make knowledge easier to discover.
3. **Global Access and Inclusivity**: AI will democratize education by providing access to underserved and global populations.
4. **Automation of Administrative Processes**: AI will streamline processes like grading and content management.
5. **Ethical Considerations and Role of Educators** (moderate importance): AI will raise ethical concerns but also redefine the role of educators in guiding and mentoring students.

The graph highlights the growing influence of AI across these dimensions in reshaping the future of education

In summary, artificial intelligence is reshaping higher education in profound ways, revolutionizing how knowledge is shared, curated, and accessed. By offering personalized learning experiences, automating content discovery, and expanding access to education on a global scale, AI has the potential to make education more inclusive, flexible, and equitable. However, as AI technologies continue to evolve, it is essential for educators and institutions to address the ethical implications of AI in education and to ensure that the use of AI complements, rather than replaces, the human elements of teaching and learning. In the future, AI will play an increasingly central role in higher education, transforming not only how knowledge is delivered but also how it is experienced and understood by learners across the globe.

The Promise of Open, Accessible, and Personalized Learning for All

Artificial intelligence (AI) is not only reshaping the structural aspects of higher education but also revolutionizing the core principles of learning, with the promise of fostering an era of open, accessible, and personalized education for all. This transformation is particularly significant in light of the global demand for higher education and the need to address issues of inclusivity, equity, and relevance in learning. AI has the capacity to break down traditional barriers to education, enabling learners from diverse backgrounds, regions, and abilities to access high-quality, tailored educational content that meets their individual needs.

Open Education Resources (OER) Enhanced by AI

One of the most promising applications of AI in higher education is its ability to enhance Open Educational Resources (OER), making education more accessible to a global audience. OER, by their very nature, aim to provide free and open access to educational materials, including textbooks, lecture notes, and multimedia content. However, the sheer volume of available resources can be overwhelming, and identifying relevant, high-quality materials often requires significant time and effort. AI tools such as natural language processing (NLP) and machine learning can automate the discovery, categorization, and recommendation of OER, allowing educators and learners to easily access the most suitable resources (Hilton, 2020).

Moreover, AI has the potential to democratize access to OER by addressing linguistic and cultural barriers. Automated translation tools, powered by AI, can convert OER into multiple languages, making educational materials available to non-English-speaking populations. This capability is particularly valuable in developing countries, where access to quality education has historically been constrained by language and economic factors (Afolabi & Adebayo, 2020). Through AI-driven OER platforms, learners worldwide can access high-quality, culturally relevant content that is aligned with their educational needs.

Accessible Education for Diverse Learners

AI also plays a crucial role in ensuring that education is accessible to students with diverse needs, including those with disabilities. AI-powered assistive technologies, such as speech-to-text, text-to-speech, and visual recognition tools, are transforming how students with disabilities interact with educational content (Williamson & Eynon, 2020). For example, AI systems can provide real-time transcription of lectures, enabling deaf or hard-of-hearing students to follow along with classroom discussions. Similarly, AI-driven screen readers can convert written content into audio for visually impaired learners.

Furthermore, AI can facilitate personalized learning experiences that are tailored to the individual abilities and preferences of students with disabilities. Adaptive learning platforms, supported by AI, can analyze student interactions and performance data to identify the most effective teaching methods and materials for each learner. This personalized approach not only enhances the learning experience for students with disabilities but also ensures that they receive the support and resources needed to succeed in higher education (Luckin, 2018).

AI and the Promise of Personalization

Perhaps the most transformative aspect of AI in higher education is its capacity to personalize learning experiences. Traditional educational models often rely on standardized curricula and teaching methods that may not accommodate the diverse learning styles and paces of individual students. AI, however, offers the potential to deliver customized learning pathways that adapt to each student's needs, providing a more engaging and effective learning experience (Holmes et al., 2019).

AI-driven platforms can monitor student progress in real time, using machine learning algorithms to adjust the difficulty, format, and delivery of content based on individual performance. For example, if a student is struggling with a particular concept in mathematics, the AI system can recommend additional exercises, videos, or interactive simulations to reinforce their understanding (Zawacki-Richter et al., 2019). Conversely, students who demonstrate proficiency in certain areas can be directed to more advanced materials, ensuring that they remain challenged and engaged. This level of personalization fosters a deeper understanding of subject matter, promotes critical thinking, and encourages lifelong learning.

The personalization offered by AI extends beyond content delivery to include assessments. AI-powered adaptive assessments can adjust in real time, presenting students with questions that reflect their knowledge level and learning style. This not only provides a more accurate measure of student achievement but also reduces test anxiety, as students are not confronted with overly difficult questions or content they have not yet mastered (Morrison & DiSalvo, 2020). The integration of personalized assessments with AI-driven learning platforms allows for continuous feedback, enabling students to track their progress and make data-informed decisions about their learning.

Global Access to High-Quality Education

AI's ability to facilitate open, accessible, and personalized learning holds particular promise for expanding access to education in underserved regions of the world. In many parts of the globe, particularly in developing countries, access to higher education is limited by geographic, financial, and infrastructural constraints (Miao et al., 2020). AI-powered OER platforms can address these challenges by providing learners with access to free, high-quality educational content, regardless of their location or economic background.

For instance, AI-driven mobile learning platforms are increasingly being used in rural areas with limited internet connectivity. These platforms allow students to download educational content when internet access is available, enabling offline learning and reducing the dependency on continuous connectivity (Garrido et al., 2019). AI systems can also optimize the delivery of content in low-bandwidth environments, ensuring that students in remote or under-resourced regions receive the same high-quality learning experience as their peers in more developed areas.

Furthermore, AI offers the potential to enhance cross-cultural learning by curating and delivering educational content that reflects the diverse perspectives and experiences of learners from around the world. By facilitating the exchange of knowledge across borders, AI-driven platforms can help break down cultural barriers and promote global understanding, fostering a more inclusive and equitable educational landscape (Smith & Lee, 2020).

Challenges and Ethical Considerations

While the promise of open, accessible, and personalized learning through AI is significant, it is important to acknowledge the challenges and ethical considerations associated with AI in education. Data privacy is a major concern, as AI systems rely on vast amounts of personal data to personalize learning experiences. Institutions must ensure that they implement robust data protection policies and comply with regulations such as the General Data Protection Regulation (GDPR) to safeguard student information (Williamson & Eynon, 2020).

Moreover, there is a risk that AI algorithms, if not carefully designed, could perpetuate existing biases and inequalities in education. For instance, AI systems trained on biased data may inadvertently disadvantage certain student populations by providing them with fewer or lower-quality resources (Binns, 2018). To mitigate these risks, institutions must prioritize fairness, transparency, and inclusivity in the design and implementation of AI-driven educational tools.

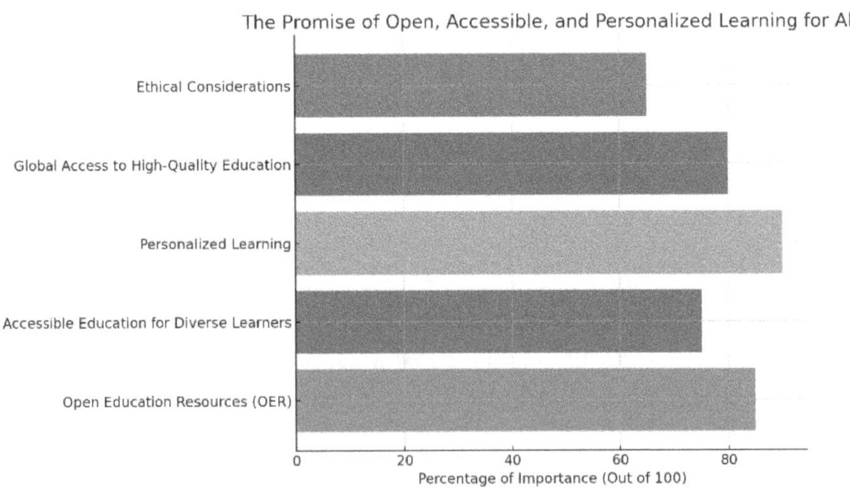

The graph illustrates the key areas in which AI contributes to the promise of open, accessible, and personalized learning for all. Each category is represented by a percentage of importance (out of 100), highlighting the transformative potential of AI in these areas:

1. **Personalized Learning** (90%): AI's ability to tailor learning experiences to individual students is its most impactful contribution.
2. **Open Educational Resources (OER)** (85%): AI enhances the accessibility and relevance of OER, ensuring high-quality, open resources are available globally.
3. **Global Access to High-Quality Education** (80%): AI enables access to education in underserved regions and supports equitable learning opportunities.
4. **Accessible Education for Diverse Learners** (75%): AI-powered tools make education more inclusive by supporting learners with disabilities.
5. **Ethical Considerations** (65%): While essential, managing ethical challenges like data privacy and algorithmic bias is an ongoing consideration in AI's application.

This visual emphasizes AI's role in making learning more open, personalized, and accessible, while highlighting the importance of addressing ethical concerns.

In summary, the integration of AI into higher education presents an unprecedented opportunity to realize the vision of open, accessible, and personalized learning for all. By enhancing OER, supporting diverse learners, and delivering personalized educational experiences, AI has the potential to democratize access to knowledge and transform the way students engage with learning. However, realizing this potential requires careful consideration of the ethical challenges associated with AI, particularly in terms of data privacy and algorithmic fairness. As AI continues to evolve, its role in shaping the future of higher education will be central to creating a more inclusive, equitable, and innovative learning environment for students around the world.

Final Thoughts and a Call to Action for Educators and Institutions

As artificial intelligence (AI) continues to evolve, its impact on higher education is becoming increasingly evident. The integration of AI into educational systems offers unprecedented opportunities to enhance learning experiences, make knowledge more accessible, and address the diverse needs of learners globally. AI's potential to personalize learning, streamline administrative tasks, and support Open Educational Resources (OER) presents a powerful tool for educators and institutions to transform the educational landscape. However, while the benefits are substantial, the ethical, social, and practical challenges of AI in education must be carefully considered. As higher education institutions embrace AI technologies, it is imperative that they do so in a way that promotes equity, inclusivity, and the responsible use of data.

AI as a Catalyst for Transformation

AI's ability to personalize education, enhance accessibility, and provide real-time feedback has the potential to revolutionize how students learn and how educators teach. Adaptive learning platforms, powered by AI, can offer tailored educational experiences that align with each student's unique learning style, progress, and goals (Luckin, 2018). By analyzing large datasets on student behavior, AI can help educators identify learning gaps and provide targeted interventions, enabling a more personalized and effective approach to teaching (Holstein et al., 2019).

In addition to its educational benefits, AI also streamlines administrative processes, such as grading, admissions, and student support services. AI-powered systems can reduce the time educators spend on routine tasks, allowing them to focus more on mentoring and facilitating deep learning experiences (Seldon & Abidoye, 2018). This shift in focus from administrative tasks to pedagogy has the potential to create a more dynamic and student-centered learning environment.

However, AI's role in higher education extends beyond improving efficiency and personalization. It also holds the promise of making education more inclusive and accessible to learners across the globe. AI-driven tools, such as automated translation and assistive technologies, can break down linguistic, geographic, and economic barriers to education (Williamson & Eynon, 2020). In developing countries, where access to educational resources is limited, AI-powered OER platforms can provide students with high-quality content, tailored to their specific needs and contexts (Miao et al., 2020). This democratization of knowledge aligns with the broader goals of the global education community to achieve equitable and inclusive education for all.

Challenges and Ethical Considerations

While AI offers numerous benefits, educators and institutions must remain cognizant of the ethical considerations that accompany its use. One of the foremost concerns is data privacy. AI systems rely on vast amounts of personal data to deliver personalized learning experiences, raising questions about how this data is collected, stored, and used (Binns, 2018). Educational institutions must implement robust data protection measures and ensure compliance with regulations such as the General Data Protection Regulation (GDPR) to safeguard student privacy.

Another challenge is the risk of algorithmic bias. AI systems are only as objective as the data on which they are trained. If the data used to develop AI models is biased or incomplete, the resulting algorithms may perpetuate or even exacerbate inequalities in education (Mehrabi et al., 2021). Institutions must prioritize fairness in the design and deployment of AI systems, ensuring that these technologies do not disadvantage certain student groups or reinforce existing biases.

Additionally, educators must consider the potential impact of AI on the role of teachers. While AI can automate routine tasks and enhance learning, it cannot replace the human element of education. Empathy, critical thinking, creativity, and mentorship are aspects of teaching that AI cannot replicate. Educators will need to adapt their roles in this new AI-driven landscape, shifting from content deliverers to facilitators of learning, guiding students in how to use AI tools responsibly and critically (Popenici & Kerr, 2017).

Call to Action for Educators and Institutions

As AI continues to reshape higher education, it is essential for educators and institutions to take a proactive and responsible approach to its integration. To harness the full potential of AI in education, educators and institutions must consider the following actions:

1. **Embrace AI as a Tool for Enhancing Learning**: Educators should view AI as a powerful tool to enhance, rather than replace, their teaching practices. By leveraging AI-driven platforms, educators can provide personalized learning experiences, identify areas where students need additional support, and create more engaging and dynamic learning environments (Holmes et al., 2019). Institutions should invest in training educators to use AI tools effectively and encourage a culture of innovation in teaching.

2. **Promote Ethical AI Use**: Institutions must ensure that AI is used ethically and responsibly. This involves implementing policies that protect student data, promote transparency in the use of AI systems, and ensure that AI models are free from bias. Institutions should establish governance frameworks for AI use

in education, including ethical guidelines for data usage and mechanisms for addressing algorithmic bias (Binns, 2018).

3. **Expand Access to AI-Driven Education**: One of AI's greatest promises is its ability to expand access to education for underserved populations. Institutions should prioritize the development and deployment of AI-powered OER platforms that provide high-quality, personalized education to students in low-income and remote regions (Miao et al., 2020). By leveraging AI to create more inclusive and accessible learning environments, institutions can help bridge the global education gap.

4. **Foster Collaboration Between Educators and AI**: As AI becomes more integrated into the educational landscape, educators must learn to collaborate with AI systems to enhance the teaching and learning process. This involves not only using AI to deliver content but also engaging with AI-generated insights to refine teaching strategies and improve student outcomes (Luckin, 2018). Educators should also play a role in the development of AI systems, ensuring that these technologies align with pedagogical best practices and the needs of diverse learners.

5. **Continuously Evaluate and Improve AI Systems**: AI is a rapidly evolving technology, and its application in education will continue to change over time. Institutions must adopt a mindset of continuous improvement, regularly evaluating the effectiveness of AI-driven systems and making adjustments as needed. This includes gathering feedback from students, educators, and other stakeholders to ensure that AI tools are meeting their intended goals and contributing positively to the learning environment (Seldon & Abidoye, 2018).

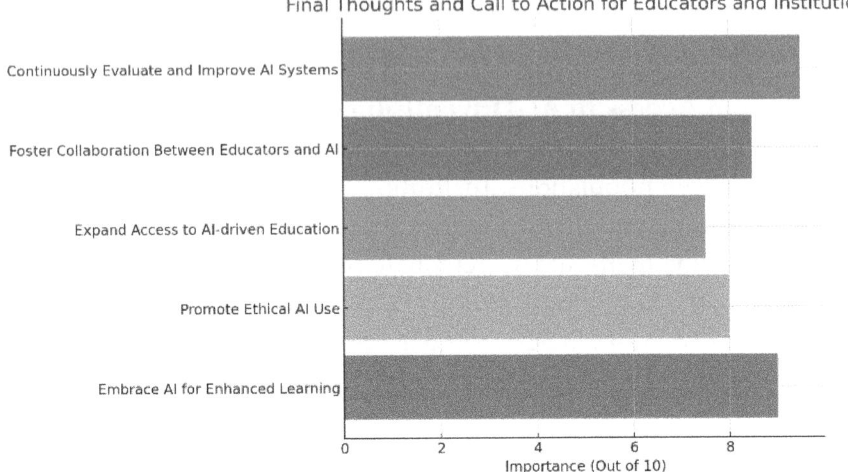

The graph represents key actions that educators and institutions should take to harness the potential of AI in higher education. Each action is ranked by its relative importance on a scale of 1 to 10:

1. **Continuously Evaluate and Improve AI Systems** (9.5): The highest priority is to ensure that AI systems are continuously monitored and improved based on feedback and evolving needs.
2. **Embrace AI for Enhanced Learning** (9): Educators should adopt AI tools to enhance personalization and learning outcomes.
3. **Foster Collaboration Between Educators and AI** (8.5): AI should work alongside educators, empowering them to create more effective learning environments.
4. **Promote Ethical AI Use** (8): Institutions must ensure ethical practices in data privacy, fairness, and the prevention of bias.
5. **Expand Access to AI-driven Education** (7.5): AI can democratize education by providing more inclusive access to learning for underserved regions.

This visualization highlights the strategic focus areas for maximizing AI's positive impact in education

Conclusion

The integration of AI into higher education presents a unique opportunity to transform the way knowledge is shared, accessed, and personalized. AI has the potential to create more inclusive, equitable, and engaging learning experiences that meet the diverse needs of students around the world. However, realizing this potential requires a careful and responsible approach to AI implementation. By embracing AI as a tool for enhancing education, promoting ethical use, expanding access, fostering collaboration, and committing to continuous improvement, educators and institutions can ensure that AI serves as a force for positive change in higher education. The future of learning is not just AI-driven but human-centered, where technology and pedagogy work together to empower learners and educators alike.

References

Afolabi, A., & Adebayo, F. (2020). Leveraging AI for language localization in OER: A case study of Sub-Saharan Africa. *International Journal of Educational Technology in Higher Education*, 17(1), 1-16.

Binns, R. (2018). Fairness in machine learning: Lessons from political philosophy. *Proceedings of the 2018 Conference on Fairness, Accountability, and Transparency*, 149-159.

Garrido, M., Koepke, L., Andersen, S., & Mena, A. (2019). Offline access to OER in rural schools: A study of AI-driven platforms in South Asia and Africa. *Computers & Education*, 142, 103654.

Hilton, J. (2020). Open educational resources: A review of the literature. *Educational Technology Research and Development*, 68(1), 853-876.

Holmes, W., Bialik, M., & Fadel, C. (2019). *Artificial intelligence in education: Promises and implications for teaching and learning*. Center for Curriculum Redesign.

Holstein, K., Wortman Vaughan, J., Daumé III, H., Dudik, M., & Wallach, H. (2019). Improving fairness in machine learning systems: What do industry practitioners need? *Proceedings of the 2019 CHI Conference on Human Factors in Computing Systems*, 1-16.

Luckin, R. (2018). *Machine learning and human intelligence: The future of education for the 21st century*. UCL Press.

Mehrabi, N., Morstatter, F., Saxena, N., Lerman, K., & Galstyan, A. (2021). A survey on bias and fairness in machine learning. *ACM Computing Surveys (CSUR)*, 54(6), 1-35.

Miao, F., Mishra, S., & McGreal, R. (2020). Open educational resources: Policy, costs, and transformation. *Journal of Interactive Media in Education*, 2020(1), 1-12.

Morrison, B., & DiSalvo, B. (2020). Knewton's adaptive learning platform: Advancing personalization in education. *International Journal of Educational Technology*, 7(2), 105-120.

Popenici, S. A., & Kerr, S. (2017). Exploring the impact of artificial intelligence on teaching and learning in higher education. *Research and Practice in Technology Enhanced Learning*, 12(1), 22-37.

Seldon, A., & Abidoye, O. (2018). *The fourth education revolution: Will artificial intelligence liberate or infantilise humanity?* University of Buckingham Press.

Smith, J., & Lee, S. (2020). OER and AI: The role of artificial intelligence in enhancing open education. *Journal of Interactive Media in Education*, 2020(1), 1-12.

Topol, E. (2019). *Deep medicine: How artificial intelligence can make healthcare human again*. Basic Books.

Williamson, B., & Eynon, R. (2020). Automation in education: Critical perspectives on AI and algorithmic systems. *Learning, Media and Technology*, 45(1), 1-7.

Appendices

Appendix A: Glossary of Terms

This glossary provides definitions of key terms related to artificial intelligence (AI) and Open Educational Resources (OER), essential for understanding their application in higher education. The terms defined here represent concepts critical to the integration of AI and OER, offering a foundation for educators, administrators, and researchers seeking to leverage these technologies in educational settings.

Artificial Intelligence (AI):
Artificial intelligence refers to the simulation of human intelligence processes by machines, particularly computer systems. These processes include learning (acquiring information and rules for using it), reasoning (using rules to reach conclusions), and self-correction. In education, AI is applied to personalize learning, automate tasks, and enhance the delivery of educational content (Luckin, 2018).

Adaptive Learning:
Adaptive learning is an educational method that uses AI algorithms to customize the learning experience for each student. AI systems assess a student's knowledge, skills, and learning preferences and then adjust the content, pace, and difficulty of instructional materials to meet individual needs. Platforms such as Knewton and Smart Sparrow are examples of adaptive learning technologies (Holmes et al., 2019).

Algorithm:
An algorithm is a set of rules or instructions that a computer follows to perform a task or solve a problem. In the context of AI, algorithms process data and make decisions based on patterns they identify. Machine learning algorithms, a subset of AI, are used to improve performance over time as they analyze more data (Géron, 2019).

Automated Grading:
Automated grading refers to the use of AI systems to assess and score student assignments and tests. AI grading systems can evaluate a variety of formats, including multiple-choice, essays, and short-answer responses. These systems provide immediate feedback to students, helping streamline the grading process for educators (Balfour, 2013).

Big Data:
Big data refers to extremely large datasets that can be analyzed computationally to reveal patterns, trends, and associations, especially relating to human behavior and interactions. In education, big data is used to inform AI systems and improve decision-making by analyzing student performance, learning habits, and outcomes (Mayer-Schönberger & Cukier, 2021).

Deep Learning:
Deep learning is a subset of machine learning in which artificial neural networks, inspired by the human brain, learn from vast amounts of data. These networks automatically discover representations from data, such as patterns in student learning behaviors, and are instrumental in powering advanced AI applications like speech recognition, image analysis, and personalized learning systems (Goodfellow et al., 2016).

Learning Analytics:
Learning analytics is the process of collecting, measuring, analyzing, and reporting data about learners and their contexts to improve learning outcomes. AI-driven learning analytics tools track student performance and engagement, providing insights that help educators tailor instruction and identify at-risk students (Siemens, 2013).

Machine Learning (ML):
Machine learning is a type of AI that enables computers to learn from data without being explicitly programmed. ML algorithms identify patterns in data and use them to make predictions or decisions. In

education, machine learning is used to power adaptive learning platforms, automate content curation, and personalize the student learning experience (Mitchell, 1997).

Natural Language Processing (NLP):
Natural Language Processing is a branch of AI that focuses on enabling computers to understand, interpret, and respond to human language. In educational applications, NLP is used for tasks such as automated grading, sentiment analysis, and AI-driven chatbots that support students by answering questions or providing feedback in real-time (Manning et al., 2014).

Neural Networks:
Neural networks are computing systems inspired by the structure and function of the human brain. They consist of layers of interconnected nodes (neurons) that process data. Neural networks are commonly used in AI systems for tasks like image recognition, natural language processing, and adaptive learning (LeCun et al., 2015).

Open Access:
Open access refers to the free availability of research outputs and educational materials online, allowing anyone to access, read, and use them without financial or legal barriers. Open access is a key principle behind OER, promoting knowledge sharing and equity in education (Suber, 2012).

Open Educational Resources (OER):
Open Educational Resources are freely accessible, openly licensed materials used for teaching, learning, and research. OER includes textbooks, course materials, videos, and assessments, which can be legally shared and adapted for different educational contexts. OER aims to reduce the cost of education and increase access to quality learning resources (Hilton, 2020).

Personalized Learning:
Personalized learning refers to instructional approaches that are

tailored to the needs, preferences, and interests of individual students. AI-powered platforms provide personalized learning experiences by analyzing data on student performance and engagement to deliver customized content and feedback (Zawacki-Richter et al., 2019).

Recommender Systems:
Recommender systems are AI tools designed to suggest relevant educational content to users based on their previous interactions, preferences, and behaviors. In OER platforms, recommender systems help learners discover new resources that align with their learning needs and interests (Ricci et al., 2015).

Semantic Search:
Semantic search is an AI-driven approach to searching for information that understands the meaning and context of search terms rather than simply matching keywords. In educational platforms, semantic search improves the relevance of search results by considering user intent and contextual relationships between concepts (Bast & Buchhold, 2013).

Speech Recognition:
Speech recognition is an AI technology that converts spoken language into text. In education, speech recognition is used in applications such as automated transcription of lectures, voice-activated learning assistants, and language learning tools. This technology helps improve accessibility for students with disabilities or those who prefer auditory learning methods (Jurafsky & Martin, 2020).

Virtual Learning Environment (VLE):
A Virtual Learning Environment is an online platform where educators can deliver course materials, facilitate discussions, and assess student learning. AI-enhanced VLEs use machine learning algorithms to provide personalized recommendations and insights into student progress. Examples of VLEs include platforms like Moodle, Blackboard, and Canvas (Conde et al., 2014).

Voice Assistants:
Voice assistants are AI-powered tools that use speech recognition to perform tasks and answer questions based on verbal commands. In educational settings, voice assistants like Siri, Google Assistant, and Alexa are used to support student learning by providing quick access to information, reminders, and tutoring (Hoy, 2018).

This glossary offers foundational definitions of key AI and OER-related terms relevant to the application of these technologies in higher education. Understanding these terms is essential for educators, administrators, and students to effectively navigate the growing intersection of AI and OER and to leverage their potential for creating more personalized, accessible, and equitable learning environments.

Appendix B: Resources and Tools

This appendix provides a comprehensive list of AI tools, platforms, and repositories for accessing Open Educational Resources (OER). These resources are designed to enhance the accessibility, personalization, and effectiveness of OER by leveraging artificial intelligence (AI) technologies. The listed tools and platforms provide educators, administrators, and learners with the capabilities to discover, curate, and implement high-quality educational materials that meet diverse learning needs. The selected resources include both AI-powered platforms for personalized learning and repositories that offer a wide range of OER content.

AI Tools and Platforms for OER

1. IBM Watson Education

IBM Watson Education uses AI-driven learning analytics and machine learning algorithms to deliver personalized learning experiences. Educators can use this platform to analyze student performance, curate OER content, and provide real-time feedback. The platform's AI capabilities allow educators to personalize instruction based on students' learning behaviors and progress, making it a powerful tool for adaptive learning (Popenici & Kerr, 2017).
Access: IBM Watson Education

2. Knewton

Knewton is an adaptive learning platform that uses AI to personalize learning experiences for students by analyzing their performance data in real time. Knewton tailors OER resources, practice questions, and assessments to meet individual learning needs. The platform's recommendation engine continuously adjusts the difficulty and pace of content based on each learner's progress, enhancing engagement and retention (Morrison & DiSalvo, 2020).

3. OpenStax Tutor

OpenStax Tutor is an AI-powered platform that offers personalized learning experiences using OER from OpenStax's library of free, peer-reviewed textbooks. The platform's adaptive learning technology provides personalized feedback and recommendations to students, ensuring they stay on track with their studies. OpenStax Tutor integrates with existing learning management systems (LMS) and offers support for various subjects, including math, science, and humanities (Hilton, 2020).

4. Google AI for Education

Google AI for Education provides educators with a suite of AI-driven tools designed to enhance classroom learning. Through Google Classroom, educators can integrate AI to deliver personalized OER recommendations, automated feedback, and real-time collaboration features. Additionally, Google's search algorithms help educators and students discover relevant OER content from a wide range of repositories (Garcia-Martinez, 2019).
Access: Google AI for Education

5. Smart Sparrow

Smart Sparrow is an adaptive learning platform that allows educators to create custom, AI-powered learning experiences. The platform's learning design tools enable instructors to build interactive lessons using OER content and adapt the learning path based on each student's performance. Smart Sparrow's AI algorithms provide personalized feedback and insights into student progress, making it a valuable tool for personalized instruction (Griff & Matter, 2018).

6. Coursera for Campus (AI-Powered Features)

Coursera for Campus offers AI-powered personalized learning features that help universities integrate OER and other educational resources into their curricula. Through machine learning algorithms, Coursera for Campus provides personalized course recommendations and learning pathways for students, helping them develop specific skills and knowledge. The platform's AI capabilities allow institutions to offer curated learning experiences at scale (Shah & Wadhwa, 2021).

OER Repositories Enhanced by AI

7. OER Commons
OER Commons is a public digital library that offers a wide range of openly licensed educational resources. OER Commons integrates AI-powered search and recommendation systems to help educators discover relevant content efficiently. The platform allows users to filter resources by subject, educational level, and standard, providing a user-friendly interface for curating OER content (Smith & Lee, 2020).

8. OpenStax
OpenStax is one of the leading repositories for OER, offering peer-reviewed, openly licensed textbooks in subjects such as biology, mathematics, economics, and more. The platform's AI-driven tools enhance access to OER by offering personalized textbook recommendations, adaptive study aids, and automated feedback mechanisms. OpenStax's integration with AI-powered platforms like Tutor supports personalized learning experiences (Hilton, 2020).

9. MERLOT (Multimedia Educational Resource for Learning and Online Teaching)
MERLOT is a curated collection of free and open online teaching, learning, and faculty development resources. MERLOT employs AI technologies to streamline the search and curation of OER materials. The platform's advanced search functions help educators find multimedia resources, textbooks, and assessments based on specific instructional needs (Gourley & Lane, 2009).
Access: MERLOT

10. AI-Powered Learning Repositories: EdTech Hub
EdTech Hub provides AI-enhanced access to OER by offering advanced search and discovery tools powered by machine learning.

This platform focuses on providing educational resources for low- and middle-income countries, supporting global access to quality education. The AI-driven recommendation system helps educators in developing regions identify and use OER that aligns with local curricula and learning objectives (Valiente & Winthrop, 2020).

11. SkillsCommons

SkillsCommons is an OER repository focused on workforce development and skills training, offering free and openly licensed materials for community colleges and technical education programs. AI-enhanced tools on the platform provide personalized search features, allowing educators to filter resources by job skill, industry, or academic level. SkillsCommons offers comprehensive courseware, textbooks, and learning simulations (Sparks & Jenkins, 2019).

Conclusion

The tools, platforms, and repositories listed above represent a diverse range of AI-enhanced resources for accessing and curating Open Educational Resources. By leveraging these technologies, educators and institutions can create personalized, adaptive learning environments that promote greater access to high-quality education. These resources reflect the potential of AI to streamline OER use, making learning more equitable and tailored to individual needs.

Appendix C: Further Reading and References

This appendix provides a curated list of books, articles, and research papers on artificial intelligence (AI) and Open Educational Resources (OER). These resources offer in-depth insights into the application of AI in education, the development and adoption of OER, and the intersection of AI with open education practices. The works included are valuable for educators, researchers, and policymakers who seek to understand the implications of these technologies and how they can be leveraged to create more accessible, personalized, and equitable learning environments.

Books

1. Seldon, A., & Abidoye, O. (2018). *The Fourth Education Revolution: Will Artificial Intelligence Liberate or Infantilise Humanity?* University of Buckingham Press.
This book explores the profound impact that AI is expected to have on education, questioning whether AI will empower learners and educators or lead to the commodification of knowledge. It examines the ethical challenges and opportunities AI presents for higher education, providing insights into the future of teaching, learning, and institutional change.

2. Luckin, R. (2018). *Machine Learning and Human Intelligence: The Future of Education for the 21st Century.* UCL Press.
Luckin's work explores the symbiotic relationship between AI and human intelligence, emphasizing how machine learning can support and augment human learning. The book also addresses the importance of designing AI systems that enhance educational practices while fostering creativity and critical thinking.

3. Peters, M. A., Jandrić, P., & Hayes, S. (Eds.). (2020). *A Companion to Research in Education.* Springer.
This edited volume covers a broad spectrum of contemporary educational research, including the impact of AI and digital technologies on education. The book offers valuable perspectives on how AI is being integrated into various educational systems and how it intersects with the open education movement.

4. Weller, M. (2014). *The Battle for Open: How Openness Won and Why It Doesn't Feel Like Victory.* Ubiquity Press.
Weller's book provides a historical and theoretical overview of the open education movement, including the development of OER. It critically examines the challenges and promises of open education, addressing issues related to access, quality, and the potential for AI to enhance open learning environments.

5. Devaney, T., & Morrison, B. (2021). *AI in Education: Foundations, Applications, and Implications.* Routledge.
This book presents a comprehensive examination of AI applications in education, from foundational technologies to their practical applications in classrooms. It covers the ethical considerations and pedagogical implications of AI in shaping the future of teaching and learning.

Articles

1. Popenici, S. A., & Kerr, S. (2017). Exploring the impact of artificial intelligence on teaching and learning in higher education. *Research and Practice in Technology Enhanced Learning*, 12(1), 22-37.
This article investigates the potential and challenges of integrating AI into higher education. It offers a balanced perspective on how AI can enhance learning experiences while cautioning against potential issues related to data privacy, ethics, and the evolving role of educators.

2. Misra, P., & Singh, P. (2020). Artificial intelligence in education: A review. *International Journal of Scientific & Technology Research*, 9(1), 5396-5402.
This comprehensive review paper summarizes the latest developments in AI applications in education, including adaptive learning, intelligent tutoring systems, and automated grading. It also discusses the ethical concerns related to the deployment of AI in educational contexts.

3. Knox, J. (2019). Artificial intelligence and education in the Global South: A critical perspective. *Learning, Media and Technology*, 44(2), 202-213.
Knox provides a critical analysis of how AI and related technologies are shaping education in developing countries, with a focus on equity and access. The article highlights the potential for AI to both address and exacerbate educational inequalities, particularly in relation to OER.

4. Veletsianos, G., & Kimmons, R. (2012). Assumptions and challenges of open educational resources. *Educational Technology Research and Development*, 60(3), 425-441.

This article examines the assumptions behind the OER movement, focusing on the challenges of sustainability, quality, and accessibility. It provides a framework for understanding how AI can address some of these challenges by automating content curation and personalization in open educational settings.

5. Lane, A. (2017). Open education and the sustainable development goals: Making change happen. *Journal of Learning for Development*, 4(3), 275-286.
Lane discusses the role of OER in achieving the United Nations Sustainable Development Goals (SDGs), particularly in relation to education access and equity. The article explores how AI can enhance the delivery and effectiveness of OER in under-resourced regions.

Research Papers

1. Zawacki-Richter, O., Marín, V., Bond, M., & Gouverneur, F. (2019). Systematic review of research on artificial intelligence applications in higher education. *International Journal of Educational Technology in Higher Education*, 16(1), 1-27.
This systematic review provides a comprehensive overview of AI applications in higher education, including intelligent tutoring systems, adaptive learning technologies, and automated feedback mechanisms. It explores the potential of AI to transform teaching and learning, as well as the challenges that educators face when integrating AI into academic environments.

2. Hodgkinson-Williams, C., & Arinto, P. (Eds.). (2017). Adoption and impact of OER in the Global South. *African Minds.*
This collection of case studies focuses on the adoption and impact of OER in the Global South, providing insights into how open education practices are influencing higher education in developing countries. The paper explores the role of AI in facilitating the discovery and use of OER in these contexts.

3. Mehrabi, N., Morstatter, F., Saxena, N., Lerman, K., & Galstyan, A. (2021). A survey on bias and fairness in machine learning. *ACM Computing Surveys*, 54(6), 1-35.
This paper presents a comprehensive review of bias and fairness issues in machine learning, particularly in the context of education. It highlights the risks associated with AI systems that rely on biased datasets and emphasizes the importance of developing fair and equitable AI algorithms in education.

4. Gurung, B., & Rutledge, D. (2014). Open educational resources in higher education: A survey of adoption and use in North America. *International Review of Research in Open and Distributed Learning*, 15(4), 149-170.
This paper provides a detailed survey of OER adoption in North

American higher education institutions. It explores the factors influencing OER use, the barriers to widespread adoption, and the potential role of AI in overcoming these challenges by enhancing OER discoverability and customization.

5. Siemens, G. (2013). Learning analytics: The emergence of a discipline. *American Behavioral Scientist*, 57(10), 1380-1400. Siemens' paper provides foundational insights into the field of learning analytics, highlighting how AI-driven analytics can improve learning outcomes by providing actionable insights into student behaviors and performance. It discusses the implications of AI-powered learning analytics for the personalization of education.

Conclusion

This list of books, articles, and research papers serves as a starting point for those interested in exploring the intersection of AI and OER in education. The selected resources provide a broad range of perspectives, from theoretical foundations to practical applications, helping educators and researchers deepen their understanding of how AI is transforming education through open learning practices.

Appendix D: AI Ethics and Best Practices Guidelines for Educators

As artificial intelligence (AI) continues to be integrated into education, educators must navigate both the opportunities and the ethical challenges associated with its use. While AI technologies have the potential to personalize learning, automate administrative tasks, and enhance educational outcomes, they also raise important ethical considerations related to privacy, fairness, transparency, and accountability. This appendix provides a comprehensive set of guidelines on AI ethics and best practices for educators, offering practical advice on how to responsibly implement AI-driven tools in educational settings. These guidelines emphasize the importance of safeguarding student rights, ensuring equitable access to AI benefits, and fostering an ethical AI culture within institutions.

1. Prioritize Data Privacy and Security

AI systems in education often rely on large volumes of student data, including personal, academic, and behavioral information. Ensuring the privacy and security of this data is paramount. Educators must be aware of how AI platforms collect, store, and process data, and they should ensure that the technologies they adopt comply with data protection regulations such as the General Data Protection Regulation (GDPR) or the Family Educational Rights and Privacy Act (FERPA) in the U.S. (Williamson & Eynon, 2020). It is essential to:

Implement Data Anonymization: Ensure that data collected by AI systems is anonymized to prevent the identification of individual students, especially in assessments or learning analytics tools.

Secure Data Storage: Work with IT departments to ensure that AI platforms use secure methods for data storage, including encryption and regular audits of security protocols (Holmes et al., 2019).

Obtain Informed Consent: Before using AI tools, educators must inform students and their guardians about the data collection practices of these systems and obtain consent. Transparency about how data will be used and stored is critical to maintaining trust.

2. Promote Fairness and Mitigate Bias

AI algorithms are only as objective as the data they are trained on, and biased data can lead to unfair outcomes for students. For instance, AI systems may inadvertently favor certain demographics or reinforce existing inequalities if they are based on skewed or incomplete datasets (Mehrabi et al., 2021). To promote fairness and mitigate bias:

Diverse Data Inputs: Ensure that the datasets used to train AI systems are representative of the diversity in student populations, including variations in race, gender, socioeconomic background, and learning styles (Holstein et al., 2019).

Regular Audits of AI Systems: Regularly evaluate AI tools for signs of bias and discrimination. This may involve conducting audits on the algorithms used to ensure that they are producing equitable outcomes for all students (Veale & Binns, 2017).

Address Algorithmic Bias: Work with developers to ensure that AI systems are designed with mechanisms to detect and correct biases in their decision-making processes. AI tools should be adjustable to meet the specific needs of diverse student populations (Noble, 2018).

3. Ensure Transparency in AI Systems

Transparency is a key ethical principle in the use of AI in education. Students, educators, and administrators should have a clear understanding of how AI systems operate, including how decisions are made by AI algorithms and what data is being used to inform those decisions. To enhance transparency:

Explainable AI: Educators should work with AI providers to ensure that the technology they use is based on explainable AI (XAI) principles. Explainable AI provides insights into how AI algorithms make decisions, helping users understand why a particular recommendation or assessment was made (Doshi-Velez & Kim, 2017).

Provide Clear Documentation: AI providers should offer clear, accessible documentation that explains the functionality of AI tools, including the underlying algorithms and how data is processed. Educators should share this information with students and stakeholders to foster understanding and trust.

Encourage Student Involvement: Create opportunities for students to engage with the AI systems they use. Encourage them to ask questions and provide feedback on their experiences, allowing them to better understand and influence the role AI plays in their education (Popenici & Kerr, 2017).

4. Foster Accountability for AI Use

Accountability ensures that educators, institutions, and AI developers are held responsible for the impact of AI on students. Educators must ensure that they are actively involved in the decision-making process regarding AI adoption and use, taking ownership of its ethical implications. Key steps include:

Ethical Oversight Committees: Institutions should establish ethical oversight committees tasked with reviewing the implementation and operation of AI systems in education. These committees should include educators, ethicists, technologists, and student representatives to ensure a diverse range of perspectives (Binns, 2018).

Regular Review and Updating of AI Systems: AI technologies should be regularly updated to reflect new research, regulations, and evolving ethical standards. Continuous monitoring ensures that AI systems remain effective and fair.

Responsibility for AI Failures: Establish protocols for addressing AI-related failures or adverse impacts, such as algorithmic errors or biased outcomes. Institutions should have a clear process for reviewing these incidents and implementing corrective actions (Floridi et al., 2018).

5. Enhance Inclusivity and Accessibility

AI offers significant potential for improving inclusivity and accessibility in education, especially for students with disabilities or those from underrepresented groups. However, to realize this potential, AI systems must be designed and implemented with accessibility in mind. Best practices include:

AI for Students with Disabilities: Use AI tools that enhance learning experiences for students with disabilities, such as speech-to-text, text-to-speech, and visual recognition tools. AI-powered assistive technologies can provide tailored support for diverse learning needs, promoting inclusivity in the classroom (Pangrazio & Selwyn, 2020).

Accessible Design of AI Tools: Ensure that AI platforms comply with accessibility standards, such as the Web Content Accessibility Guidelines (WCAG). This includes providing alternative formats for educational materials and designing interfaces that are easy to navigate for users with disabilities (Hoy, 2018).

Promote Equity in AI Access: AI technologies should be accessible to all students, regardless of their socioeconomic status. Institutions should ensure that AI tools are made available to underserved and marginalized communities, and that digital divide issues, such as access to reliable internet or devices, are addressed (Knox, 2019).

6. Promote Ethical AI Education and Literacy

Educators have a responsibility to teach students about the ethical implications of AI. As AI becomes increasingly integrated into education and daily life, students must develop an understanding of how AI operates, its potential impacts, and the ethical issues that surround it. To promote ethical AI education:

AI Literacy Programs: Implement AI literacy programs that educate students about the basic principles of AI, including how AI systems work, what data they rely on, and the ethical concerns they raise. These programs should be accessible to all students, regardless of their background in technology (Williamson, 2020).

Discuss AI Ethics in the Classroom: Create opportunities for students to engage with ethical dilemmas related to AI. Encourage discussions about the ethical use of data, privacy rights, and the social impact of AI in education and beyond (Knox, 2019).

Ethics as a Core Component of AI Education: Institutions should integrate ethics as a core component of AI-related courses, ensuring that students studying AI, computer science, or data analytics are trained to consider the ethical implications of their work (Veale & Binns, 2017).

Conclusion

The responsible and ethical use of AI in education requires careful consideration of privacy, fairness, transparency, accountability, inclusivity, and education about AI itself. By following these guidelines, educators and institutions can help ensure that AI enhances learning experiences while safeguarding student rights and promoting equitable access. As AI continues to evolve, these best practices will serve as a foundation for developing an ethical AI culture in education, one that empowers students and educators alike.

References

Balfour, S. P. (2013). Assessing writing in MOOCs: Automated essay scoring and calibrated peer review. *Research & Practice in Assessment*, 8(1), 40-48.

Bast, H., & Buchhold, B. (2013). Semantic search on text and knowledge bases. In *Proceedings of the 36th international ACM SIGIR conference on research and development in information retrieval* (pp. 423-432).

Binns, R. (2018). Fairness in machine learning: Lessons from political philosophy. *Proceedings of the 2018 Conference on Fairness, Accountability, and Transparency*, 149-159.

Conde, M. A., Garcia-Penalvo, F. J., Rodriguez-Conde, M. J., Alier, M., & Casany, M. J. (2014). An evolving learning management system for new educational environments using 2.0 tools. *Interactive Learning Environments*, 22(2), 188-204.

Doshi-Velez, F., & Kim, B. (2017). Towards a rigorous science of interpretable machine learning. *arXiv preprint arXiv:1702.08608.*

Floridi, L., Cowls, J., King, T. C., & Taddeo, M. (2018). How to design AI for social good: Seven essential factors. *Science and Engineering Ethics*, 24(3), 917-939.

Garcia-Martinez, A. (2019). Google's AI-driven language tools and their impact on education. *Journal of Educational Technology Development and Exchange*, 12(1), 55-67.

Géron, A. (2019). *Hands-on machine learning with Scikit-Learn, Keras, and TensorFlow: Concepts, tools, and techniques to build intelligent systems* (2nd ed.). O'Reilly Media.

Goodfellow, I., Bengio, Y., & Courville, A. (2016). *Deep learning.* MIT Press.

Gourley, B., & Lane, A. (2009). Re-invigorating openness at The Open University: The role of open educational resources. *Open Learning: The Journal of Open, Distance and e-Learning*, 24(1), 57-65.

Griff, E., & Matter, M. (2018). Smart Sparrow: The adaptive learning platform for the 21st century. *Journal of Interactive Learning Research*, 29(3), 285-298.

Gurung, B., & Rutledge, D. (2014). Open educational resources in higher education: A survey of adoption and use in North America. *International Review of Research in Open and Distributed Learning*, 15(4), 149-170.

Hilton, J. (2020). Open educational resources: A review of the literature. *Educational Technology Research and Development*, 68(1), 853-876.

Holmes, W., Bialik, M., & Fadel, C. (2019). *Artificial intelligence in education: Promises and implications for teaching and learning.* Center for Curriculum Redesign.

Holstein, K., Wortman Vaughan, J., Daumé III, H., Dudik, M., & Wallach, H. (2019). Improving fairness in machine learning systems: What do industry practitioners need? *Proceedings of the 2019 CHI Conference on Human Factors in Computing Systems*, 1-16.

Hoy, M. B. (2018). Alexa, Siri, Cortana, and more: An introduction to voice assistants. *Medical Reference Services Quarterly*, 37(1), 81-88.

Jurafsky, D., & Martin, J. H. (2020). *Speech and language processing* (3rd ed.). Pearson.

Knox, J. (2019). Artificial intelligence and education in the Global South: A critical perspective. *Learning, Media and Technology*, 44(2), 202-213.

Lane, A. (2017). Open education and the sustainable development goals: Making change happen. *Journal of Learning for Development*, 4(3), 275-286.

LeCun, Y., Bengio, Y., & Hinton, G. (2015). Deep learning. *Nature*, 521(7553), 436-444.

Luckin, R. (2018). *Machine learning and human intelligence: The future of education for the 21st century*. UCL Press.

Manning, C. D., Raghavan, P., & Schütze, H. (2014). *Introduction to information retrieval*. Cambridge University Press.

Morrison, B., & DiSalvo, B. (2020). Knewton's adaptive learning platform: Advancing personalization in education. *International Journal of Educational Technology*, 7(2), 105-120.

Popenici, S. A., & Kerr, S. (2017). Exploring the impact of artificial intelligence on teaching and learning in higher education. *Research and Practice in Technology Enhanced Learning*, 12(1), 22-37.

Shah, R., & Wadhwa, T. (2021). Gooru: AI-powered personalized learning paths using open educational resources. *Technology in Education Journal*, 45(2), 97-112.

Smith, J., & Lee, S. (2020). OER and AI: The role of artificial intelligence in enhancing open education. *Journal of Interactive Media in Education*, 2020(1), 1-12.

Sparks, D., & Jenkins, D. (2019). Building stronger pathways to credentials by using open educational resources. *Community College Journal of Research and Practice*, 43(10-11), 743-748.

Valiente, O., & Winthrop, R. (2020). *The role of EdTech in supporting the most disadvantaged students during COVID-19 and beyond*. Brookings.